100 WA
Kent

compiled by

JIM SHEAN

The Crowood Press

First published in 1995 by
The Crowood Press Ltd
Ramsbury
Marlborough
Wiltshire SN8 2HR

British Library Cataloguing-in-Publication Data
A catalogue record for this book is
available from the British Library

ISBN 1 85223 872 0

All maps by Janet Powell

Typeset by Carreg Limited, Ross-on-Wye, Herefordshire

Printed by Redwood Books, Trowbridge, Wiltshire

CONTENTS

35.	Bishopsbourne	5m	(8km)
36.	Challock and Molash	5m	(8km)
37.	Westwell	5m	(8km)
38.	Bethersden	5m	(8km)
39.	Hothfield	5m	(8km)
40.	...and longer version	8m	($12\frac{3}{4}$km)
41.	East Peckham and Beltring	5m	(8km)
42.	...and longer version	$9\frac{1}{2}$m	(15km)
43.	High Halden and St Michael's	5m	(8km)
44.	Biddenden	5m	(8km)
45.	Lower Rainham Riverside	$5\frac{1}{2}$m	($8\frac{3}{4}$km)
46.	St Margaret's and Kingsdown	$5\frac{1}{2}$m	($8\frac{3}{4}$km)
47.	Ivychurch	$5\frac{1}{2}$m	($8\frac{3}{4}$km)
48.	Waltham and Sole Street	$5\frac{1}{2}$m	($8\frac{3}{4}$km)
49.	Hastingleigh	$5\frac{1}{2}$m	($8\frac{3}{4}$km)
50.	Deal and Sandwich Bay	6m	($9\frac{1}{2}$km)
51.	Hadlow	6m	($9\frac{1}{2}$km)
52.	Ide Hill	6m	($9\frac{1}{2}$km)
53.	Iwade	6m	($9\frac{1}{2}$km)
54.	Conyer Route 1	6m	($9\frac{1}{2}$km)
55.	Tonbridge	6m	($9\frac{1}{2}$km)
56.	...and longer version	9m	($14\frac{1}{4}$km)
57.	New Pound and Shipbourne Forest	6m	($9\frac{1}{2}$km)
58.	Hogben's Hill	6m	($9\frac{1}{2}$km)
59.	Elham	6m	($9\frac{1}{2}$km)
60.	Little Chart and Westwell Leacon	6m	($9\frac{1}{2}$km)
61.	Egerton	6m	($9\frac{1}{2}$km)
62.	Frittenden	6m	($9\frac{1}{2}$km)
63.	Ruckinge and Ham Street	6m	($9\frac{1}{2}$km)
64.	Bilsington	6m	($9\frac{1}{2}$km)
65.	Laddingford	6m	($9\frac{1}{2}$km)
66.	Shadoxhurst	6m	($9\frac{1}{2}$km)
67.	East Malling	$6\frac{1}{2}$m	($10\frac{1}{4}$km)
68.	Chilham	$6\frac{1}{2}$m	($10\frac{1}{4}$km)
69.	Rhodes Minnis	$6\frac{1}{2}$m	($10\frac{1}{4}$km)
70.	Boughton Lees	$6\frac{1}{2}$m	($10\frac{1}{4}$km)

71.	Sissinghurst Castle	6½m	(10¼km)
72.	Conyer Route 2	7m	(11km)
73.	Keston, Downe and Farnborough	7m	(11km)
74.	Hollingbourne	7m	(11km)
75.	Penshurst and Chiddingstone	7m	(11km)
76.	Lympne and Royal Military Canal	7m	(11km)
77.	Dungeness	7m	(11km)
78.	...and longer version	11½m	(17½km)
79.	The Stour Valley Walk	7m	(11km)
80.	Grafty Green and Boughton Malherbe	7m	(11km)
81.	Preston and the Stour Rivers	7m	(11km)
82.	Upstreet and Sarre	7m	(11km)
83.	Borough Green and Basted	7½ m	(12km)
84.	Allhallows Marshes	7½m	(12km)
85.	Gravesend and Shorne Marshes	7½m	(12km)
86.	Graveney and Faversham Creek	7½m	(12km)
87.	Cliffe and the Thames Estuary	7½m	(12km)
88.	Eastry and Worth	7½m	(12km)
89.	...and longer version	11m	(17½km)
90.	The Isle of Harty	8m	(13km)
91.	Wye and Crundale	8m	(13km)
92.	Shorne Wood Country Park	8m	(13km)
93.	East Farleigh	8½m	(13½km)
94.	Newenden	8½m	(13½km)
95.	Kent Water	9m	(14½km)
96.	Markbeech, Hever and Penshurst	9m	(14½km)
97.	Westerham and Toys Hill	9m	(14½km)
98.	Reculver and the Wantsum	9½m	(15¼ km)
99.	Stone-in-Oxney and Appledore	9½m	(15km)
100.	Lyminge and Brabourne	11m	(17½km)

Publisher's Note

We very much hope that you enjoy the routes presented in this book, which has bee compiled with the aim of allowing you to explore the area in the best possible way on foot.

We strongly recommend that you take the relevant map for the area, and for thi reason we list the appropriate Ordnance Survey maps for each route. Whilst the detail and descriptions given for each walk were accurate at time of writing, the countrysid is constantly changing, and a map will be essential if, for any reason, you are unabl to follow the given route. It is good practice to carry a map and use it so that you ar always aware of your exact location.

We cannot be held responsible if some of the details in the route descriptions ar found to be inaccurate, but should be grateful if walkers would advise us of any majo alterations. Please note that whenever you are walking in the countryside you are o somebody else's land, and we must stress that you should *always* keep to establishe rights of way, and *never* cross fences, hedges or other boundaries unless there is clear crossing point.

Remember the country code:

Enjoy the country and respect its life and work
Guard against all risk of fire
Fasten all gates
Keep dogs under close control
Keep to public footpaths across all farmland
Use gates and stiles to cross field boundaries
Leave all livestock, machinery and crops alone
Take your litter home
Help to keep all water clean
Protect wildlife, plants and trees
Make no unnecessary noise

The walks are listed by length - from approximately 3 to 12 miles - but the amount o time taken will depend on the fitness of the walkers and the time spent exploring an points of interest along the way. Nearly all the walks are circular and most offe recommendations for refreshments.

Good walking.

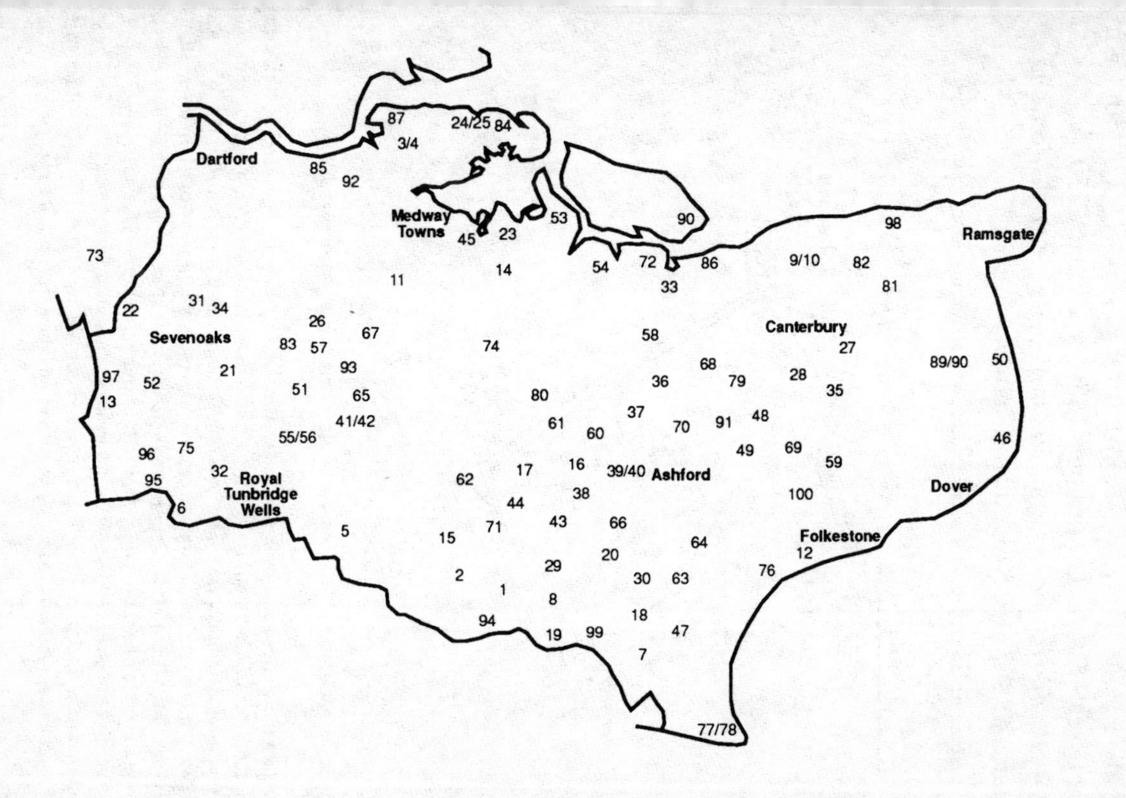
Dartford
Medway Towns
Sevenoaks
Royal Tunbridge Wells
Ashford
Canterbury
Ramsgate
Dover
Folkestone

Walk 1 ROLVENDEN 3m (5km)

Maps: OS Sheets Landranger 188; Pathfinder 1250.

A walk offering panoramic views over fields and woodland.

Start: At 845313, Rolvenden Church.

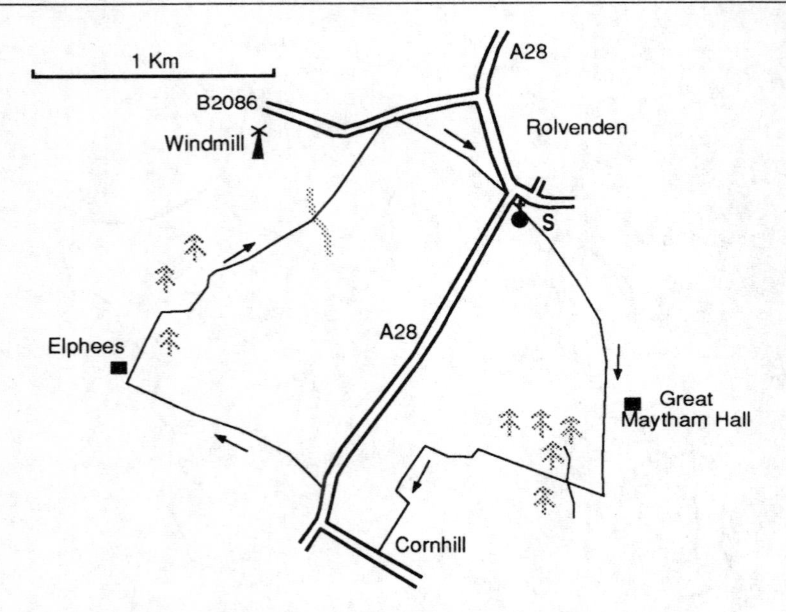

On street parking is available close to the church, but please park tidily.

Go into the churchyard, walk past the war memorial, on your right, and, just past the church, bear left to a path fork. Keep right and continue to reach a kissing gate. Go through and gradually bear left, crossing through fields, reach a stile. Go over and follow the fenced path beyond through woodland, passing, on your left, the grounds of **Great Maytham Hall**. Continue to reach another stile. Cross, turn right and walk along the edge of a field, going downhill through trees to reach a stream.

Cross the stream by way of a footbridge, then go uphill to reach a stile. Cross and maintain direction along the right-hand edge of two fields. Cross another stile turn left and go around a pond. Now go right and head towards a large oak tree in the middle of the field. When you reach the tree, turn left and continue to a stile. Cross into the next into field and walk straight ahead. Cross another stile, turn left and then soon turn right, walking beside a vineyard. Go through a gate and cross a footbridge over a stream to reach a lane. Turn right, following the lane which leads to the A28.

Cross, with great care, and turn right along the edge of the main road for about 50 yards, then turn left through a gate. Go straight ahead, following a path beside a fence to reach a gate. Go through and follow the right-hand edge of a field to reach another gate. Turn right, immediately going through another gate. The path beyond leads uphill, passing Elphees, on the left, and a pond, on the right. Cross a stile and follow the waymarker arrow around the left edge of a field to reach a partially concealed stile in the far left-hand corner. Go over and turn right, going through a gateway. Now go diagonally left across a field, and in the far left corner cross a footbridge, a stile and then another footbridge. Turn left into another field, go through a wooden gate and go diagonally right across another field. Cross over a strengthened section of fence on to a road.

Turn right, then almost immediately right again, over a stile into a field. Head diagonally left to go through a gap in the hedge and follow the left-hand edge of the playing field beyond. Cross a stile and continue along a driveway to reach the High Street in **Rolvenden**. Now retrace your steps to the start of the walk.

POINTS OF INTEREST:

Great Maytham Hall – The Hall was once the home of author Frances Hodgson Burnett. The gardens are said to have been the inspiration for her book *The Secret Garden.*

Rolvenden – No visit to this charming village would be complete without a trip around the excellent C M Booth Motor Museum in the High Street. The Star Inn in the village is a Grade II listed building and was formerly the village poor house.

REFRESHMENTS:

The Star Inn, Rolvenden.

The Bull, Rolvenden.

Walk 2 **BENENDEN** 3m (5km)

Maps: OS Sheets Landranger 188; Pathfinder 1250.

A charming walk through open fields and parkland.

Start: At 807329, the Post Office in The Street, Benenden.

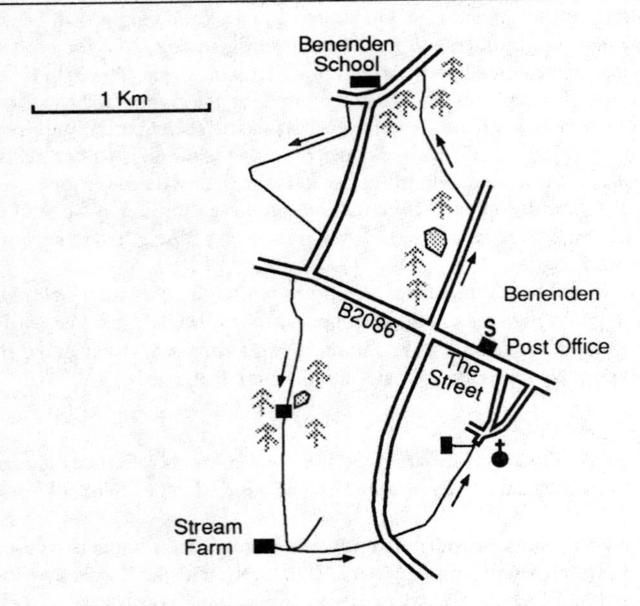

The best place to park for this route is the car park next to the village hall.

From the Post Office, **Benenden,** walk westwards to reach a cross-roads (of the B208 with a minor road). Turn right in the direction of Benenden Hospital. Go downhil passing a pond on your left, then uphill to reach a stile on the left. Cross and g diagonally right across a field to reach a gate in the right-hand corner. Go through an follow a track running between fences to reach another gate. Go through and bear le across the corner of a field to reach a stile. Cross and walk alongside tennis court then turn left along a tarmac drive and continue beside the **Benenden School** building

Just after a turning on the left, and before the main school building, turn le through a gate on to a track. Walk forward, cross a stile and turn right into a fiel following a yellow arrow waymarker. A second waymarker arrow indicates the route to a stile in the right-hand corner. Do not cross: instead, turn left and head downhill along the boundary of the field. At the next corner, cross a stile and follow the edge of a playing field to reach a driveway. Turn right and follow the drive to reach a road (the B2086).

Turn right, but soon turn left (crossing the road with care) along a signed footpath between hedges. After 150 yards, go over a stile on the left and turn right to follow the right-hand edge of a field. Cross another stile and walk along the border of another field. Go through a group of trees and walk past a pond on the left. Now go through a gate in the right-hand corner of the field and follow the right-hand boundary of the next field, downhill, to reach a gate on to a track near Stream Farm. Turn left, soon going through a gate on to a track. When the track bears left, continue straight on, going uphill on a path between hedges.

Go over a stile on to a road and cross to the stile opposite. Cross and follow a path diagonally to the right corner of a field. Go through a kissing gate and along the tarmac path beyond. Bear right, go through a gate and follow the track beyond for about 50 yards, then turn right along a driveway. Very soon, just before Benenden Church, turn left into a lane and follow it back to The Street, from where it is a short step back the start of the walk.

POINTS OF INTEREST:

Benenden – This secluded, very pretty, village, set among Kent's hop fields, has a fine green and some exquisite timbered houses.

Benenden School – Formerly Hemsted Manor House, but now a girls school, the building is a delight, and claims to have once been visited by Queen Elizabeth I. The Princess Royal, amongst other members of the current royal family, was educated here.

REFRESHMENTS:

The King William IV, Benenden.
The Bull, Benenden.

Walks 3 & 4 — COOLING AND CLIFFE — $3^1/_2$m ($5^3/_4$km) or $8^1/_2$m ($13^1/_2$km)

Maps: OS Sheets Landranger 178; Pathfinder 1177.

A choice of two walks between, and around, two villages.

Start: At 756759, Cooling Church.

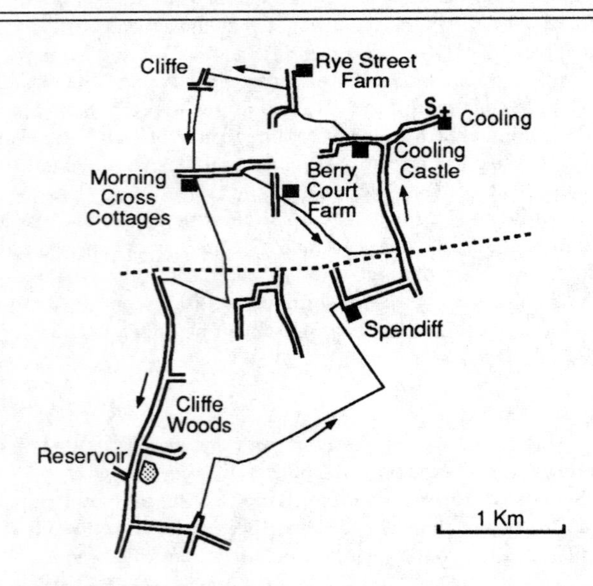

From **Cooling Church**, turn left and follow the road as it goes first left, then right. Go past Cooling Castle, on your right, and just after the end of the castle grounds, turn right over a stile and follow the path beyond, going diagonally right. The path now meanders towards the bend in a road. On reaching the road, turn right and follow it to the southern end of Rye Street Farm. Now go over a stile on the left and follow the path beyond, part of the Saxon Shore Way, into Cliffe. Walk alongside some houses, then turn left and follow a road in the front of those houses to reach a point where a track goes straight ahead and a path bears left. Take the track and follow it to the road near Morning Cross Cottages.

The shorter route turns left here. Go along the road until it turns left. There, take a path on the right, in the bend of the road, and follow it down to the road by Berry

Court Farm. Turn left, and at the end of the farm buildings, opposite a house called Redbarn, turn left on to another path which goes diagonally to the right. Cross over at a cross-paths, and again when a track crosses. Maintain direction until you reach the railway line. Now turn left and walk parallel to the railway line to reach a minor road. Turn left, rejoining the longer route.

The longer walk goes straight on, following Well Penn Road to reach a railway crossing. Go over and maintain direction along the track as it zig-zags away from the railway to eventually reach a road. Turn right along a path that goes gently downhill, back towards the railway line. You reach another road just as you arrive at the railway: turn left along this road for about $1^1/_2$ miles, going past Cliffe Woods and a large reservoir on the left to reach Lee Green Road, also on the left. Take this to reach a crossing where a road goes right and a track goes left. Follow the track through an orchard and into a wood, continuing to reach the outskirts of Cliffe Woods. Now follow the track as it performs a semi-circle around the bottom corner of the village to emerge, once again, into woodland. Continue to follow the track as it goes uphill and then crosses the hillside and down. After about $^1/_2$ mile you reach a minor road: turn left along a track that leads downhill and through a field to reach the rear of the dwellings at Spendiff. Join the track that runs between the buildings to reach a road. Continue along the road, turning left with it. Follow the road across the railway line to rejoin the shorter route.

Follow the road to reach a T-junction opposite **Cooling Castle**. Turn right and retrace your steps back to Cooling and the start of the walk.

POINTS OF INTEREST:

Cooling Church – In the churchyard there are a number of lozenge gravestones said to have been the inspiration for similar graves in Charles Dickens' *Great Expectations*.

Cooling Castle – The castle was built by Sir John de Cobham in 1381. Later it was the residence of John Oldcastle, thought by many to have been the original Falstaff. Sir John was hanged in 1417 as a Lollard, as the supporters of John Wycliffe were known. Although the castle is not open to the public, much of interest can be seen from the road.

REFRESHMENTS:

The Horseshoe and Castle, Cooling.
The Six Bells, Cliffe.
The Evening Star, Cliffe.
The Staff of Life, Cliffe.

Walk 5 **LAMBERHURST AND SCOTNEY CASTLE** $3^{1}/_{2}$m ($5^{3}/_{4}$km)
Maps: OS Sheets Landranger 189; Pathfinder 1249.
A pleasant walk, offering excellent views, on the hills around Lamberhurst.
Start: At 677362, the car park adjacent to the Chequers Inn, High Street, Lamberhurst.

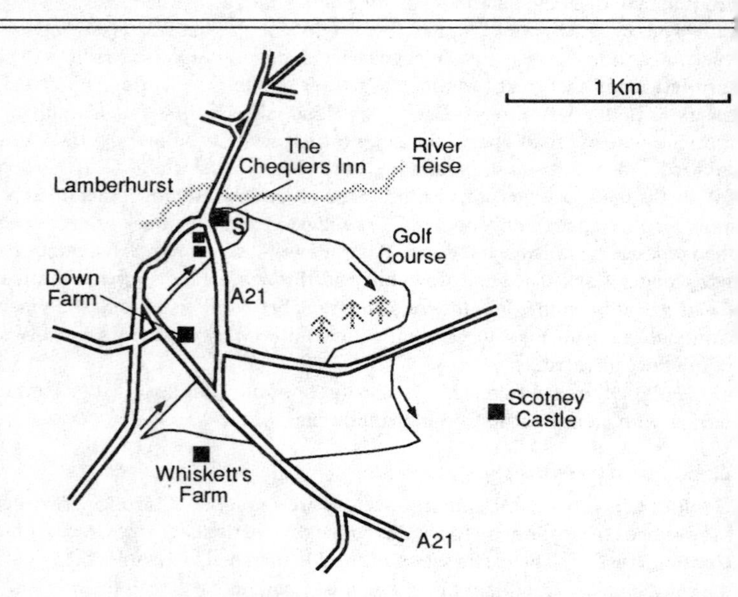

Walk to the rear of the car park and go through the gate. Go across two playing fields to reach a stile at the far right corner of the second field. Cross and go along the footpath beyond, following it across a golf course fairway. Climb a wooden barrier and continue in the direction indicated by a yellow waymarker, crossing a second fairway. Go over the stile ahead, and cross farmland to reach a concrete track. Follow this uphill, and at the top cross a stile on the right and follow the left-hand edge of the field beyond.

Cross another stile, marked **Scotney Castle** Estate, and soon go left through a gap in the fence. Turn right and follow the meandering edge of another field, as indicated by the yellow waymarkers. Cross a stile, bear right and go up to a green arrow which indicates the Woodland Walk. Follow this route through the woods to reach a tarmac lane. Turn left, and after several hundred yards go right through a gate into a field, following a signed footpath to Kilndown. Continue by going left and downhill through a field to reach a stone bridge. Do not cross: instead, turn right along a grassy track, go through a gate and across another field. Go through a gate and turn right along a lane to reach the main A21.

Cross, with great care, and take the signed footpath into the field opposite. Keep to the right-hand edge of the field for 100 yards, then go right through a gap in the hedge into another field. Turn left and follow the field boundary, then cross the driveway of Whiskett's Farm into another field. Follow the track running along the field's left-hand side until it bears left, then go along the footpath ahead. Cross a field, then climb the wire fence, using the struts provided, and turn right.

Follow a footpath to reach a lane, turn left and continue uphill on to Sand Road. Turn left and continue for 100 yards, then turn right along a concrete track towards a signed footpath. Go slightly right, and downhill, through vineyards, following a grassy path. Cross a stile and the field beyond, then bear left to go through a gate. Go down a slope, then bear left along a footpath to once again meet the A21. Cross over, again with great care, turn left and then soon turn right along a driveway, as indicated by a footpath sign. Cross a stile and walk for about 20 yards before turning left along a track which leads into the playing fields. Now retrace your steps to the car park in **Lamberhurst**.

POINTS OF INTEREST:

Lamberhurst – This fine village has maintained much of its old character, despite the presence of the main road. The Owl House is a delightful half-timbered, 16th-century house, said to have once been the headquarters of a gang of smugglers. The House's garden is equally delightful. Another fascinating spot is Finchcocks, a museum of musical instruments.

Scotney Castle – Although not on the route, this National Trust property is worth visiting for its gardens, claimed by many to be the most romantic in England, and really setting off the fine, 14th-century moated castle.

REFRESHMENTS:

The Chequers Inn, Lamberhurst.
The Elephant's Head, Lamberhurst.
The Brown Trout, Lamberhurst.
There is also a tea room at Scotney Castle Gardens.

Walk 6 **ASHURST** $3^1/_2$m ($5^3/_4$km)

Maps: OS Sheets Landranger 188; Pathfinder 1248.

A walk through rolling farmland with fine views over the River Medway valley.

Start: At 507389, the corner of Ashurst Hill and the road to Ashurst Railway Station.

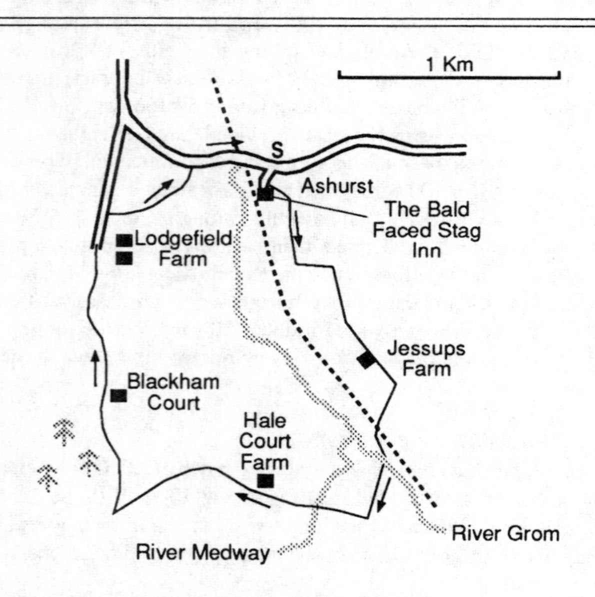

Parking for this walk is readily available in the station road.

Head along the station road, then cross a stile on the left and go diagonally right, uphill, through a field. Go through a gate in the right-hand corner, and after about 50 yards, go through another. Now go along the left-hand edge of a garden, and then through another gate. When the path beyond joins a track, go left. Walk past Jessups Farm, then turn left along a track marked as part of the **Sussex Border Path**. Go uphill, and at the top turn right along another track.

Follow this new track downhill, and at the bottom cross a stile next to a gate. Maintain direction, taking the track along the left-hand edge of a field. Go through a gateway and continue, downhill, to reach a sign for Sussex Border Path East. Turn right and head downhill through a field. Go through a gate, then pass under the railway and go through another gate. Bear left to follow the path through a field, continuing to a footbridge over the River Grom, a tributary of the Medway. Cross and continue through a field, bearing right to reach a track marked as part of the **Weald Way**. Turn right, soon crossing a footbridge over a stream and continuing to cross a bridge over the River Medway.

Follow the track until it turns right near Hale Court Farm. There, go straight on. Cross two very close stiles, continue for 50 yards and then go through a gate on the right. Soon you go through another gate and then walk through a field to reach a stile in the right-hand corner. Cross and turn left along a winding concrete path which leads uphill through two gates to reach a junction. Turn right and follow the signed drive in the direction of Blackham Court. After crossing a small bridge over a stream, leave the track as it bears right and continue up a grassy slope.

When you reach a hedgerow, bear left and walk with the hedge on your right. Go through a gate, walk between fences and then follow the left-hand edge of a field to reach a gate at the far left-hand corner. Go through, turn right and follow the edge of a field to reach a gate on to a lane. Turn left, but very soon go down a set of steps on the right, marked with a footpath sign. These lead to Lodgefield Farm. Follow a concrete track through a gate and into a field. Go diagonally left to reach a stile and go over into another field. Follow the field's left-hand edge downhill, and at the bottom go into the field on the left. Follow the right boundary to reach a stile. Go over and turn right to reach the A264. Turn right and follow the road with great care. Go under the railway bridge and make the last few steps to reach the curiously-named Bald Faced Stag Inn, and the start.

POINTS OF INTEREST:

Sussex Border Path – This fine long distance footpath – even if it is in a neighbouring county! – links Emsworth with Rye, a distance of 150 miles.

Weald Way – The second of the two long distance footpaths followed on this walk links Gravesend with the South Downs Way, joining the latter to the north of Eastbourne.

Ashurst Church – Dedicated to St Martin of Tours, the church has two 17th-century sundials. A place of pilgrimage in Tudor times because of a crucifix which was said to have miraculous powers.

REFRESHMENTS:

The Bald Faced Stag Inn, Ashurst.

Walk 7 **BROOKLAND** $3^1/_2$m ($5^3/_4$km)

Maps: OS Sheets Landranger 189; Pathfinder 1271.

A pleasant walk from this fine marsh village, often on quiet country roads.

Start: At 989258, Brookland Church.

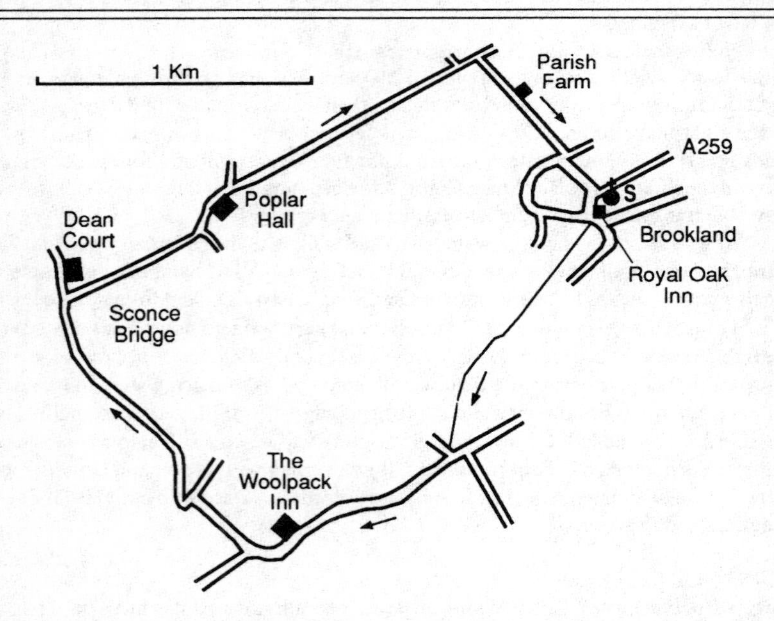

From the church, which is an essential place to visit, turn left and head away from the main centre of the village. Go past a turning on the right, continuing to reach a T-junction, and the Royal Oak Inn. Go straight across the road to reach a gate. Go through and follow the signed path beyond as it leads away to the right. When, very soon, the path forks, at the boundary of the field, take the left-hand branch. Follow this path for about $^1/_2$ mile as it goes, firstly, to the boundary ahead, and then straight on to the next. When you cross into the third field the path once again divides: take the left-hand branch and follow it as it leads to the corner of the field to join a road, with Hook House on your left.

Turn right along the road, following it as it crosses White Kemp Sewer to reach the Woolpack Inn, one of the most isolated inns on Romney Marsh as well as one of the finest. Just beyond the inn, the road turns right to join the A259. If you were to turn left here you would head into East Sussex, so go straight on (heading north-westwards), with great care still beside the A259. Soon, you will reach a minor road on the left. Take this, swinging around the **Philippine Village Craft Centre** in a loop, still beside the A259. The craft centre is on the site of a former army camp. Stay with the road, following it to Sconce Bridge which crosses back over White Kemp Sewer. Soon after crossing the bridge you will reach a turning on the right: take this, soon passing the buildings of Dean Court, on the left.

Continue along the road to reach a fork. Take the left-hand branch, soon passing Poplar Hall, on your right. Next, you pass Saddler's Wall Lane, on your left. Walk along the road for about 600 yards, passing a turning to the left to reach one on the right. Take this, soon passing Parish Farm, on your left, and continuing to reach a cross-roads, where four turnings are connected by a short stretch of road. Take the road directly opposite and follow it back into **Brookland**. When you reach a T-junction you will see the church ahead.

POINTS OF INTEREST:

Philippine Village Craft Centre – A strange collection of buildings in Philippine style. The Centre often looks closed but in the summer receives many visitors. In June, it hosts a Philippine Festival and is invaded by many hundreds of Philippino exiles.

Brookland – The village lies on a slight rise that was once an island in Walland Marsh. The village church, dedicated to St Augustine, is arguably the finest on Romney Marsh. The remarkable building dates from the 12th or 13th century and has a separate three-tiered, timber belfry made of massive beams salvaged from ships that came to grief in Rye Bay. Inside, the church has several treasures. Of particular interest is the lead font, which is Norman and decorated with the signs of the zodiac.

REFRESHMENTS:

The Royal Oak, Brookland.
The Woolpack Inn, on the route.

Walk 8 **SMALLHYTHE** $3^1/_2$m ($5^3/_4$km)

Maps: OS Sheets Landranger 189; Pathfinder 1250.

A short, pleasant walk around this wealden hamlet, on the edge of Romney Marsh.

Start: At 894301, Smallhythe Place.

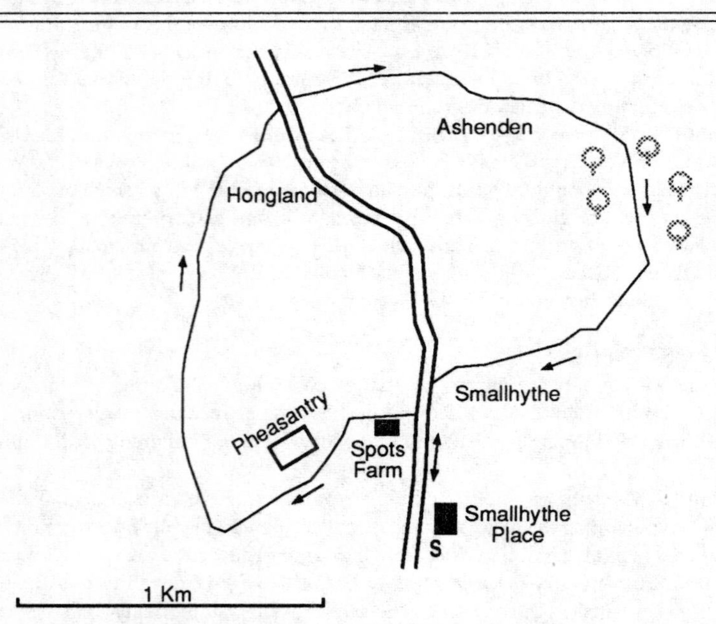

From Smallhythe Place, go back on to the main road, turn right and head towards Smallhythe. Go past the chapel, on your right, to reach the entrance to Spots Farm which houses the **Tenterden Vineyard**, on the left. Go through the gate and follow this past the farm buildings. When the driveway divides, take the left-hand branch Continue along a path that goes gradually downhill, skirting a pheasantry, then bears right to join a track that goes gently uphill. After about 200 yards, take a path that goes to the left of the track, and then runs parallel with it for 100 yards before rejoining it. Now ignore a path on the right, staying with your path as it runs along the boundary of an orchard.

Continue to reach the boundary between two orchards. Cross a stile and follow the path beyond into the heart of the orchard. Continue along the path to the far corner, crossing into the next orchard and continuing to reach a road. Turn left, cross the road, and almost immediately turn right along a track that again runs beside an orchard. Stay with this track as it bears left, but remains beside the orchard, and then continues to join the drive for Ashenden. Follow the drive to reach its junction with another going away to the left. Do not follow that drive: instead, turn right along a path, following it as it bears around to the left and goes quite steeply downhill to join a track that runs beside an orchard. At the bottom of the slope the path turns to the right and runs to the rear of the buildings of Dumbourne. Just past the buildings, cross a stile into the corner of a field, and follow the boundary of the field as it leads to the far corner. There, cross a stile into the next field and follow the path through its centre to reach a gate in the boundary ahead. Go through the gate and maintain direction to reach another gate in the opposite boundary. Go through this gate to join a track.

Follow the track across a field and into another, continuing to reach a stile on to a road. Turn left and follow the road through Smallhythe and back to **Smallhythe Place**.

POINTS OF INTEREST:

Tenterden Vineyards, Spots Farm – The farm is one of England's earliest, and best known, producers of wine. There is also an extensive herb garden. Visitors welcome between May and October.

Smallhythe Place – Dating from the 16th century, this typical Kentish yeoman's house was the harbourmaster's house when Smallhythe was a port. It is now managed by the National Trust and houses the Ellen Terry Memorial Museum. The famous Victorian actress lived here from 1899 until 1928. The museum has a collection of memorabilia of the actress, together with other theatrical momentoes.

REFRESHMENTS:

There is a tea room at Smallhythe Place.

There are also ample opportunities in nearby Tenterden.

Walks 9 & 10 **HERNE** $3^1/_2$m ($5^3/_4$km)
or $6^1/_2$m ($10^1/_4$km)

Maps: OS Sheets Landranger 179; Pathfinder 1195.

Two, mainly woodland, walks around this ancient village.

Start: At 183658, Herne Church.

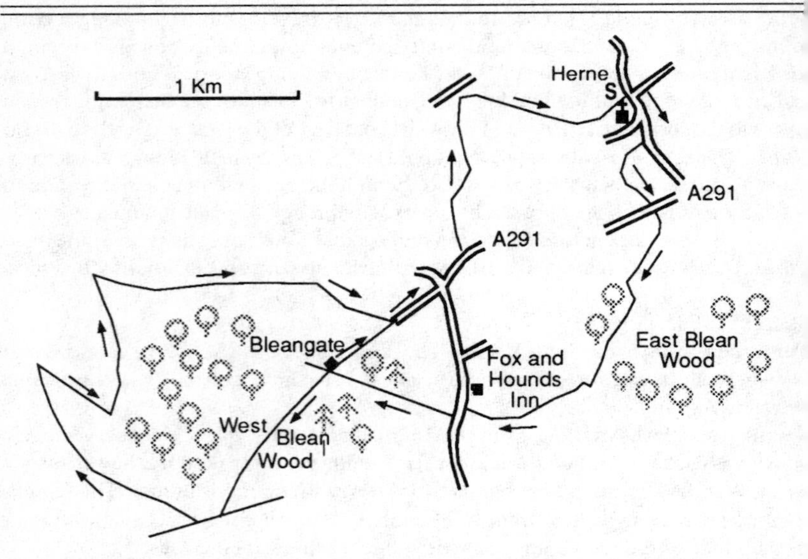

From Herne Church, walk to the main road (the A291) and turn right, southwards taking care as this can be a busy route. When the main road bears right, take the left hand turning, following it to reach a footpath on the right. Take this, following i between houses and then bearing left along the boundary of an orchard. Stay with the path to pass a row of houses, continuing to reach a road. Go straight across and follow a track that runs beside a garden, on the right, to reach a corner. There the track bears right along the boundary of a field. When the track divides, take the left-hand branch following it into a wood, part of East Blean Wood. When you emerge from the woodland the track once again forks: take the right-hand branch. Soon, another track crosses the one you are following, continue to another path fork and take the right hand track. Stay with this track as it goes past a small patch of woodland and then continues to reach a road (the A291 again), next to the Fox and Hounds Inn. Cross with great care, and turn left, but very soon go right, along another track that heads into woodland. Follow the track as it bears away slightly to the right, and then runs along a field edge, on the right, to reach Bleangate.

The shorter route turns right here, following a driveway to rejoin the longer route, which joins from the left.

The longer walk turns left and follows a path deep into West Blean Wood, a fine piece of mixed woodland. When the track divides, take the left branch and continue along it until another track crosses. This is New Road, a substantial track that leads to a group of cottages (which you do not reach): turn right on to it. After about 50 yards, turn right along a path which leads you out of the woods. When you reach the driveway of Warren Farm do not proceed along it: instead, turn sharp right along another path that returns in the direction you have just come. The path bears left and leads to the top of the delightfully named Knockhimdown Hill, and then bears left alongside a patch of woodland. Stay on this path as it goes uphill to reach a path crossing. Turn right here, going downhill and soon walking alongside woodland, on your right. You cross a track and soon reach another small patch of woods. Here, bear right and follow the path uphill to reach a minor road. Turn left along the road, rejoining the shorter walk.

Go along the road to reach its junction with the A291. Go straight ahead, with great care, following the road in the direction of Herne Common. Opposite the first house, turn left along a track that follows the boundaries of several fields and then goes gently downhill. When the track reaches a road do not join it: instead, turn sharp right along a path that crosses through several fields. Continue along the path to reach a crossing path. Here, turn left and follow the new path into the churchyard at **Herne** where the walk began.

POINTS OF INTEREST:

Herne – Now overlooked in favour of Herne Bay, its more famous seaside neighbour, Herne is a place of great charm, maintaining much of its rural character. A cluster of fine old buildings surround the church, mainly 13th century, but with a 14th-century tower that Ruskin described as 'perfect'. The church's most famous vicar was Nicholas Ridley who sang the *Te Deum* in English here, the first time it had been so sung in the country. When he was tied to the stake in Oxford, to be burnt for his 'heretical' views, his last words were 'Farwell Herne, thou worshipful and wealthy parish'.

REFRESHMENTS:

The Fox and Hounds Inn, on the route.
The Smugglers Inn, Herne.

Walk 11 **BLUEBELL HILL AND KIT'S COTY** 4m ($6^1/_2$km)

Maps: OS Sheets Landranger 188; Pathfinder 1193.

Easy walking through woodland and across open countryside, passing neolithic burial sites. Muddy in parts.

Start: At 745621, the Bluebell Hill picnic site car park.

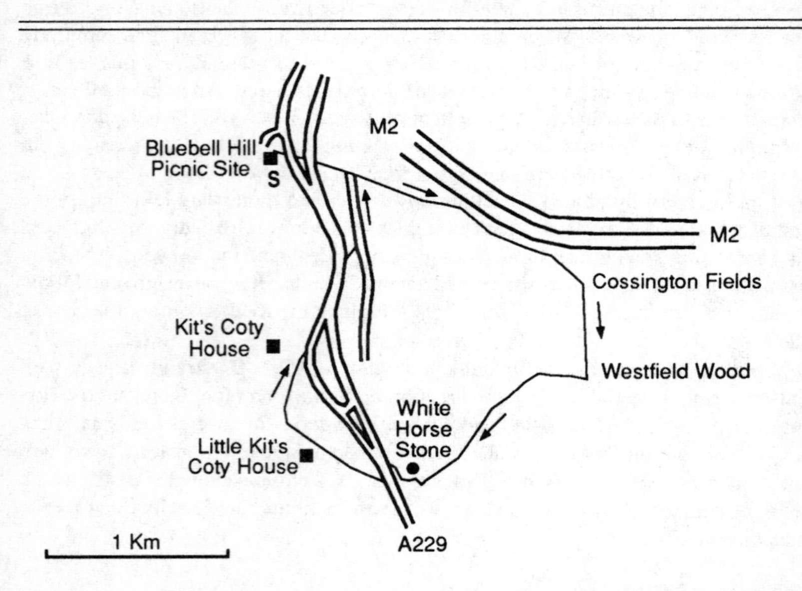

Turn right out of the car park and walk along the road, which is part of the North Downs Way. Cross the bridge over the Maidstone road and, at the Upper Bell Inn, cross another road to reach Mill Lane. Walk along the lane, but when it turns to the right leave it to follow the footpath straight ahead. Follow the path to reach two stiles: go over the right-hand one which leads to an enclosed path. Follow this into a meadow with woodland on the right. Continue straight on, ignoring paths on either side, until you reach the end of the woods.

There you will find a broad path which runs below and parallel to the bank of the M2 motorway. Follow the path as it heads towards radio masts. The right of way now bears right, crossing fields to reach a boundary at Cossington Fields. At this boundary turn right (southwards) towards Westfield Wood. From this section of the route there are excellent views across large areas of open fields. When Westfield Wood is reached, turn right rejoining the North Downs Way. The path turns left into the wood, follows the top of a ridge and then begins to descend through a fine grove of trees. The path becomes quite steep here, and can be slippery in wet weather, so care is needed. Go through a horse gap and turn right, still following the North Downs Way.

Soon, on the right-hand side of the track, you will see a huge stone, reddish in colour, known as the White Horse Stone. It was possibly deposited here by the Neolithic tomb-makers who were active in this area. When the track reaches a garage, avoid walking along the main road by turning behind the garage and following another track which leads through a tunnel under the road. Turn left, and then almost immediately right along a bridleway. The red North Downs Way marker will assist you to find the right route here. Along the new track you will soon reach a turning to the left which offers access to **Little Kit's Coty House**. The main bridleway leads down to a road junction. This can be busy, so care should be taken in crossing to the footpath on the other side. Follow the footpath up to reach **Kit's Coty House**, on the left.

Leaving the burial chamber, you will soon reach a set of steps leading up to the Old Chatham Road. Climb these and turn left to reach a footbridge that takes you safely over the main road, which runs parallel. Turn left again and climb steadily up the cutting, going through a wood to reach Warren Road, an old Roman Road. Turn left along Warren Road, continuing up to Mill Road. Turn left and retrace your steps back to the Bluebell Hill picnic site.

POINTS OF INTEREST:

Little Kit's Coty House – This Neolithic burial chamber, also known as the Countless Stones, is smaller and less well known than as its larger neighbour. Despite this it is still of interest.

Kit's Coty House – This Neolithic long barrow is the most important prehistoric site in Kent. The mound is 170 feet long, but only three uprights and the capstone now remain of the burial chamber itself. Until the mid-18th century a single large stone, known as the General's Stone, stood at the far end of the mound, but this was blown up as it got in the way of ploughing. A local legend claims the site was the burial place of a local chieftain called Catigern, though the name post-dates the tomb by many centuries. Because of reasonable state of preservation and inaccessibility, the dolmen is still occasionally the scene of ritual ceremonies.

REFRESHMENTS:

The Upper Bell Inn, on the route.

Walk 12 **HYTHE AND SALTWOOD** 4m ($6^1/_2$km)

Maps: OS Sheets Landranger 179; Pathfinder 1252.

A pleasant walk through parkland, woodland and farmland, and through part of the ancient Cinque Port town of Hythe.

Start: At 164348, in fee paying car park opposite the police station in Hythe.

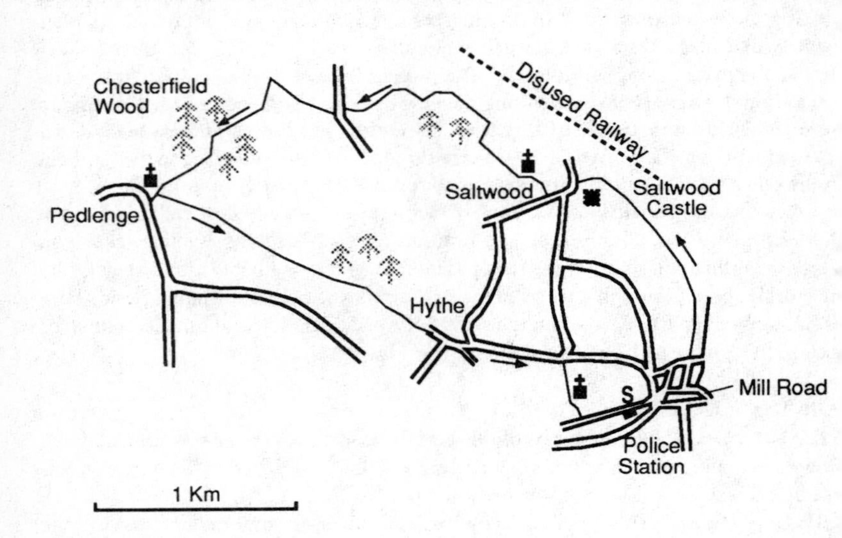

Cross to the police station and go down Sun Lane, which is signposted to the town centre. Turn right along the High Street to its end, then turn left into Station Road and immediately right into Mill Road. Turn left into Mill Lane and walk up to a junction. Cross and take the footpath by the posts opposite. At the end of the path, go left along a track to reach a stile. Cross and follow the right-hand edge of the fields beyond. Soon, **Saltwood Castle** is seen ahead.

Go past the castle to reach a road. Turn left, and after 50 yards take the signed footpath on the right, going through a kissing gate and heading towards Saltwood Church. Enter the churchyard through another kissing gate, leaving it on to a road. Turn right, and then fork right at the 'No Through Road' sign. When this road turn right, go ahead along a signed bridleway which leads uphill into woods. Continue to reach a yellow waymarked stile on the left. Cross to reach a fork and take the right branch.

Continue to a cross-paths, going straight over, in the direction indicated by the yellow waymarkers. Go through woodland, and at a junction of paths turn left to follow the path to the edge of the woods. Go over a stile into a field. Follow the field's right edge to reach the next stile, go over and continue to cross a footbridge. Now continue to reach a road. Cross the road to go through the gate opposite. Follow the grassy path beyond: after 400 yards you will reach a gate. Do not go through: instead, turn left just before it along a path which leads down into Chesterfield Wood.

Follow the main path through the woods, exiting over a stile. Follow the obscure track beyond to some buildings, then follow a lane around Pedlinge Church and go through gates back into the field you have just left, but on a different path. Continue with the fence on your right, following it as it swings to the right. After the second gate you reach a small wood on the right: where the fence and the wood end, go forward along a path to reach a gate at the corner of the wood. The path beyond this leads to a footbridge. Cross the left-hand of two bridges and enter Brock Hill Country Park on a path marked 'Permissive footpath detour'.

Walk up the slope, following the waymarkers and keeping parallel to the fence on your right. At the top, bear right to reach a stile. Go over and bear left along a path. At the path's end, turn right along a track that immediately veers left. Follow the track to arrive at the corner of a residential road. Turn right and walk towards **Hythe** churchyard, on your right. Just before the churchyard take some steps down to Oak Lane. Now go down to the High Street and retrace your steps back to the start.

POINTS OF INTEREST:

Saltwood Castle – The castle is 11th-century and was once the property of the Archbishop of Canterbury, an irony since it was from here, in 1170, that the four knights rode to Canterbury in order to murder Thomas à Becket.

Hythe – Hythe means 'haven', and has been a safe harbour since Roman times. The town was one of the Cinque Ports, lies close to the Royal Miltary Canal and is a terminus for the Romney, Hythe and Dymchurch Railway. Not surprisingly, therefore, it attracts plenty of visitors. Some visit the fine Church of St Leonard, a superb Early English church, famous for its crypt which has a macabre accumulation of skulls and other human bones.

REFRESHMENTS:

There is a variety of inns and cafés in Hythe.

Walk 13 CROCKHAM HILL 4m ($6^1/_2$km)

Maps: OS Sheets Landranger 187 and 188; Pathfinder 1208.

A pleasant walk through open fields. Some steep ascents.

Start: At 444507, Holy Trinity Church, Crockham Hill.

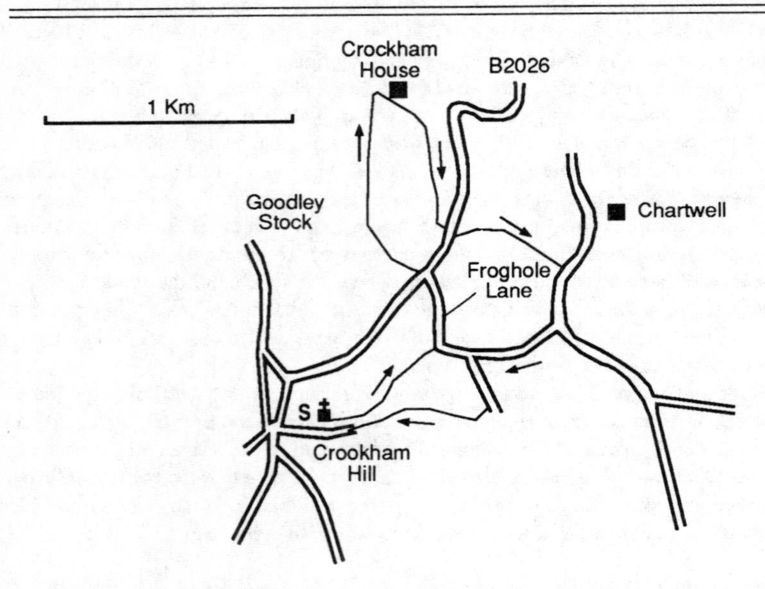

From **Holy Trinity Church** go to the car park at the top of the lane (or, alternatively begin the walk from there). At the bottom corner of the car park there is a stile which leads to a footpath through a meadow. Cross another stile and then go over a stream via a footbridge. Stay on the footpath as it follows the boundary of another field and, at the left-hand corner, cross another stile and follow the path beyond up a winding stairway, known as Buttle Steps, through gardens and on to the road known as Froghole Lane.

Turn left, uphill, to a junction. Cross over and take the footpath directly opposite. Stay with the path as it veers left to reach a fork. Take the right-hand route to walk uphill through woodland to reach, eventually, another fork. Again follow the right branch to reach an intersection of paths. Go straight on, following the path as it bears to the left. The path now widens: after about 200 yards, turn right along a footpath beside a fence.

Follow the footpath downhill, passing through a gap in a fence. At the bottom, just before a stile, where there is a sign for Froghole, turn right and walk to the entrance of April Cottage. Turn left to reach a road. Cross and take the footpath opposite, following the blue arrow waymarker. Climb uphill and at the top turn left at an intersection of paths. Continue to a fork and take the right-hand branch to walk downhill to reach a road (Mapleton Road). Here you may wish to detour to the left to visit **Chartwell.**

Turn right along the road. Go past Old Well Cottage, then turn right through a gate on to a signed footpath to a private road to Mariners. At the end of the private road, go through a gate to return to Froghole Lane. Continue along the lane to reach another lane, on the left, marked by a sign for The Coach House. Take this and at its end follow the footpath straight ahead, going through woods to reach Acremead Cottage, on the left. Turn right, and at the third stile on the right cross to go along a path through woodland that returns you to the Church car park.

POINTS OF INTEREST:

Holy Trinity Church, Crockham Hill – Octavia Hill, founder of the National Trust, is buried here, next to the altar beneath her effigy carved in marble.

Chartwell – This National Trust property was the home of Sir Winston Churchill from 1924 and the rooms have been left as they were when he was in residence. The lake is home to his famous black swans and the garden studio is decorated with his paintings.

REFRESHMENTS:

The Royal Oak, Crockham Hill.

Walk 14 **HARTLIP AND QUEENDOWN WARREN** 4m ($6^1/_2$km

Maps: OS Sheets Landranger 178; Pathfinder 1194.

A walk through Kentish villages and orchards, finishing at a nature reserve.

Start: At 839643, Hartlip Church.

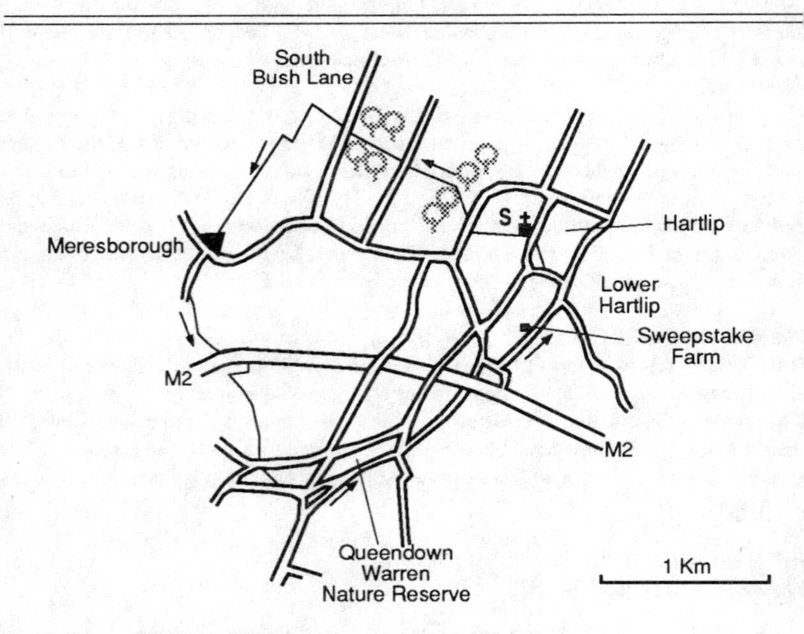

Parking is possible near the church, but please park tidily.

From the church, take the signed footpath beside the churchyard, following it into orchards. Continue to reach a small road. Turn right, but very soon turn left along a path that goes diagonally through more orchards. At the end of the orchards take the path that goes left, following it to reach a lane (Spade Lane). Cross and follow the path opposite, going through more orchards to reach South Bush Lane.

Cross and follow the path opposite, bearing to the right to reach a junction with a crossing path. Turn left along the new path which, at first, skirts an orchard. Turn right, with the path, into the orchards and then turn left, still following the path through ınd then out of the orchards. Now maintain direction to reach a road junction at the ʼillage of Meresborough. Take the road directly opposite and follow it through the ʼillage. Just beyond the village there are tracks running in either direction from the ʼoad: take the left-hand track, heading southwards, diagonally away from the road.

When the track reaches woodland, follow it as it skirts the wood edge and then uns parallel to the M2 motorway. Cross the motorway by way of a footbridge and hen double back and follow the track along the edge of the woods. At the corner, vhere the track goes straight on, turn left on to another track, following it as it goes liagonally through the woods. The track emerges on to a gentle slope that leads up to **Queendown Warren Nature Reserve**.

Enter the reserve at a junction of roads and follow a track diagonally across the Warren to reach a cross-roads. Take the second road on the left, walking along the top of the slope and then leaving Queendown Warren and going down towards the M2. Go under the motorway and then take the first road on the right. Now go first left, passing Sweepstakes Farm. Maintain direction into Lower Hartlip and take the first urning left. Now, after about 150 yards, go right along a track that bears diagonally eft to reach a point where another path joins from the right. Follow the single path eads into **Hartlip**, arriving opposite the church.

POINTS OF INTEREST:

Queendown Warren Nature Reserve – This well managed Nature Reserve preserves a worthwhile piece of old Kent.

Hartlip – This superb little village stands among orchards in a way that is quintessentially Kent. The church, restored in Victorian times, has some interesting stained glass from that period.

REFRESHMENTS:

There are inns in both Hartlip and Meresborough.

Walk 15 **CRANBROOK** 4m (6½km

Maps: OS Sheets Landranger 188; Pathfinder 1249.

A walk through farmland and woodland around the old town o Cranbrook.

Start: At 778359, the car park at the Hill, Cranbrook.

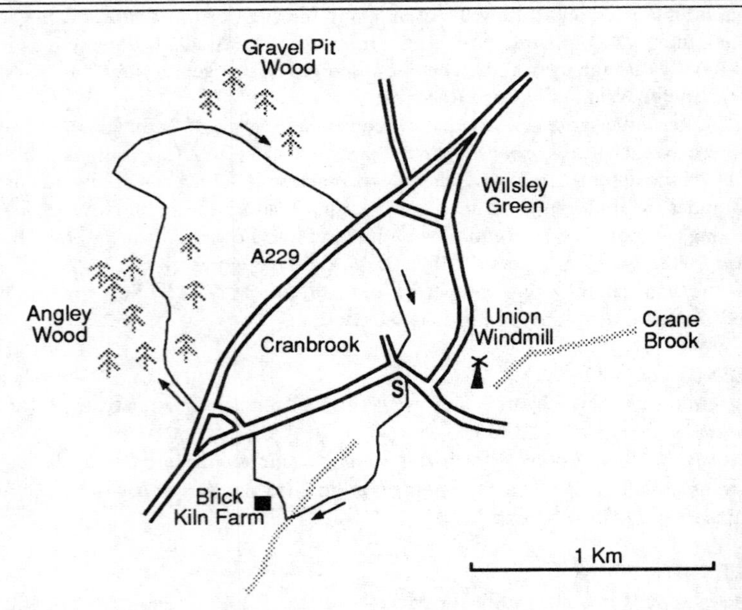

Go to the rear of the car park, which is to be found beside the B2189 in **Cranbrool** and take the path to the left of the dental surgery. Follow the path as it goes to the le of Crane Brook, from which the town at the walk's start derives its name. Now g past a footpath, on the right, which leads to a playground, continuing along your pa when it bears left. Continue to reach Bramley Drive, and very soon turn right along lane on the right. When the lane goes left, continue straight on, following a footpa into woodland.

Cross a stile and follow the right-hand edge of a field for about 100 yards reach another stile on the right. Cross and follow the path beyond into woodland. Th small stream you cross is Crane Brook. Continue along the path to reach a stile. Cro and follow the path on the left to reach a track. Turn right and follow the track to a road. Cross and follow the made-up road opposite to reach another road (the A229). Cross, with great care, and follow the footpath directly opposite, which is signed to Glassenbury.

Go past a fire warning sign, and a path on the left, to reach a fork. Follow the right-hand branch, going downhill, and swinging left, then right. When you reach the bottom, do not continue along the path as it goes sharp left: instead, take a small path on the right. When this path forks, take the left branch, going downhill. Stay with the path as it goes right at the bottom of the slope. Cross a stream to reach another fork and take the right branch, soon cross back over the stream by way of a footbridge.

The path beyond leads up a long, steep ascent through woodland, then goes out and down the other side. Go up another slope and through two kissing gates to reach a driveway. At the end of the drive go through a gateway on to the A229 road. Cross, with great care, and follow the footpath opposite. Go through another kissing gate and go diagonally right across a field. Go through a gate and follow the path beyond between playing fields. Now bear right to reach a lane. Turn left, then go through another kissing gate and pass the playground. Now take the path on the right through the churchyard to reach a junction of roads. Keep left and walk down to The Tanyard, reached on the right. Follow this back to the car park and the start of the walk.

POINTS OF INTEREST:

Cranbrook – This fine old town had a period of prosperity in the 15th century when it became a centre for weaving. The Union Windmill, which dominates the town, does not date from that time. It was built in 1816, and, at 72 foot (22m) high is claimed to be the second tallest in England. The Church of St Dunstan is often called the 'Cathedral of the Weald' and is well worth a visit. The church has a superb 13th-century porch, complete with an original oak door. Inside the church is the famous Priest's Room of Sir John 'Bloody' Baker. Sir John was Mary Tudor's Chancellor and he used this room for torturing Protestants, before they went to the stake. He was also the founder of Sissinghurst Castle.

REFRESHMENTS:

There are numerous possibilities in Cranbrook.

Walk 16 **Pluckley** 4m ($6^1/_2$km

Maps: OS Sheets Landranger 189; Pathfinder 1230.

A pleasant walk from this Wealden village.

Start: At 925454, the Black Horse Inn, Pluckley.

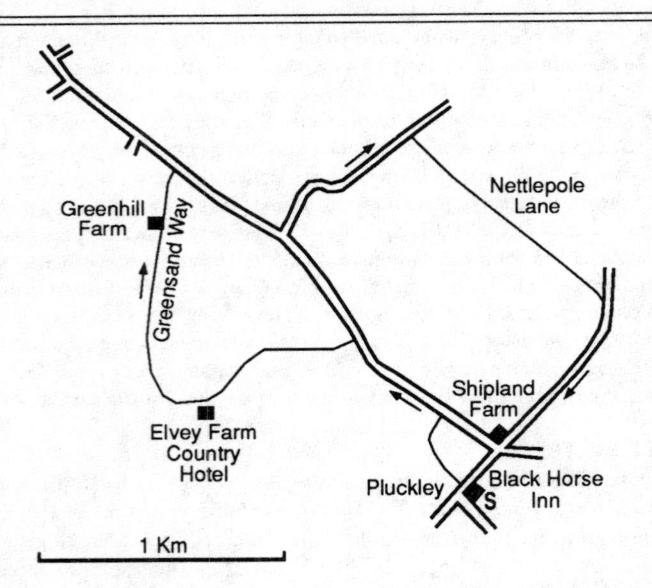

Turn right from the inn and follow the road to reach a T-junction. Go straight acros on to a track, and follow it through Shipland, bearing right beyond there to reach road. Turn left and follow the road through Kingsland, then, just as the road bea gently to the right, go left along a byway that meanders downhill and leads to th Elvey Farm Country Hotel. Pass to the right of the hotel and turn right along a pat that follows the course of a small stream. Eventually the path reaches a track leadin off from a minor road.

Do not go along the track: instead, bear right on to a path signed as the **Greensan Way**. Follow the path uphill and then through the buildings of Greenhill Farm t reach a road (New Road). Turn right and follow the road to reach Pivington Farn Now turn left along a road that runs alongside an orchard. Stay with the road as urns right, then left. About 200 yards after the left turn, turn right along a byway alled Nettlepole Lane.

The lane leads gently uphill, with patches of woodland on the left, then goes past Nettlepole Cottage, on the right, before reaching a road. Turn right and walk along he road for $^1/_2$ mile. There are substantial **orchards** on your left, with woodland visible n the distance.

Eventually the road reaches a cross-roads, with Shipland Farm on your right. Go traight across and follow the road into **Pluckley**. Continue past the houses, on your ight, to reach a turning on the left. Take this to return to the inn from which the walk tarted.

'OINTS OF INTEREST:

Greensand Way – This fine long-distance footpath has Kent and Surrey sections, the whole linking to create a superb 100 mile route from Haslemere to Yalding.

Orchards – Kent is often called the Garden of England, and has been famous as a ruit growing area since the Romans planted orchards and vineyards. To the apples ne Romans brought, the Normans added pears. Today, fruit is still crucial to the conomic well-being of the county.

'luckley – The television series *Darling Buds of May* was filmed in and around this leasant village. The village church, from where there are splendid views over the Veald, has many fine features, including some excellent stained glass. Pluckley lays laim to being one of Britain's most haunted villages, with over a dozen spectres ıcluding a pipe-smoking gipsy lady and two Lady Derings, the Red Lady and the Vhite Lady.

.EFRESHMENTS:

'he Black Horse Inn, Pluckley.
'he Dering Arms, Pluckley.
'he Rose and Crown, Pluckley.

Walk 17 **SMARDEN** 4m ($6^1/_2$km

Maps: OS Sheets Landranger 189; Pathfinder 1230.

A walk across farmland and on country roads around thi charming village.

Start: At 879424, Smarden Church.

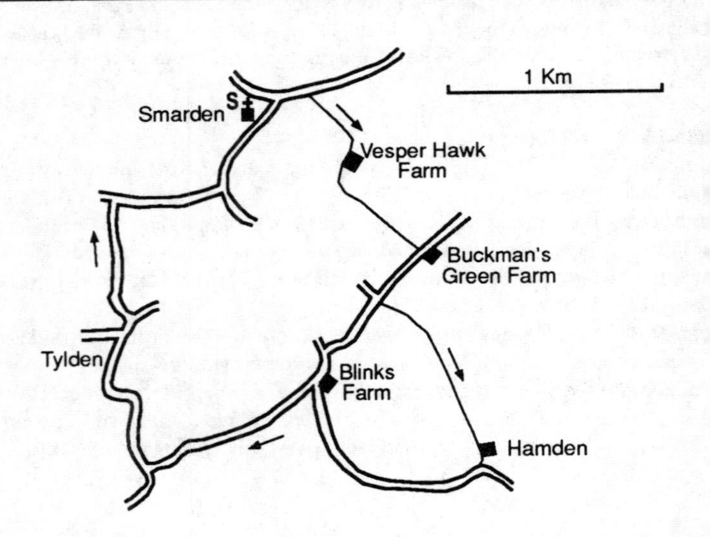

There are several points in Smarden where you might begin a walk, but Smard church has been chosen as it is a place that most walkers will wish to visit.

From the church, turn right and follow the road around to the right. Now turn l along the main street through the village. Just past the Post Office, go right alon street that leads away from the village. At the end of the street, follow the path t goes straight on, walking with a field boundary on your left. At the end of the fie there is a junction of paths. Turn left, going past the buildings of Vesper Hawk Far Shortly after passing the farm, cross a stream and continue to where another pa crosses. Turn left and then bear diagonally right towards the field edge ahead. Cr a stile and maintain direction through two more fields to reach a road oppos Buckman's Green Farm.

Turn right along the road, following it to reach a turning on the right. Directly pposite this, you turn left along a path that follows the left-hand boundary of a field nto its corner. Cross into the next field and bear diagonally right, with the path, ollowing it through the buildings of Hamden. Continue to reach a road at a bend. Go eft along the road, following it as it bears right and continuing to reach a T-junction ear Blinks Farm.

Turn left and follow this new road to reach a fork. Take the right-hand branch nd follow it into the hamlet of Tylden. Take the second turning on the left, following his road as it bears right, then left. Continue along the road, going between Thorn arm and Grigsby Farm to reach another road junction. Turn right along Biddenden Road and follow it to the next junction. Turn left and follow the road back into **marden**, bearing around to the left to return to the **church**.

OINTS OF INTEREST:

marden – This fine Wealden village has a number of well-preserved, half-timbered uildings. Arguably the best of the old buildings are the Penthouse and the cloth hall, he latter being a very fine example of the type, reflecting the wealth that immigrant lemish weavers brought with them

marden Church – This 14th-century building is sometimes called the 'Barn of Kent'. The reason is the height and structure of the wooden roof and the wide, aisleless nave, which combine to look like an old tithe barn.

REFRESHMENTS:

The Bell Inn, Smarden.
The Chequers, Smarden.
The Flying Horse Inn, Smarden.

Walk 18 **SNARGATE** 4m ($6^1/_2$km

Maps: OS Sheets Landranger 189; Pathfinder 1271.

A walk from this marsh village across open countryside.

Start: At 991287, Snargate Church.

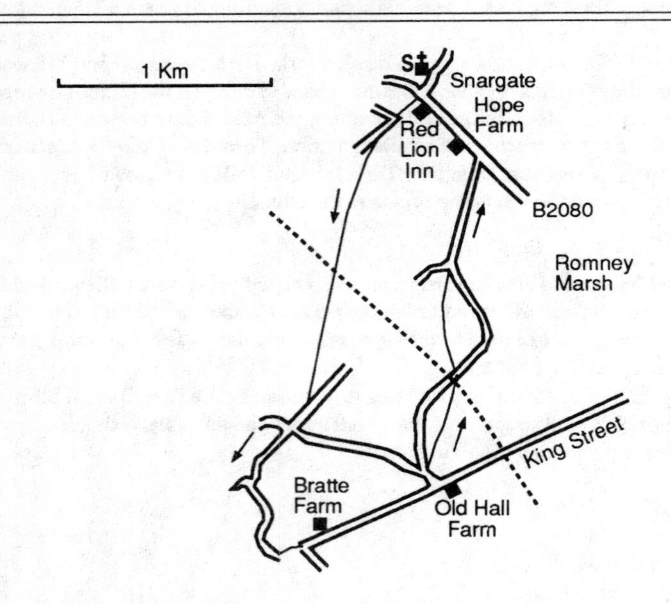

From the **church**, go on to the road and turn right. Follow the road for a short distanc to reach a T-junction, with the Red Lion Inn on the left. Go straight across the roac with care, and along the path opposite. Follow the path through a field to reach anothe road just as it turns sharply. Do not actually join the road: instead, go to the left of th turning and continue along a path that goes diagonally to the left. Follow this path t reach a stile in the centre of the field boundary ahead. Cross and head towards the le corner of the far boundary of the next field. Cross into the next field and turn right an follow its edge towards a railway line. Cross the railway and turn left, initially, the very soon go diagonally right, going just past the corner of one field and headin towards the centre of the field boundary ahead. Cross into the next field and g diagonally left, aiming for the corner where you will find a stile.

Cross the stile on to a road and turn right. Follow this minor road to reach a cross-roads. Go straight across, staying with the minor road for another 200 yards to reach a T-junction, with the road on the right bending away into a corner. Turn left and follow the road as it winds left, then right and continues to reach another T-junction. Go left and follow the road (King Street), going past a turning, on your right, and Brattle Farm, on your left. When you reach a turning on the left, with the entrance to Old Hall Farm on the right, turn left, follow the minor road to reach a fork.

Take the right-hand branch. Now, very soon, you leave the road, turning right over a signed stile and going along the path beyond. Go into a field and head diagonally left towards the far corner of the opposite boundary. At the corner, you will reach the intersection of a road and a railway line. Cross both the railway and the road and continue along the path you have been following – it bisects the road and railway at about 45 degrees – heading diagonally left of the centre of the boundary ahead to reach a stile. Cross the stile into the next field and maintain direction along the path as it heads towards the intersection of two roads in the near distance. When you reach the road, go straight ahead on the single route, following it to reach a T-junction. Turn left along a road that runs parallel to New Sewer, on the right.

Continue along the road (the B2080), with care, passing Hope Farm, on the left, and eventually reaching Snargate Bridge, on the right. Turn right, crossing New Sewer and heading back to Snargate Church where the walk began.

POINTS OF INTEREST:

Snargate Church – This interesting, in part 13th-century, building is another of the isolated churches on Romney Marsh, an area often referred to as the sixth continent. The one-time rector of the church was Richard Harris Barham, author of the *Ingoldsby Legends*. The reverend gentleman took a dim view of the Royal Military Canal, seeing it as unfit for the purpose for which it was constructed and too expensive. He wrote a satirical piece about the waterway, noting at the end that despite the scorn he had poured on it, he had to admit that it had succeeded, for while Napoleon had crossed the Rhône and the Rhine he had not, as yet, crossed the Canal.

REFRESHMENTS:

The Red Lion Inn, Snargate.

Walk 19 **WITTERSHAM AND RIVER ROTHER** 4m ($6^1/_2$km)

Maps: OS Sheets Landranger 189; Pathfinder 1271.

A walk across open country and alongside the River Rother, from this fine village.

Start: At 899274, the Post Office, Wittersham.

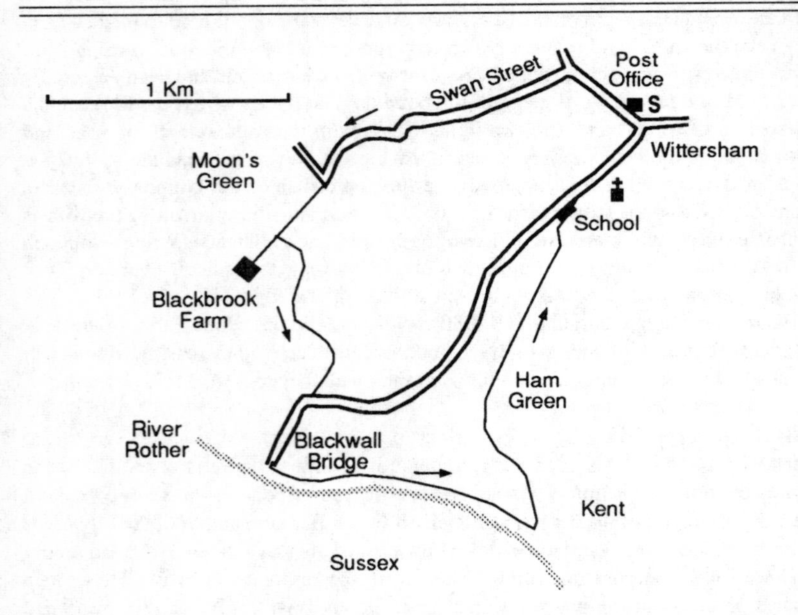

From the Post Office, go on to the main village street and turn right. **Wittersham** is a growing village and for a short distance you will be walking through its centre. When you reach a T-junction, take the turning on the left (Swan Street) and follow it as it goes past the last of the village houses. Stay on this road as it bears first to the left past Bates Farm, then to the right, past Hall Farm. When the road turns to the right again, go ahead, through a gate, and along the drive leading to Blackbrook Farm. This is a long drive: after about 200 yards, go left along a signed footpath.

Follow the path along the inside boundary of the field you are in, bearing around to the right to reach a staggered corner. Here, cross a stile on the left into the next field and follow the path as it goes to the right, eventually reaching a crossing track opposite a sewage works. Turn right along the track, following it to reach a road just as it turns. Go straight ahead, along the road, in the direction of the River Rother which you can see in the distance. Follow the road to Blackwall Bridge. Do not cross: instead, go down to the left of the bridge to join the **Sussex Border Path** which runs alongside the river. Head eastwards for a pleasant riverside walk of about $^1/_2$ mile.

Eventually the path bears left, away from the river and goes gently uphill in the direction of Ham Green. Here the path becomes a track: follow it through the buildings of Ham Green. Beyond, the track reverts to a path and divides into three separate routes. Take the centre path, following it as it takes a straight route, going gradually uphill. When you reach the boundary of a field on your left, maintain direction, but stay close to the field edge. Continue along the path to reach the rear of the village school. Here it turns left, and goes beside the school to reach a road.

Turn right, and very soon pass the main **church** of Wittersham, which is well worth a visit. Continue along the road, passing Wittersham House, on the left, and continuing to reach a T-junction. To your right here is the Ewe and Lamb Inn, while to your left is the village Post Office, the start of the walk.

POINTS OF INTEREST:

Wittersham – The village is sometimes known as the 'capital' of the Isle of Oxney. It was here that the remains of an iguanadon were found, evidence of the earliest life forms on the land that is now Kent. Just east of the village is Stocks Mill, a well-preserved post-mill dating from 1781. It is open to the public on Sundays between June and September.

Sussex Border Path – This fine long distance footpath links Emsworth with Rye, a distance of 150 miles.

Wittersham church – Parts of the building date from the 12th century, but the sandstone tower is from the 15th century. Inside, there is a fine modern window depicting a shepherd and his flock.

REFRESHMENTS:

The Ewe and Lamb Inn, Wittersham.

Walk 20 **WOODCHURCH** 4m ($6^1/_2$km

Maps: OS Sheets Landranger 189; Pathfinder 1250.

From this fine wealden village, a walk through an agricultura landscape.

Start: At 943349, Woodchurch Church.

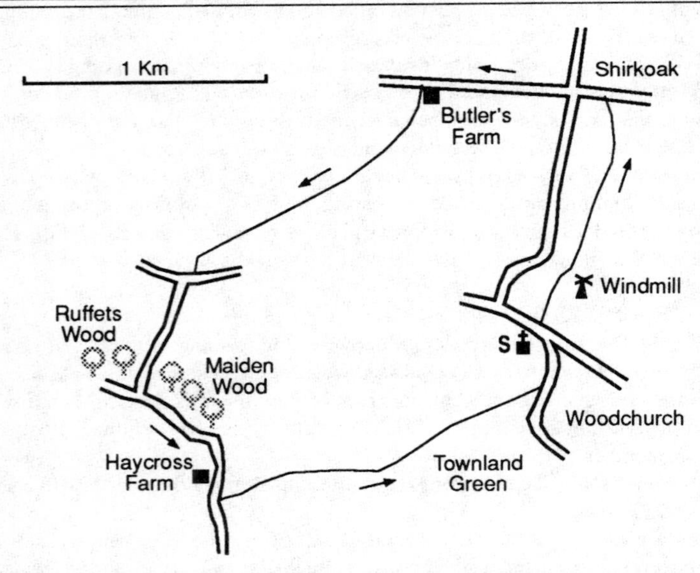

From the **church**, take the path opposite, which leads to the now disused **Woodchurc Windmill**, which can be visited. When you reach a junction of paths, take the righ hand route which bears around the buildings of Sunny Mead Farm and then heac north. Follow the path to reach a gate in the centre of the field boundary ahead. G through into the next field. In that field, the path divides: take the left-hand branc walking through the centre of the field to reach the far boundary. Cross into the ne field. Again, the path divides: take the left-hand branch, which soon leads to a roac

Turn left and follow the road to the cross-roads at Shirkoak. Cross straight ov and continue along the road to reach the entrance to King Farm, on the right. Opposi the farm drive, turn left along a signed footpath into a field. Walk to the corner, cro into the next field and go along the right-hand boundary. Half-way along that boundar go through a gate into another field and follow a path that goes diagonally across both that field and the next. Now maintain direction along the path as it crosses several fields and goes first downhill, and then uphill. Eventually the path joins another coming from the right: take this single route and follow it to a road. Turn right to reach a fork. Follow the left-hand branch, continuing past Ruffets Wood, on the right, to reach a T-junction.

Turn left and follow the road, with Maiden Wood on your left. Just past the end of the wood, and past the entrance to Haycross Farm, on your right, turn left along a footpath. Follow the path through a field and towards the woodland ahead. Cross a stile into the wood and maintain direction on the path through it. On emerging from the wood, go into a field, staying with the path as it goes gently downhill and through several fields. Eventually your path becomes the central one of three paths that join to form a single route.

Follow this single route as it goes through the area known as Townland Green and leads on to reach the main road through Woodchurch. Turn left along the road, following it back through the village, staying on the left to return to the church.

POINTS OF INTEREST:

Woodchurch Church – This fine 13th-century building has nave piers of the local Bethersden marble. It has a collection of interesting brasses and a fine Norman font. It's steeple, just over 100 feet high, is Kent's leaning tower, although much more gently than its Italian counterpart.

Woodchurch Windmill – This former smock mill was in use until 1926. It is open to the public and houses an exhibition of milling machinery and a collection of old photographs.

REFRESHMENTS:

The Stonebridge Inn, Woodchurch.
The Bonny Cravat, Woodchurch.

Walk 21 **SHIPBOURNE** $4^1/_2$m ($7^1/_4$km)

Maps: OS Sheets Landranger 188; Pathfinder 1208.

A walk through woodland and fields, including historical sites.

Start: At 592523, verge parking on The Common, Shipbourne.

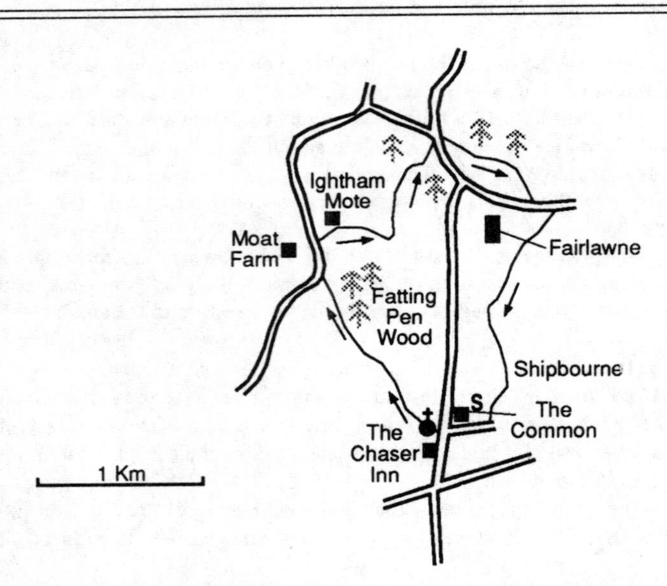

From The Common, walk along Upper Green Road to reach the St Giles' Church. Go through the churchyard to reach a gate. Go through and take the footpath on the right. Follow the edge of a field, leaving it at its far right-hand corner, as waymarked by a yellow post. Follow the footpath through another field, and again leave in the right-hand corner, where there is another waymarked post. Turn left and follow a track through another field to reach a stile. Go over into the strangely named Fatting Pen woods. Go through the woods and cross another stile into a field. Follow the right-hand edge of the field, crossing a stile into the next field and continuing along the left-hand edge to reach a road.

Turn right and follow the road to Ightham Mote, passing Mote Farm, to the left on the way. Enter **Ightham Mote** through the iron gate and follow the drive as it bears right, past the house. Continue straight ahead, going uphill and through several fields before turning left through a wooden gate on to a footpath. Follow the path to woodland, continuing through the trees to reach a gate. Go through and turn right, with care, along a road. Soon, turn left along a bridleway which leads to Fairlawne Estate. Continue through the woods, leaving through a gate into a field.

Follow the right-hand edge of the field to a path fork. Turn right, then cross a stile into another field. Keep to the left boundary of this field, and at the far corner cross a stile into a lane. Turn left along the lane to reach a stile on the right. Go over this, back into the grounds of **Fairlawne**. Go right and walk downhill, crossing two more stiles to reach a yellow signpost which points to another, similarly marked, stile. Cross this, then leave Fairlawne over another waymarked stile and walk down a slight slope to reach a made-up track beside ponds.

Follow a signed footpath on the left, to Shipbourne, and keep to the right at a fork in the lane. After going past the old mill house, go through a wooden gateway and cross a small bridge over a stream. Now head uphill towards some houses, and when the path forks keep going straight ahead, between gardens, to reach a drive. Turn right to follow the driveway, and then a lane, back to the start.

POINTS OF INTEREST:

Ightham Mote – The property is owned by the National Trust and is open to the public at standard Trust times. The Mote is a beautiful medieval moated manor house which includes a magnificent Great Hall and a 13th-century chapel.

Fairlawne – The former family home of Sir Harry Vane, a member of the Long Parliament, who was executed by Royalists after the Restoration. Sir Harry's ghost is said to haunt Fairlawne on the anniversary of his execution.

REFRESHMENTS:

The Chaser Inn, Shipbourne.

There is a tea room at Ightham Mote.

Walk 22 CUDHAM AND DOWNE $4^1/_2$m ($7^1/_4$km)

Maps: OS Sheets Landranger 187; Pathfinder 1208 and 1192.

A walk through historical villages and across open, often steep, countryside.

Start: At 445598, Cudham village car park.

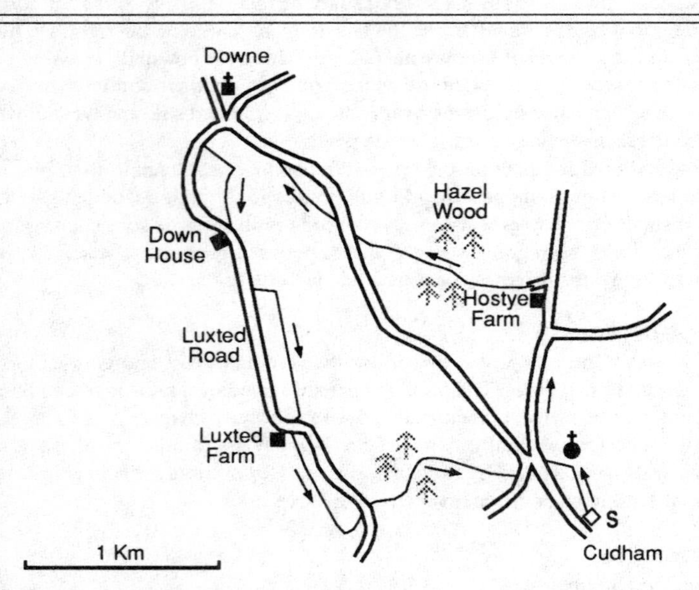

Follow the signed footpath out of the car park to the village church. Go left through the churchyard and out to Church Approach. Turn right along the road to reach Hosteye Farm on the left. Just past the farm, turn left along the driveway, where the bridleway to Downe is signed. When the driveway bears right, continue along the bridleway, going downhill and crossing a stile to join the signed Cudham Circular footpath.

Continue along the footpath, then climb wooden steps through woods. Now follow the CC sign along a track to reach Cudham Road. Turn right along the road, then cross over to turn left along a signed footpath which runs parallel to the lane. The path eventually rejoins Cudham Road near Christmas Tree Farm. Turn left along the road to reach the village of Downe. At the road junction in the village, turn left into Luxted Road. Walk past two groups of cottages and then turn left along a signed footpath.

Walk between flint walls, following yellow waymarker arrows which will then direct you around the edge of a field. Climb a stile on the left, and turn right along a footpath which skirts the edge of a field to reach a kissing gate. Go through into another field and go diagonally across it to reach a stile. Go over and turn left to reach Luxted Road again, near the entrance to **Down House**.

Continue along the road for another 200 yards, then turn left over a stile and follow the signed footpath beyond across a field. Go right as indicated, and at the right-hand corner of the field cross another stile. Follow the right-hand edge of the field beyond until you reach another stile. Cross on to a narrow path and follow it to a stile. Cross to reach Luxted Road yet again.

Turn right, soon leaving the road by turning left along the driveway to Luxted Farm: the drive is marked by a footpath sign. At the end of the drive, cross a stile and walk along the left boundary of the field beyond. Cross another stile and continue down the left-hand side of another field to eventually reach a third stile. Cross and continue for several hundred yards to reach another stile. Cross on to a signed footpath and follow it to reach Luxted Road for the last time.

Cross the road and take the footpath opposite, going between fenced gardens and on into woods. A series of steep wooden steps leads down a slope to a stile. Cross and follow the path beyond through open fields. Cross another stile and ascend a hill. At the top, cross another stile and turn left into Church Hill. Continue along Cudham Lane and then retrace your steps back to the start.

POINTS OF INTEREST:

Down House – This was the home of Charles Darwin until his death in 1882. It now houses a Darwin Museum which is open on all afternoons except Mondays and Fridays. Fittingly, nearby Downe Bank is a Site of Special Scientific Interest.

REFRESHMENTS:

The George and Dragon Inn, Downe.
The Queens Head Inn, Downe.
The Blacksmiths Arms, Cudham.

Walk 23 UPCHURCH AND LOWER HALSTOW $4^1/_2$m ($7^1/_4$km)

Maps: OS Sheets Landranger 178; Pathfinder 1194.

A route around, and between, two villages, including riverside and open country walking.

Start: At 844675, the church at Upchurch.

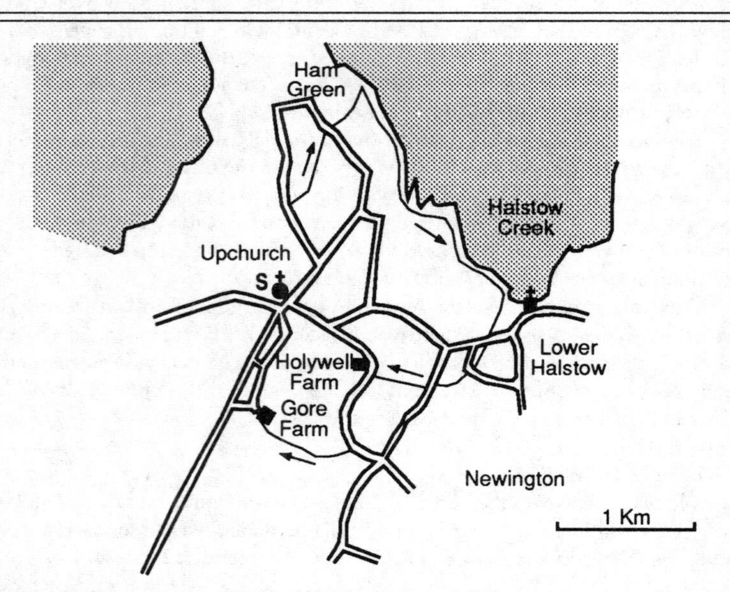

Parking is possible near the church, but please park tidily.

Leave **Upchurch**, heading north along the village road. Go past the village hall and a row of houses, and continue to reach Poot Lane on the left. Turn left along this for 250 yards to reach a stile on the right, marked with a waymarker for the **Saxon Shore Way**. Cross the stile and follow the waymarkers to reach a lane at Ham Green. Cross over and follow the track opposite that runs beside Ham Green Farm and continues to the shore of the Medway Estuary.

When you reach the water, turn right along a path, enjoying a pleasant riverside walk of about $1^1/_2$ miles with expansive views across to the Isle of Sheppey. Parts of this route can be quite muddy following inclement weather, but a through route is always possible. Eventually the path leads inland, following **Halstow** Creek, on your left. Follow the path to reach a road almost opposite the Three Tuns Inn. Cross over and follow a road between houses, then turn right along a footpath that runs behind the houses. Follow the path to reach a minor road.

Turn right, but very soon turn left along a footpath, following it when it bears right to reach a road near Westfield Cottages. Cross over and take a path along the right-hand edge of a field to reach a road at Holywell Farm. Turn left and follow the road, ignoring two paths that go off to the right. When the road forks, take the right-hand branch in the direction of **Gore Farm**. Follow a path through the farm buildings, which are open to the public, to reach a road.

Turn right and follow the road into Upchurch, taking care as it can be busy. At the cross-roads, cross over to return to the start.

POINTS OF INTEREST:

Upchurch – The fine medieval Church of St Mary the Virgin, is where Sir Francis Drake worshipped as a child.

Saxon Shore Way – This ancient long distance route was originally used by the Romans moving armies to defend against Saxon invaders. Today the 140 mile route from Gravesend to Rye is taken by more peaceful walkers.

Lower Halstow – The creek beyond the village is from where the Romans are said to have exported oysters and pottery. It offers excellent views across the Medway to Deadman's Island and Chetney Island.

Gore Farm – At the farm the various buildings have been converted to accommodate a variety of shops.

REFRESHMENTS:

The Three Tuns Inn, Lower Halstow.

The Crown, Upchurch.

Gore Farm Tea shop.

Walks 24 & 25 **ALLHALLOWS-ON-SEA** $4^1/_2$m ($7^1/_4$km) or $7^1/_2$m (12km)

Maps: OS Sheets Landranger 178; Pathfinder 1178.

A walk alongside the Thames Estuary and across marshland.

Start: At 841784, the centre of Allhallows-on-Sea.

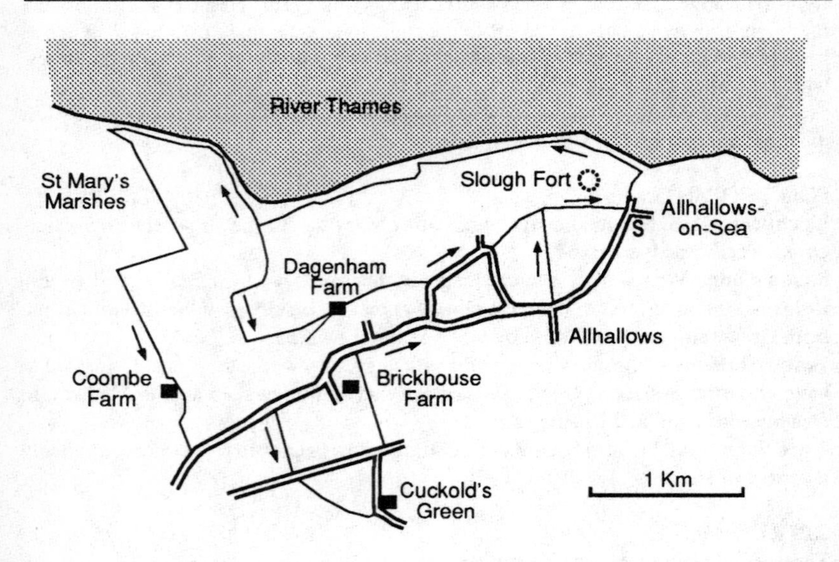

From the start point, continue north, through the chalets, and caravans to the river's edge. Turn left along the path that runs beside the **Thames Estuary**. From it there are expansive views across the river mouth towards Essex. Very soon, on the right, you will see some fine beaches, the reason why the village expanded as a holiday resort. Continue along the path for about $1^3/_4$ miles, to reach a path, on the left, that heads inland, away from the river.

The shorter route takes this path to the left. Go through a field, following the boundary on the left, and, at the field's end, turn right, still on the path. When the path divides, take the left branch, following it to the end of the field. Turn left and follow the field edge to the corner. There, go straight across the field ahead. Cross a track and maintain direction to reach Dagenham Farm. Go through the farm buildings and continue to reach a road, Homewards Road. Go ahead, along the road until it bears right. There, go straight on, following a path that leads past Slough Fort. Just before the fort, the longer route rejoins from the right.

The longer route takes the right-hand path, climbing on to the sea wall and following it as it bears around to the left. When another wall comes in from the left, between two ditches, turn on to this and head inland. When the wall ends, maintain direction to reach a junction of tracks. Turn right. At a corner of a field another path goes to the left: follow this down to Coombe Farm. Follow the farm drive to a road. Turn left. After about 500 yards a minor road joins from the left: take a path on the right here, following it to reach a road. Cross and follow the path opposite. This bears left, then continues to a point where another path joins from the right. Follow the single path, which very soon reaches a road. Turn left, passing Orchard House and Cuckold's Green to reach a T-junction. Turn right, then very soon turn left along a track heading northwards. Go past Brickhouse Farm, continuing to reach a road. Turn right and follow the road for $^3/_4$ mile, taking great care as it can be busy. When you reach the turning on the right for Allhallows, take the track on the left and follow it northwards. The track leads to a track junction where the shorter route is rejoined.

Turn right and follow the track past the entrance to **Slough Fort**. Continue along the track back to **Allhallows-on-Sea** and the start of the walk.

POINTS OF INTEREST:

Thames Estuary – Close to the mouth of Yantlett Creek, to the east of Allhallows-on-Sea, lies an obelisk which marks the limit of authority of the Port of London over the River Thames. Close by is an Elizabethan iron beacon erected when the possibility of invasion seemed very high.

Slough Fort – Excavations of this ancient fort have revealed Roman artefacts.

Allhallows-on-Sea – The creation of Allhallows-on-Sea followed the boom in seaside tourism, but the expected crowds did not materialise and the railway built to carry them was closed. The old track bed can still be seen, to the east of the village.

REFRESHMENTS:

The British Pilot, Allhallows.

The Rose and Crown, Allhallows.

The best idea on this route is to bring your own and enjoy a picnic somewhere along the way.

Walk 26 **OFFHAM** 4½m (7¼km)

Maps: OS Sheets Landranger 188; Pathfinder 1209.

A walk across open fields and through woodland.

Start: At 659574, at the eastern end of the village of Offham.

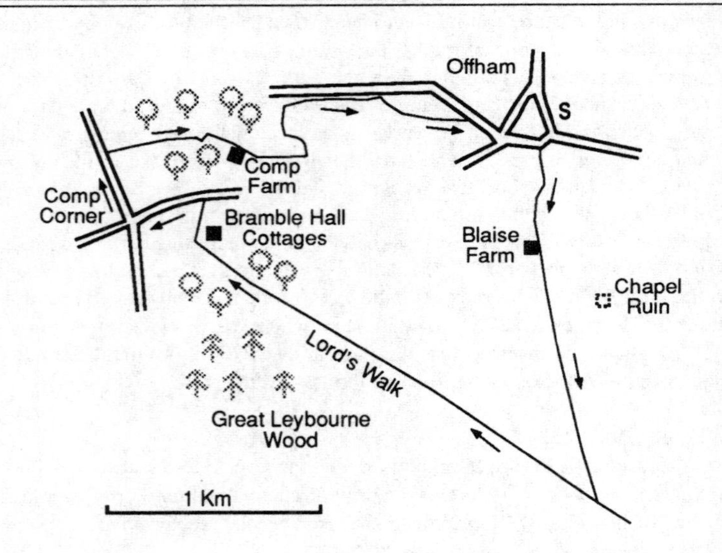

At the eastern end of Offham there is a T-junction. Head southwards from this, then soon, turn left along a track that heads due south, away from the village. Follow the track past Blaise Farm, maintaining direction to pass the remains of the Chapel of St Blaise, away to the left. Stay with the track, between fields, but when it takes a left turn, go straight ahead, following the right-hand boundary of a field.

When the path reaches woodland, do not follow it: instead, take the track, known as Lord's Walk, that goes very sharp right, follow it along the edge of Great Leybourne Wood. Eventually Lord's Walk leads into the woods. Follow it into orchards and through to Bramble Hall Cottages. Turn right to pass in front of the cottages, and continue to reach a road. Turn left and follow the road to the cross-roads at Comp Corner. Turn right along the road for about 400 yards, then go right along a signed footpath, following it across orchards and beside the buildings of Comp Farm.

Continue along the path to reach Hook Wood, following the wood's boundary as the path becomes a track. Continue along the track towards a road. Just before reaching the road the track turns right and runs parallel to the highway: stay with it, but go ahead along a path when the track bears right. Soon the path reaches a minor road on the right. Take this, and follow it as it skirts a quarry and turns left. The road becomes a path: continue along it to reach a road near **Offham.** Turn right at this road and follow it to a crossroads, where you go straight on. From here you can return to the start

POINTS OF INTEREST:
Offham – This village dates from Saxon times and derives its name from Offa. In 832AD, the village was presented to the Church by King Ethelwulf of Kent. On the village green, there is a quintain or tilting-post, the only remaining example in England. The device was used by knights in the days of jousting for practising with the lance. The pivot allowed the target to swing around when hit and so unseat an inexperienced knight. Each May Day the ancient usage is revived.

REFRESHMENTS:
The Red Lion, Offham.
The King's Arms, Offham.

Walk 27 **PATRIXBOURNE** $4^1/_2$m ($7^1/_4$km)

Maps: OS Sheets Landranger 189; Pathfinder 1211.

A walk from this pretty village on the outskirts of Canterbury through Kentish orchards.

Start: At 189552, Patrixbourne Church.

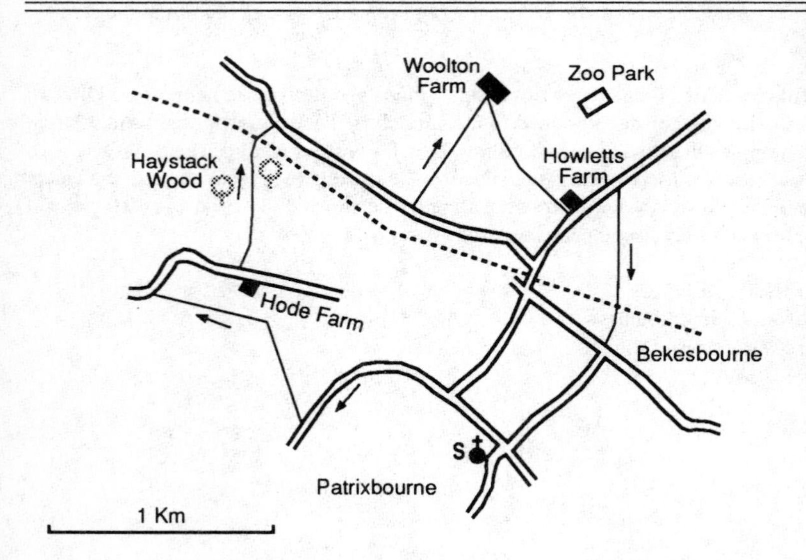

From the church turn left along the road to reach a cross-roads. Turn left and walk through the village of Patrixbourne to reach another cross-roads. Go straight across, following the road as it bears around to the left, and ignoring the North Downs Way which continues straight on from the bend. Continue along this small country road as it goes gently uphill. At the top of the slope, turn right through a gate and follow the path beyond across an orchard to reach the corner of a field, with the buildings of Hode Farm visible ahead.

Turn left and follow a new path through the orchard to reach a minor road. Turn right along this road, following it when it bears right towards Hode Farm. Just before you reach the front of the farm buildings, on your right, go left along a path that leads through more orchards and into Haystack Wood. Go through the wood, continuing beyond it to reach a railway line. Cross the line and bear right to reach a road. Turn right and follow the road for about $^1/_2$ mile, then go through a gate on the left and follow a track up to Woolton Farm. Just before reaching the farm buildings, turn sharp right along a path and follow it down to a track that runs alongside Howletts Farm and on to reach a road. On your left during this section of the walk, you can see the buildings of **Howletts Zoo**.

Turn left along the road. If you wish to visit the zoo park, follow the road to reach the main entrance, on the left. The walk does not go that far, turning right over the second of two stiles and following the path beyond diagonally right to reach the railway line again. Cross the railway and join a track that leads to the hamlet of **Bekesbourne**. When you reach the main village road, turn right, and then almost immediately left. The roads here effectively create a staggered cross-roads.

Follow the minor road back towards **Patrixbourne**. When you reach the next cross-roads go straight across to return to the village church where the walk began.

POINTS OF INTEREST:

Howletts Zoo – This is one of the two zoo parks in Kent owned by John Aspinall.

Bekesbourne – This hamlet was the site of an archbishop's palace, destroyed by the Roundheads during the Civil War. All that remains is the gatehouse, wherein Archbishop Cranmer took refuge following the death of Edward VI. More recently, Ian Fleming lived in the village and drew inspiration for many of his James Bond novels.

Patrixbourne – The mix of old and new houses in the village is a delight, a real success of rural planning. The church, where the walk starts, is in Perpendicular style. It is best known for its magnificent Norman doorway, under the tower, some exceptional carvings – look, especially, for those on the priest's door – and some fine 16th-century Swiss stained glass.

REFRESHMENTS:

None on the route, so bring your own or head for Littlebourne, to the north-east, or Canterbury itself.

Walk 28 **Lower Hardres and Pett Bottom** $4^1/_2$m ($7^1/_4$km)

Maps: OS Sheets Landranger 189; Pathfinder 1211.

A walk between rural hamlets, mainly on quiet country roads.

Start: At 151526, the Granville Inn, Lower Hardres.

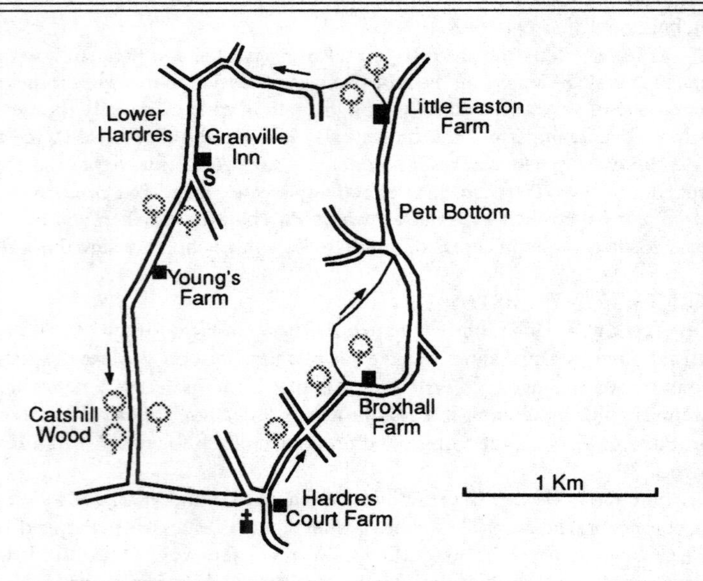

From the inn, turn left along the village street to reach a road fork. Take the right-hand branch, a minor road that, at first, leads through woodland, and then goes gradually uphill and past Young's Farm. Next, the road goes through Catshill Wood, another pleasant patch of woodland and continues to reach a T-junction. Turn left along a minor road signposted to Lower Hardres Court. The road goes gradually uphill, passing Bowhill Shaw, on the left, and then a road, also to the left. Now, just as the road bears right, at the corner of the churchyard on the right, turn left along a minor road running between houses.

Follow the road past the buildings of Hardres Court Farm, then alongside St Andrew's Wood, on your left, to reach a small cross-roads. Go straight across and continue along the road until it bears right in front of Broxhall Farm. At the point at which the road turns, turn left along a path, following it along the edge of Broxhall

Wood to reach the corner of a field. Cross a stile into the right-hand field and continue beside the left-hand boundary. Maintain direction as you cross two further fields, continuing to reach a road at a T-junction. Cross and follow the road opposite into Pett Bottom.

Go through the hamlet, passing the Duck Inn, and following the road as it runs between open fields to reach Little Easton Farm. There, turn left along a track that runs between the farm buildings. When the track divides three ways, turn left along a path which runs alongside Whitehill Wood. Turn left with the path as it follows the boundary of the wood, and then, very soon, cross on to a path on the right which leads into the woods.

Follow this path through the woods for only a short distance to reach a road at a point where it bends. Turn right and follow the road, with woods on your right, as it goes gradually downhill. Ignore the farm road, on the right, for North Court Farm, bearing left with the road as it leads into **Lower Hardres**. Go past the school to reach the main village street. Turn left along this to retrace your steps back to the start of the walk.

POINTS OF INTEREST:

Lower Hardres – The village stands close to the top of the North Downs, one of the two sections of Downland which define the county of Kent. The chalk uplands of the North Downs end dramatically at Dover, where the chalk creates the famous white cliffs.

REFRESHMENTS:

The Granville Inn, Lower Hardres.
The Duck Inn, Pett Bottom.

Walk 29 **TENTERDEN** $4^1/_2$m ($7^1/_4$km)

Maps: OS Sheets Landranger 189; Pathfinder 1250.

A short, pleasant walk around the fine wealden town, a corporate member of the Cinque Ports.

Start: At 884334, St Mildred's Church, Tenterden.

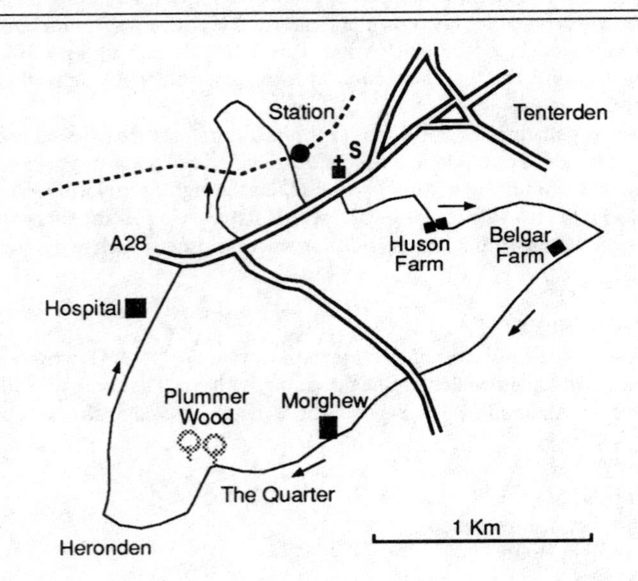

From the churchyard of St Mildred's, go on to the main road (the A28) throug Tenterden. Cross, with care, and take the path opposite, following it between buildings Now take a path to the left, following it past a school, with the leisure centre opposite to reach a track. Turn right and follow the track to reach the entrance to Huson Farm on the left. Turn left here and follow the track as it eventually reduces to a path, the runs to the rear of a built up area and finally reaches a junction with another track.

Turn right and follow the track past Belgar Farm, continuing to reach a road. G straight across and along a path that goes through a field to reach a gate in its fa boundary. Go through into the next field. Continue past a pond, on your right, an then the buildings of Morghew, ignoring the turning off to the right. Maintain directio as the path becomes a track, continuing past an area known as The Quarter. Follo the track across country, passing the southern end of a patch of woodland, Plummer Wood. The track then curves slightly, going very gently downhill and then bears right to reach Heronden.

Just past Heronden, turn right along a path, following it uphill. Cross a ditch and then go past Plummer Farm. Maintain direction along the path to pass the rear of Westwell Hospital. Continue on when another path joins from the left, going on to join the drive that leads to the hospital. Eventually you will reach a junction of tracks. Turn right, very soon reaching a road. Here, you again turn right. Cross and follow the road in the direction of **Tenterden**. Go past a road on the right, signed to Smallhythe, then turn left along a path that runs between some of the fine houses in this part of the town.

The path leads to a track: follow this to the railway line of the **Kent and East Sussex Railway**, one of the few private railway lines in existence in Kent. Cross the railway and follow the path to reach another path going off to the right. Take this path, soon joining a paved track that runs past Pittlesden Manor Farm and on to the private railway's station. Here, cross the line again, and follow the path as it leads back into Tenterden. When you reach the main road, turn right and retrace your steps to St Mildred's church and the start of the walk.

POINTS OF INTEREST:

Tenterden – This charming Cinque Ports town is often referred to as the capital of the Weald. There is much to see in the town, with highlights being St Mildred's Church, the town museum and the Kent and East Sussex Railway. The church dates from the 15th century and is over 100 feet high. The town is the probable birthplace of William Caxton, the original printer.

Kent and East Sussex Railway – A privately run service that operates steam trains down the Rother Valley, from Tenterden. The service runs from Easter onwards, mainly at weekends.

REFRESHMENTS:

Every taste is catered for in Tenterden.

Walk 30 KENARDINGTON AND WAREHORNE $4^1/_2$m ($7^1/_4$km)

Maps: OS Sheets Landranger 189; Pathfinder 1250.

A walk between two villages, through woodland and beside the Royal Military Canal.

Start: At 989325, Warehorne Church.

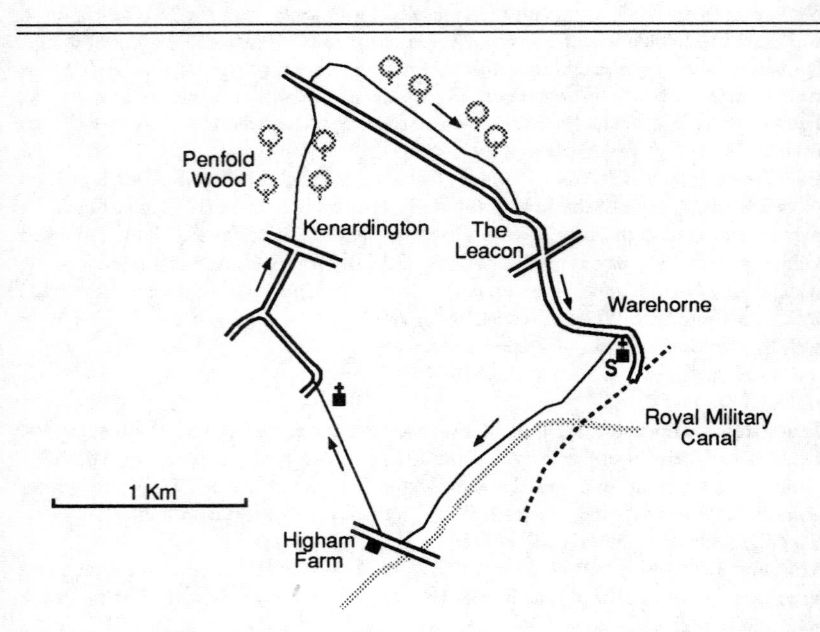

Go into the churchyard at Warehorne and walk to its rear. Now go along a footpath that immediately divides. Take the right-hand branch and follow it as it passes the buildings of Tinton Manor Farm, on your right. Cross a field boundary and continue to reach the **Royal Military Canal**. Turn right along the track that runs beside the canal, following it for nearly a mile to reach a road crossing both the track and the canal. Turn right along this road, heading away from the canal. Just past the entrance to Higham Farm, on your left, turn right over a signed stile and follow the path beyond which heads slightly diagonally to the right through a field to reach Kenardington church, which stands about a mile outside the village.

Maintain direction along the path as it goes past the church, out of the churchyard and through a field to reach a road at a bend. Turn right and follow the road as it bears to the left. Stay with the road to reach a T-junction. Turn right and walk into Kenardington, going past farms on either side to reach another T-junction. Cross, turn left, then almost immediately right along a signed footpath. The path initially follows the left-hand boundary of a field, then goes across the corner to reach a patch of woodland, Penfold Wood. Now maintain direction, following the path as it goes through the wood to reach a road. Cross and follow another path that leads diagonally to the right. Ignore various paths that lead away to reach the edge of another patch of woods. Here, turn right and follow a path that runs along the woodland boundary for about 800 yards. The path then moves away from the woods to follow the boundary of a field to reach a road.

Turn left and walk to a cross-roads at The Leacon. Take the road directly opposite, signed for Warehorne, and follow it as it leads back into the village. Go past the Post Office and the Woolpack Inn before reaching the church and the start of the walk.

POINTS OF INTEREST:

Royal Military Canal – The canal was built during the Napoleonic Wars as both a defence and to transport troops and supplies. Some areas of the canal are now being renovated and the whole is increasingly a haven for many species of water birds. Beyond the Canal lies Romney Marsh, a huge expanse of flat marshland that has been turned into grazing land by the excavation of a vast array of dykes.

REFRESHMENTS:

The Woolpack Inn, Warehorne.
The Worlds Wonder Inn, Warehorne.

Walk 31 **Otford** 5m (8km)

Maps: OS Sheets Landranger 188; Pathfinder 1208.

A walk through and around the ancient village of Otford, including some steep hill walking, but with excellent views.

Start: At 525593, the car park in High Street, Otford.

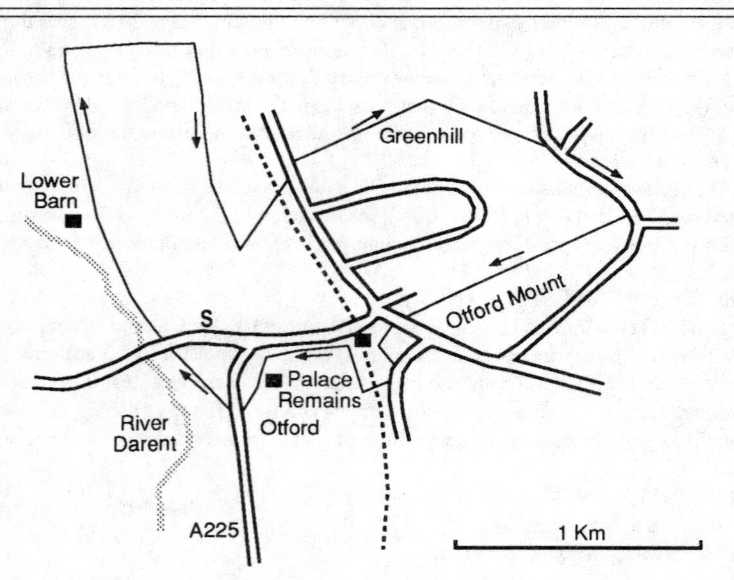

From the car park in **Otford**, turn right along High Street and walk past the Horns Inn. Here, the Darent Valley Path is marked by a yellow arrow: turn right along it, following the bank of the River Darent to pass Little Oast. Continue along the path, passing Lower Barn and going through a golf course to reach a made-up road. Turn right, uphill, for about 200 yards to reach a footpath, on the right, by a stone marker. At this point you leave the **Darent Valley Path** which goes up to the left.

Follow the path back through the golf course, cross a stile and walk down the right-hand side of the field beyond. Go over another stile and continue towards a barn, Just before reaching it, turn left along a footpath, going diagonally across a field to reach a railway line. Cross, with great care, by means of stiles to reach a narrow path. Follow it to reach Shoreham Road, the A225. Cross, with care, and turn left along it to soon reach a stile, on the right, leading to a footpath. Take this, rising quite steeply between fields and meadows to reach woodland at the top of Greenhill.

Follow the path into the wood to reach a path fork. Take the right-hand branch, continuing through the woods to reach open grassland. Now go left, uphill, along the edge of the wood. Cross a stile and the field beyond, by the TV mast. Go over another stile back into woodland and pass a farm to reach a made-up road. Turn right, passing Paine's Farm, on the right, and Mount Farm, on the left. Now turn right along a footpath which goes through further woodland and across the corner of a field to join the North Downs Way.

Follow the Way down wooden steps to reach the Pilgrim's Way. Cross this and turn right, then left into Chalk Pit. Follow the path around a playing field and then bear right to reach a road. Turn left and follow the path to its conclusion. Now turn right for about 20 yards, and then right again on to another footpath. Cross the railway line, again with great care, and again by means of stiles. After crossing the second stile turn right to reach a T-junction. Turn left, heading away from the railway station.

Go through the churchyard to reach the War Memorial and a pond. Turn left towards the remains of **Otford Palace**, and then right again into Palace Field. At the end of the path, cross the road and turn left. Now take the footpath on the right, following it back to the High Street. From there, retrace your steps back to the start.

POINTS OF INTEREST:

Otford – This village, clustered around its duck pond, has many historical connections. Roman remains have been found in profusion, Henry VIII camped here with one of his Queens and 5,000 followers and D H Lawrence visited the wife of the poet Edward Thomas.

Darent Valley Path – The Memorial Chalk Cross at Shoreham can be seen from this section of the Walk.

Otford Palace – The Palace, of which only these few remains survive, is said to have been offered to Henry VIII by Archbishop Cranmer. Ever the gracious King, Henry turned it down because it was too damp!

REFRESHMENTS:

The King's Arms, Otford.
The Crown Inn, Otford.
The Horns Inn, Otford.

Walk 32 **SPELDHURST** 5m (8km

Maps: OS Sheets Landranger 188; Pathfinder 1228.

A pleasant walk around this attractive village, with some fairl gentle ascents.

Start: At 554415, Speldhurst village hall car park.

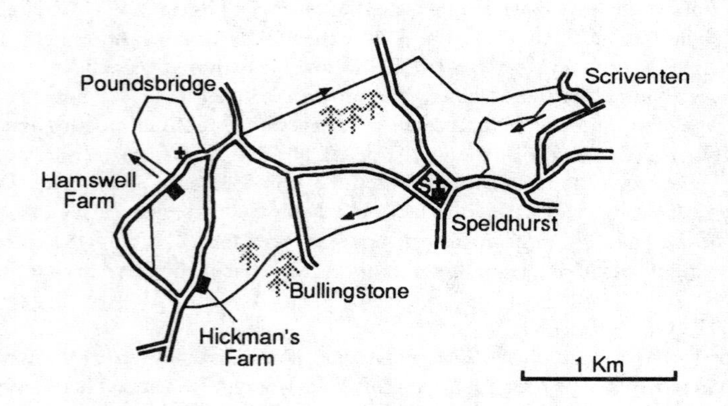

From the car park go into St Mary's Lane and follow it to Northfields Road. Tur right to the junction with Penshurst Road. Turn left and after about 50 yards, take th signed footpath on the right. Follow the path across open fields, continuing along i when it becomes enclosed to reach a road. Turn right, then left beside Old Bullingstone Keep right at a fork and cross a footbridge. The path beyond goes uphill, then level off: cross a stile in a fence, with a house on your right, and continue to reach anothe stile. Go over to reach a road.

Cross to the turning opposite, and when the road bears left, go right through gate. Soon, bear diagonally left across a field and go through another gate. Go over stile in a hedge and cross the next field to reach another stile about 50 yards left of th farm buildings. When you reach the road, turn right, go past Hamswell Farm and the take the signed footpath on the left, crossing a stile into a field. Keep to the right, going around the field edge. Soon the River Medway will appear on your left: cross a stile into the next field and continue beside the river to reach a footbridge. Do not cross; instead, turn right, away from the river. Go through a gate and bear right along a track to the far left-hand corner. Go through another gate and continue to a road. Poundsbridge Church is on your right.

Turn left to a junction, and turn left again. Continue to the next junction and turn right past a half-timbered house. Now go left over a stile into a field and walk with the hedgerow on your right. Cross a series of stiles as you go through fields for about $^3/_4$ mile to reach a road. Turn left, and almost immediately right along a signed path, going past a house. This surfaced track bears right, with a stream on the left, and leads across a bridge and up to a farm area. Go over a stile by a gate and continue to another stile on the left beyond a footpath sign on a tree. Cross and continue to another stile. Cross and bear left to yet another stile which leads to a road.

Turn right, and just after the lodge of Scriventon, turn right up some steps to reach a stile. Cross and continue with the hedge on your right. Cross two further stiles and then turn left along a lane. Turn right along a footpath between trees, and cross a footbridge into a field. Turn right and walk around the field edge to a reach a stile. Cross and turn left along a concrete drive, following it until it turns right. There, cross a stile on the left, and bear right to reach another stile on to a road.

Turn right and go up into Speldhurst, passing **St Mary's Church** on the left. Follow Penshurst Road, then turn right into Northfields Road to return to the start.

POINTS OF INTEREST:

St Mary's Church, Speldhurst – Within the church there are some remains of the original 14th-century building, although the present building is Victorian. The excellent stained glass windows are by the pre-Raphaelite artist Burne-Jones.

REFRESHMENTS:

The George & Dragon, Speldhurst.

Walk 33 **OARE AND FAVERSHAM** 5m (8km

Maps: OS Sheets Landranger 178; Pathfinder 1195.

A walk following the shores of two creeks and on public road through part of Faversham.

Start: At 006629, street parking in Oare.

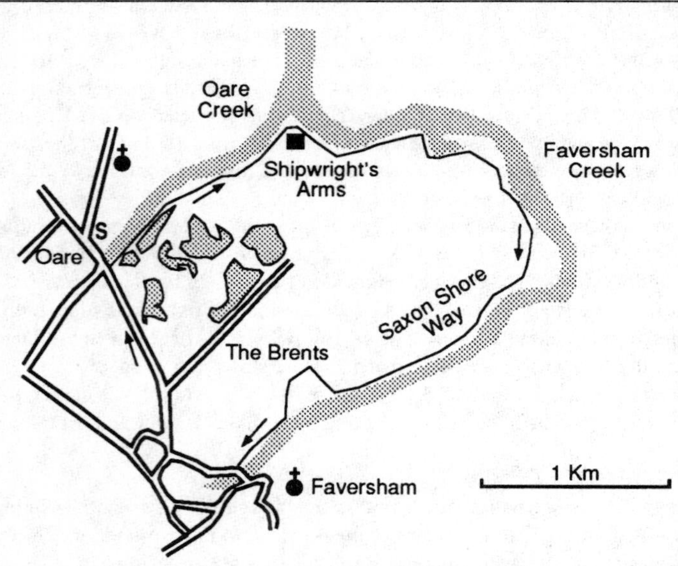

From Oare follow the road back towards Faversham to reach a cross-roads by the hea of Oare Creek, an inlet of the River Swale. Turn left and continue by the side of th creek. When the road goes to the right, cross to a signed footpath on the left whic follows the creek's shoreline. This is part of the **Saxon Shore Way**.

Follow the route along the shore, going past the Shipwright's Arms, where th creek becomes Faversham Creek. Continue for a pleasant walk of about 2 miles following this waterside path, with open country to your right to reach the outskirts o Faversham. Now go around the edge of a factory to reach its entrance. There, take footpath to the right to reach a footbridge. Cross the bridge to return to the edge of th creek.

At the southern end of the creek the road reaches a junction: cross the bridge on the left and follow the road into the centre of **Faversham**. Here you may choose to explore the central part of the town, from where you can rejoin the road for Oare at several places. If you prefer to return immediately, then when the road reaches a junction, with a church opposite, turn right and follow the road back to the start.

POINTS OF INTEREST:

Saxon Shore Way – This ancient long distance route was originally used by the Romans moving armies to defend against Saxon invaders. Today the 140 mile route from Gravesend to Rye is taken by more peaceful walkers.

Faversham – This is an ancient town, both the Romans and the Saxons having had settlements here. From its later, medieval, period the town boasts the largest collection of charters of any town in Britain. The centre of the town has retained many of its old buildings, a number being of considerable architectural interest. The Church of St Mary of Charity is in Early English style, while the Masonic Lodge, once the town's Grammar School, is Tudor. Perhaps the finest collection of fine old buildings is in Market Place, many of them dating from Tudor and Stuart times.

REFRESHMENTS:

The Shipwright's Arms, on the route.
There are various inns and cafés in Faversham.

Walk 34 **KEMSING** 5m (8km

Maps: OS Sheets Landranger 188; Pathfinder 1208 and 1192.

Moderately easy walk crossing parts of the North Downs.

Start: At 555587, Kemsing village car park, behind th
Wheatsheaf Inn.

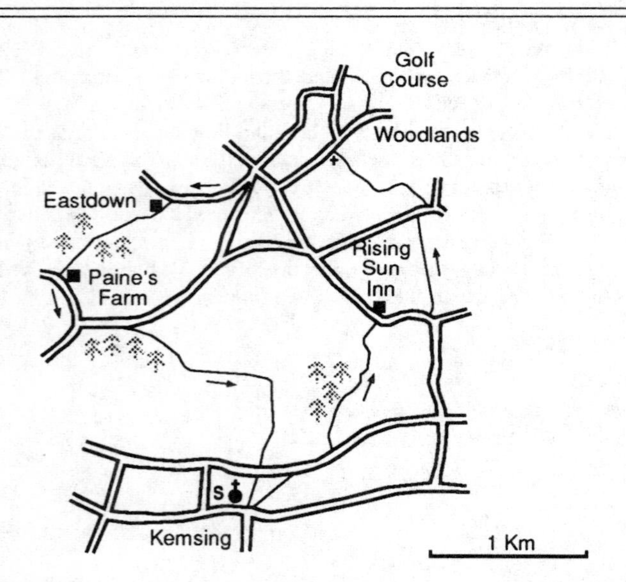

Leave the car park and go left along the High Street, then left again into Church Lane When you reach the churchyard, go right and diagonally across the recreation groun opposite. Go along the top boundary, walking parallel to the road, on a path tha becomes enclosed and leads to the road. Turn right along the road until you reach house called Woodlea.

Turn left here, along a signed footpath going uphill. Cross a stile and, as th hillside opens up, bear diagonally left and cross two more stiles. Now bear right uphill, and cross another stile in a corner. Turn right along a path, following it to stile. Cross, turn left and head for another stile in the corner of the field. Cross and keeping the hedgerow on your right, continue to reach a road opposite the Rising Su Inn.

Turn right and follow the road to a point just before a junction. There, opposite a building, go left over a stile and follow the signed footpath beyond into woods. Go through the woods and cross a golf course fairway to reach a stile. Cross and follow the hedge to the right to reach a road by the church at Woodlands. Turn right, and very soon left over a stile. Cross a field with trees on the right, cross a stile and go left, with the fence on your left, to reach some trees. Bear right across another fairway and continue with trees on your right. When the trees bear away to the right, keep ahead along a fairway, heading for the corner of woodland. Go down to a stile and cross on to a lane.

Turn left to a junction. Turn right along a road to a cross-roads. Turn left, then go right at a fork. Now follow the road to reach the house called Eastdown. There, turn left over a stile, then go right, behind the house. Go diagonally across a field to reach a stile in the corner. Cross and go through woods to reach the open hillside. Go down and slightly left to reach a stile into woods. Go through the woods, then follow the fence on your left, crossing several stiles, to reach a road.

Turn left past Paine's Farm, and at a junction go left again, but soon cross a stile on the right on to a section of the **North Downs Way**. Follow the Way to a drive and turn right. Now go left through the gates of Otford Manor and follow the drive to reach a stile on the left. Cross, bear right and walk parallel to the drive as far as a stile on the left. Cross into a field and go diagonally to reach a stile in a fence. Cross and turn right. When you reach a telegraph pole, veer left, cross a stile and follow a hedged path. Now go downhill along a narrow path which leads to open hillside.

Turn left on a path which leads to a grassy slope and bear right there to walk downhill to a gate. Turn left, and at the next gate go right and down to a road. Cross to the footpath opposite and bear left to go down to the recreation ground. Bear right through the churchyard to reach a path, following it to an opening into the car park where the walk began.

POINTS OF INTEREST:

North Downs Way – This was Britain's eleventh long distance footpath – now called National Trails – opening in 1978. It is 141 miles long and links Farnham to Dover.

REFRESHMENTS:

The Rising Sun Inn, on the route.

There are also several possibilities in Kemsing.

Walk 35 **BISHOPSBOURNE** 5m (8km)

Maps: OS Sheets Landranger 189; Pathfinder 1211.

A gently sloping walk mainly on quiet country roads.

Start: At 188526, Bishopsbourne Church.

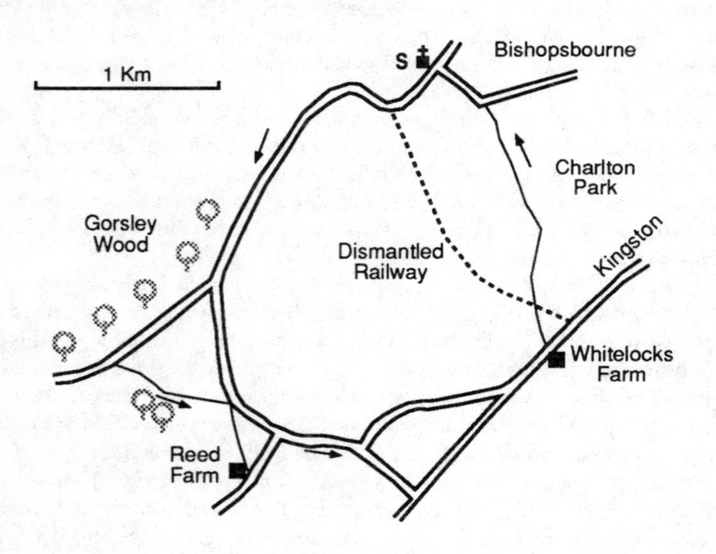

There is on-street parking near the church, but please park tidily.

Turn right from Bishopsbourne church and follow the road as it crosses a dismantled railway. Once across the railway the road turns right, then, soon after, left: continue along it to reach a fork. Take the right-hand branch, following the road as it runs alongside Gorsley Wood, on the right. After about $^1/_2$ mile, turn left along a signed path that, initially, has a clump of woodland on the left. Follow the path across a field, now with woodland on the right.

Continue along the path as it bears left and away from the woodland. Cross two fields separated by stiles and continue to reach a road. Do not join the road: instead, turn right along an extension of the path. Cross into another field and, almost immediately, cross over into another. Now follow a lesser path to reach the buildings of Reed Farm. Go through the farm to reach a road. Turn left and walk to a T-junction. Turn right and follow the road as it bears left, then right. Take the first turning on the left, and go along this new road, with an orchard on the right. Eventually the road meets another coming from the right. Bear left and follow the road to the outskirts of Kingston.

When you reach the entrance to Whitelocks Farm, on the right, turn left along a path between houses. Follow the path as it goes very gradually downhill and then crosses the dismantled railway crossed earlier in the walk. Once over the railway, head diagonally left to the far corner of a field to reach a stile. Cross and turn right. Very soon you join a more substantial footpath. Now turn left over a stile into the grounds of Charlton Park.

Follow the path beyond the stile across the parkland to join a track. Maintain direction along the track, following it into **Bishopsbourne** to emerge on the main village road near the Post Office. Turn left to reach a T-junction. Turn left again to reach the church where the walk began.

POINTS OF INTEREST:

Bishopsbourne – The village church is an intriguing place with some interesting 17th-century Flemish glass in the south chapel. Oswalds, the old rectory to the north-east of the church, was the home of Joseph Conrad, the novelist, from 1919 until his death in 1924. In an earlier rectory, the Reverend Richard Hooker lived, and wrote his monumental work *Ecclesiastical Polity*. He was offered the living at Bishopsbourne by Queen Elizsabeth I in order that he could concentrate on his writing.

REFRESHMENTS:

The Mermaid, Bishopsbourne.

Walk 36 **Challock and Molash** 5m (8km)

Maps: OS Sheets Landranger 189; Pathfinder 1211.

A walk through farmland and forest.

Start: At 012508, the Halfway House Inn, Challock.

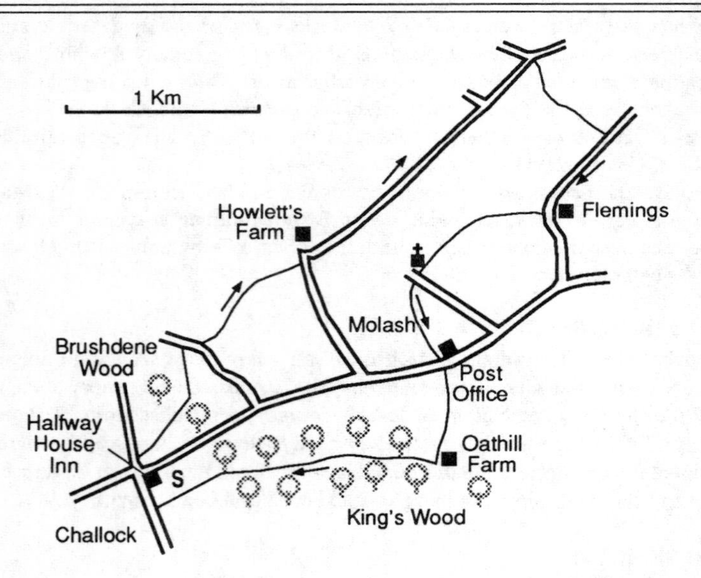

Leave the inn car park and turn left along the road, soon reaching a cross-roads. Turn right here, very carefully, as this is the main Faversham to Ashford road (the A251) and can be busy. At the end of the used car lot, turn right along the signed footpath and follow it into Brushdane Wood. Stay on the path as it goes gently downhill and then bears left to emerge from the wood into an orchard. Maintain direction, following the path as it heads for the far corner of the orchard to reach a road. Turn right, but very soon turn left along a track that runs through another orchard.

This track meets the boundary of a field on your right: follow this for a short while until it bears right. There, bear left and then follow the path to the right and cross into a field. Follow the field's left-hand boundary to reach a road. Turn left and when the road goes right, close to Howlett's Farm, go with it, staying with it for just over a mile as it goes gently downhill. When the road reach a T-junction, turn sharp right and go diagonally between the two roads along a path that runs alongside the left-hand edge of a field to reach a stile on the left. Cross the stile into another field. Go diagonally across the field, heading for the right-hand side of the buildings at Little Bower, to reach a road.

Turn right, along the road to reach Flemings, on your left. At the end of the house, turn right along a path, following it along the left edge of a field. When the field edge bears left, stay with it. Maintain direction at the end of the boundary to walk uphill into another field. Walk along the right-hand boundary of this field, eventually entering the churchyard of **Molash Church**. Walk through the churchyard and out on to a road. Turn right, and almost immediately left along a track. After a few yards go through a gate on the left into an orchard. Head diagonally through the orchard, then go past buildings to reach a road (the A252) near Molash Post Office.

Cross the road, with great care, and go along the track opposite, following it past the War Memorial. Continue to reach a junction of tracks at Oathill Farm. Turn right, soon reaching **King's Wood**, where the track becomes a forest path. There are many paths leading into the woods, all of them enabling you to explore this delightful stretch of woodland. However, this walk maintains direction, staying on the same path for about $^3/_4$ mile. When you emerge from the woods, continue along a field edge until it turns left. There, continue straight on to reach the junction of two fields. Cross a stile into the right-hand field and follow its left-hand boundary to reach a gate. Go through a gate on to the main road. Turn right, with great care, and you will very soon arrive back at the Halfway House Inn at Challock.

POINTS OF INTEREST:
Molash Church – Although much restored, there is enough medieval work left here to make an exploration worthwhile.
King's Wood – This extensive area of woodland is a delight. The lucky, or very patient, visitor may encounter deer.

REFRESHMENTS:
The Halfway House Inn, Challock.
The George Inn, Molash.
A good alternative would be to take a picnic and enjoy it in King's Wood.

Walk 37 **WESTWELL** 5m (8km)

Maps: OS Sheets Landranger 189; Pathfinder 1230.

A walk from the village across wooded Downland.

Start: At 991475, Westwell Church.

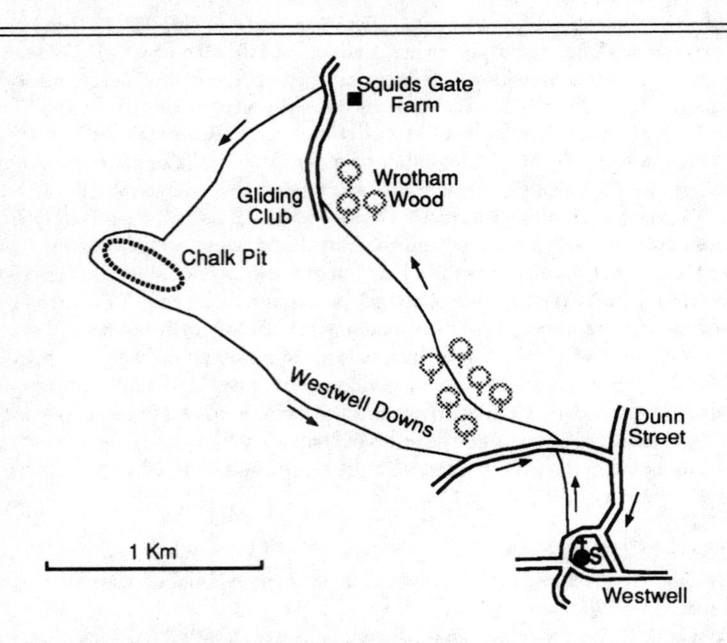

Turn right from the church and very soon you will reach a cross-roads. Turn right and walk along the road until it bears right. There, take the path that runs along the left-hand side of a row of houses. Continue uphill to reach a road. Go straight across and follow the path opposite. Very soon the path forks: take the left-hand branch following it as it leads on to **Westwell Down** and into woodland. The path bears diagonally right, then emerges from the woods into a field. Aim towards the far right corner, going over a stile there into another field. Now maintain direction, going uphill through two more fields, then entering another patch of woodland.

Go through the woodland, Wrotham Wood, and when you emerge walk, at first parallel to a minor road. Next, leave the path to join the road, continuing along it to reach the entrance to Squids Gate Farm. Now, as the road bears away to the right, go left along a byway that runs along the boundary of a large band of woods. To your left is a gliding club, and you may sometimes see aircraft floating above. When you reach the end of the woodland, your route bears left, around the edge of a chalk pit. Continue past the works for this pit, on your right.

Follow the byway/road downhill towards Westwell. Go past the first turning on the left, staying with the road as it bears left and, eventually, reaches a T-junction. Turn right, go past Westwell Court and retrace your steps back to the **church** and the start of the walk.

POINTS OF INTEREST:

Westwell Down – This is an extensive stretch of wooded downland, offering excellent views. The Down is traversed by the North Downs Way – the route past the chalk pit follows the line of the National Trail – and it is easy to see why the chalk ridges were such a popular route. With the lack of tree cover – at least, in comparison to the densely forested Weald at the foot of the Downs – the ridge was easier, safer and more direct.

Westwell – This Downland village has two greens, one beside the pub, the other by the church.This latter building has some work from the 13th century remaining despite the attempts of the restorers, including a Jesse window and a stone vaulted chancel.

The village also has a very pretty windmill and a mill-pond that goes right up to the houses around it.

REFRESHMENTS:

The Wheel Inn, Westwell.

Walk 38 **Bethersden** 5m (8km

Maps: OS Sheets Landranger 189; Pathfinder 1230.

A straightforward walk through farmland.

Start: At 928403, Bethersden Church.

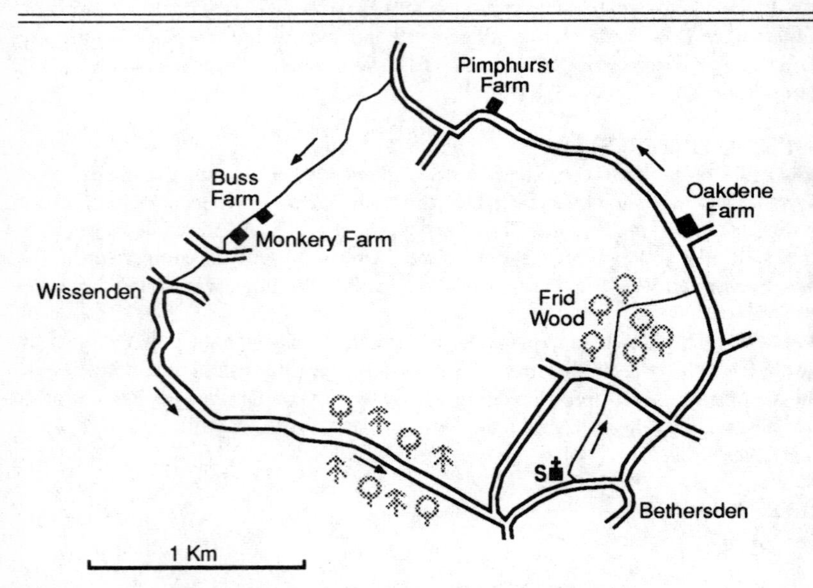

Take the path on the left-hand side of the church. The path very soon divides: take th right-hand branch and cross into a field. Go through the heart of the field, continuin through the buildings of a saw mill to a road. Turn left, and almost immediately tur right on to a track that leads into Frid Wood. When the track emerges from the wood stay with it, bearing right to walk alongside another part of the same woodland. Th track becomes a path: continue along it to reach a fork. Take the right-hand branch following it to a gap in the field boundary. Go through into the next field and cross t reach a road.

Turn left, following the road to a junction near Oakmead Farm. Go straight o (heading north-westwards), soon passing the drive to Frid Farm, on the left. Continu along the road, a most pleasant route, with open farmland on either side. Go pas Pimphurst Farm, on the right, continuing along the road as it bears left to reach junction. Ignore the turning to the left, continuing to reach a row of houses, also on the left. Now take the track that runs beside the houses. At the end of the track, cross on to a path. Follow the path across a field to reach a stile in the boundary ahead. Cross and follow the left-hand boundary of the next field. Cross into the next field near a pond. Go past the pond and then walk through the buildings of Buss Farm. Continue through Monkery Farm to reach a road.

Turn right along the road, but when it turns sharp right, maintain direction along a path that leads through fields to Wissenden. The path reaches the road in Wissenden at a T-junction. Go directly ahead, following the road past several farm entrances and into a substantial piece of woodland, the woods being on both sides of the road. The road leads back towards **Bethersden**: go past a turning on the left, continuing to reach a T-junction. Turn left and follow the road through the village to return to church.

POINTS OF INTEREST:

Bethersden – The village is famous for its marble quarries. From these, stone was taken for the construction of Canterbury and Rochester Cathedrals. Although now mainly restored, the village church has retained its fine 15th-century tower. The Stevenson brothers Rocking Horse workshop in the village offers demonstrations of this fascinating craft. Horses from the village have found their way to nurseries and fun-fairs all around the world.

REFRESHMENTS:

The Bull Inn, Bethersden.
The George, Bethersden.

Walks 39 & 40 **HOTHFIELD** 5m (8km) or 8m ($12^3/_4$km)

Maps: OS Sheets Landranger 189; Pathfinder 1230.

Walks across open countryside around this village, mainly on quiet country roads.

Start: At 971451, the Thanet Arms, Hothfield.

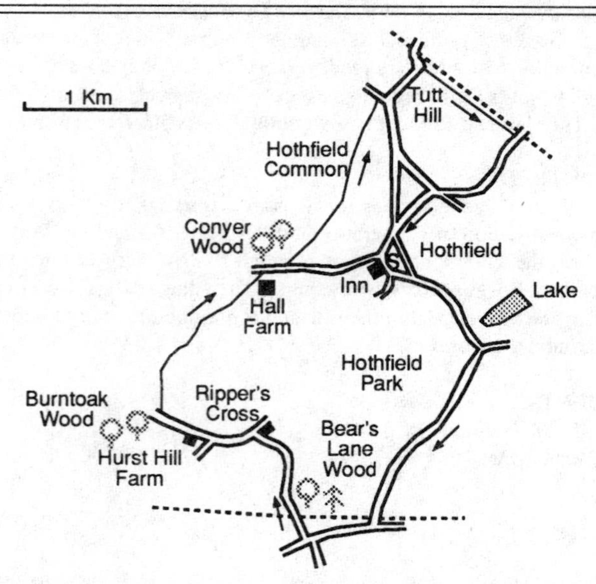

From the Thanet Arms, turn right and follow the road through Hothfield. When the road forks, take the lesser turning on the left. Go past the Post Office, continuing along the road, Waterfall Road, as it leads away from the village. Go past a path into the woodland of **Hothfield Park**, on the right, then cross a stream. Go past a lake and a small waterfall, on your right. Soon after, you reach a turning on the right, take this, following the road past West Lodge and Worten Home Farm. Continue along the road to go over the railway line, and, almost immediately, to reach a T-junction.

Turn right and walk along the road, going past a turning on the left. Soon after, turn right, opposite the entrance to Bridge Farm, on to another minor road that recrosses the railway line. Continue along the road, Bear's Lane, with Bear's Lane Wood on your right-hand side. The road bears around to the left and then reaches the junction at Ripper's Cross. Turn left and follow the road to a fork. Take the right-hand branch, following the road past Hurst Hill Farm, on the left. A little further on, Burntoak Wood begins on your left: turn right there, along a byway. Follow the byway as it goes gently downhill, going past a small patch of woodland on the left, then past the pond called Egg Hole and crossing the River Stour. Go through the buildings of Hall Farm, continuing to a gate. Go through this on to a road. Turn left towards Hothfield.

The shorter walk continues along the road, with Conyer Wood on the left, to reach a fork, with, on the left, a school, and beyond it, Hothfield Common. Take the right-hand branch, following it back to the Thanet Arms.

The longer route crosses the road and takes a path that begins just to the right of Conyer Wood. Follow the path through the centre of the field to reach the far boundary. Go through a gate into the next field and maintain direction, staying with the path as it heads on to **Hothfield Common**. The path is now signed as part of the Greensand Way: continue along it until another path crosses. Here, the Greensand Way goes left. Do not follow it: instead, stay on your path, following it across the Common, passing Froghole Toll and Butler's Toll to reach a road (the A20) opposite the hamlet of Tutt Hill. Cross, with great care, turn right briefly and take the first turning on the left. Follow the road to the railway line. Do not cross: instead, go right to join a path that runs parallel to the railway for some distance. When you reach the next road, turn right and follow it back to the main road. Cross, again with great care, and follow the road opposite towards Hothfield. At the next junction, with a school on the right, you rejoin the shorter route. Turn left to return to the Thanet Arms and the start of the walk.

POINTS OF INTEREST:

Hothfield Park – Within the Park is the village's 13th-century church. It holds the magnificent tomb of Sir John Tufton who was responsible for rebuilding part of the church after it had been partially destroyed by lightning in 1598.

Hothfield Common – This managed area of 250 acres of open land and woodland is a Nature Reserve, preserving the flora and fauna of this unique greensand area of the Vale of Kent, which lies between the North Downs and the Weald.

REFRESHMENTS:

The Thanet Arms, Hothfield.

Almost as good would be to take a picnic and to stop on Hothfield Common.

Walks 41 & 42 **East Peckham and Beltring** 5m (8km) or $9^1/_2$m (15km)

Maps: OS Sheets Landranger 188; Pathfinder 1229.

A choice of walks between two villages, partially alongside the River Medway.

Start: At 662488, the Addlestead Tavern, East Peckham.

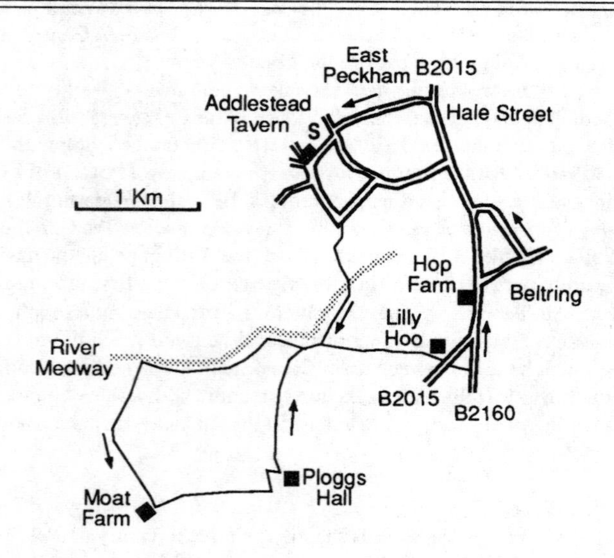

From the tavern, head southwards, almost immediately reaching a cross-roads. Continue straight on, following the road out of East Peckham and down to Snoll Hatch. When the road turns left, continue straight on along a track that goes between the houses ahead. The track now bears right and continues to a bridge over the **River Medway**. Cross the bridge, staying with the track as it goes around to the left. Now walk along the riverside tow path for nearly $^1/_2$ mile before joining another track that turns sharply to the left.

The shorter walk follows this track away from the river. Maintain direction, ignoring all paths leading off in either direction. The track goes past Lilly Hoo, and soon after reaches a road (the B2015). Cross, with care, and continue along a track that leads to another road (the B2160). Turn left along this road, following it with great care as it can be very busy. Go ahead at a road junction – where the B2015 joins from the left – and continue past the **Whitbread Hop Farm**, on your left. Continue to reach a turning to Beltring on the left. Take this road (Beltring Road), following it through the tiny hamlet. Just after the last of the houses, turn left along a road that leads back to the main B2015, reaching it opposite an industrial estate. Turn right and follow the road, again with great care, as it goes through the west side of East Peckham and continues up to Hale Street. Go past Arnold's Lodge Farm, then go left, at the next road turning, along Church Lane. Follow this road to reach a T-junction. Turn left, then soon after turn right and follow the road back to the Addlestead Tavern and the start of the walk.

The longer walk continues along the riverside path for another mile to reach Ford Green Bridge. Here, turn left and head away from the river along a path that leads across a dike. Continue to reach a crossing of paths at Hammer Dyke. Take the left-hand path, following it through several fields to reach the rear of the buildings of Moat Farm. Now find a path that leads away to the left and follow it as it leads to, and over, the far boundary of the field. Continue through two more fields, then, just after crossing into a third field, turn right, then left to reach Ploggs Hall. Go to the front of the building to reach the driveway, which goes to the left. Turn right at the first available opportunity, and, after a few yards, turn left along a path that heads back towards the river, going through several fields and across several dikes. Go past a path leading off to the left, continuing to reach a crossing of paths. Turn right here, rejoining the shorter walk which is followed back to the start.

POINTS OF INTEREST:

River Medway – The river has played a very important part in the history of Kent, carrying timber and iron from the Weald downstream and, later, supplying water for the hop growers to make beer. So important was it that it is the traditional barrier between the Men of Kent, to the east, and the Kentish Men, to the west. On this route the river flows gently through very pleasant countryside.

Whitbread Hop Farm, Beltring – This is a working hop farm which also houses a museum and craft centre. There are 25 oast houses on the site, sadly no longer used to dry hops. It is open to the public April-September.

REFRESHMENTS:

The Addlestead Tavern, Bullen Lane, East Peckham.

Walk 43 HIGH HALDEN AND ST MICHAEL'S 5m (8km)

Maps: OS Sheets Landranger 189; Pathfinder 1250.

A walk through countryside around these two Wealden villages, near Tenterden.

Start: At 901373, High Halden Church.

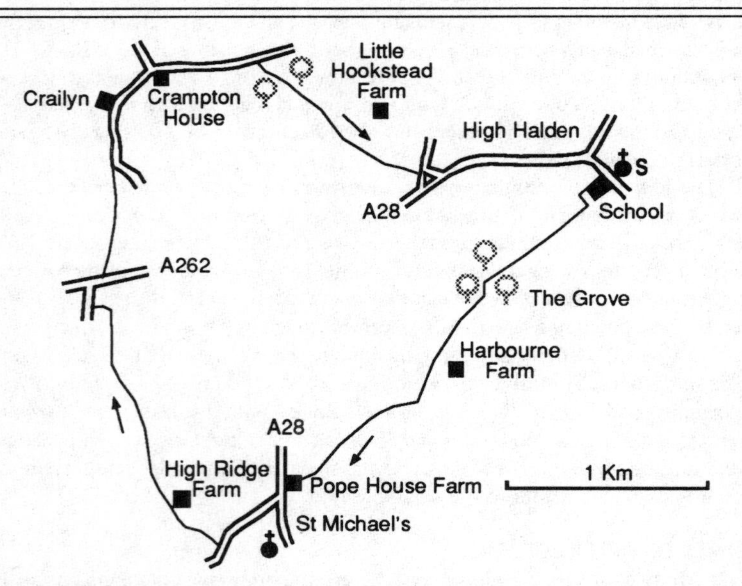

From **High Halden Church** go to the road and, directly opposite, take a path that runs between the Post Office and the village school. Very soon the path turns left, and then right. Continue along it as it goes through two fields and then leads into a patch of woodland, The Grove. You emerge from the woods just as the path becomes part of a four-way junction. Carefully choose your route: you want to follow the second turning, going slightly to the right from where you join the junction. This path goes to the rear of Harbourne Farm, not through the buildings, and then continues to reach a fork.

Take the right-hand branch, a track, and continue along it, going slightly uphill and through the buildings of Pope House Farm to reach a road (the A28). Turn left and very soon cross over, with great care, and take a turning on the right. Follow this road past houses to reach a signed footpath on the right. Follow this path past High Ridge Farm, to the right, continuing very pleasantly through open farmland for about a mile, going through several fields, and finally reaching a road. Turn right, almost immediately reaching a T-junction with the A262. Turn right, and then, very soon, cross, with great care, to turn left along a signed footpath that bears diagonally right to cross a dismantled railway. Follow the left-hand boundary of the field beyond to reach the opposite corner, and go through to a road.

Turn left and follow the road as it curves round, going past Crailyn, on the left. Continue past a turning, also on the left, and then past Crampton House, on the right. When you reach a patch of woodland, away to the right, turn right along a path that bears diagonally left through it, then joins a track which runs to the rear of Little Hookstead Farm. Once beyond the farm, the path begins to ascend slowly, crossing several fields to reach some houses. Stay with the path, going alongside a house to reach a road. Take the road directly ahead, following it to its T-junction with the A28.

Turn left and follow the road back into High Halden, taking great care as this is a busy road, a section of the main Ashford to Tenterden route. When the road forks, cross, with even greater care, and take the right-hand turn which very soon leads back to High Halden Church where the walk began.

POINTS OF INTEREST:

High Halden – This pleasant Wealden village, on the main route between Ashford and Tenterden, has a fine village green and some, now converted, oast houses, a typical Kentish landmark. The church has a fine timber tower built in about 1300 and is unique in Kent. There is also much fine internal timber work.

REFRESHMENTS:

The Chequers Inn, High Halden.
The Fat Ox, St Michael's.

Walk 44 **Biddenden** 5m (8km)

Maps: OS Sheets Landranger 188 and 189; Pathfinder 1250.

A walk through farmland around this delightful village.

Start: At 849384, Biddenden Church.

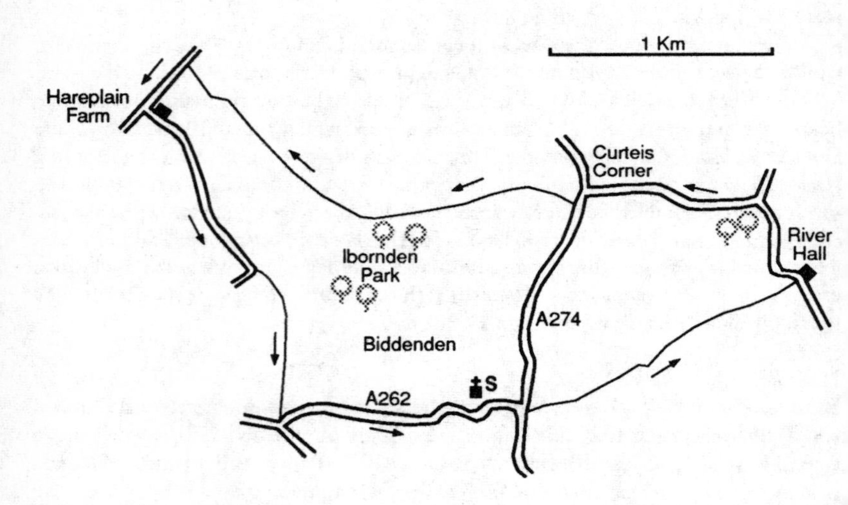

From the **church** go on to the main road (the A262) and turn left, walking through the village to reach a T-junction with the A274. Go straight across, with great care, and follow a track that runs between houses and out into open countryside. The track becomes a path: continue along it, heading diagonally left towards the right-hand corner of a field. There, another path joins from the left: follow the path as it bears round to the right. Now follow the field boundary and cross a stile into the next field. Turn left, walking along the field's left-hand edge. Now go to the centre of the far boundary, cross between two small ponds, with the boundary on your left. About half-way along, go through a gate and continue, now walking beside the right-hand boundary.

When the field boundary turns right, continue on towards the corner ahead and to the right. Cross into the next field and bear left to reach a road near more ponds.

Turn left along the road, going past the entrance to River Hall, on your right. The road meanders between fields and eventually reaches a T-junction. Turn left and follow the road, with a small patch of woodland on your left. Continue along the road to reach a T-junction at Curteis Corner. Turn left, and then very soon right along a path that runs beside a house and then goes into a field. Head for the far left-hand corner of the field, cross through a group of trees and continue on, following the right-hand boundaries of several fields. When you reach the edge of Iborden Park, stay with the path as it follows the boundary. This is a good spot to detour for a picnic if you have brought your own refreshments.

Continue through a small part of the Park near its driveway entrance, and then ignore various paths going off to the right as you walk alongside an orchard to reach a road. Turn left along the road, but turn first left. Follow the new road, soon passing Hareplain Farm. Continue along the road for about $^1/_2$ mile until it turns to the right. There, take the track going straight on. The track becomes a path: keep following it, continuing when it becomes a track again. Follow the track to reach a road (the A262).

Turn left along the road, with great care, following it back into **Biddenden**.

POINTS OF INTEREST:

Biddenden Church – The church dates mostly from the 13th century. There is a Jacobean oak pulpit, and many fine brasses inside.

Biddenden – There are many fine old houses in this beautiful village, including old weavers' cottages and a superb medieval cloth hall with seven gables. The village sign commemorates two famous inhabitants, the 'The Maids of Biddenden'. The maids were the Siamese twin sisters, Eliza and Mary Chulkhurst, who were joined at the shoulder and hip. It is unclear when the sisters were born. Usually it is quoted as 1100, but some experts believe this to be a misreading of 1500. The sisters lived for 34 years and left money in their wills for the distribution of bread and cheese to the village poor. This is the basis of the Chulkhurst Charity, the gift of bread and cheese to village pensioners on Easter Monday each year.

REFRESHMENTS:

The Three Chimneys, Biddenden.
The Red Lion, Biddenden.

Walk 45 **Lower Rainham Riverside** $5^1/_2$m ($8^3/_4$km)

Maps: OS Sheets Landranger 178; Pathfinder 1194.

Easy walking, mainly along river estuary.

Start: At 807684, the car parking area at Sharp's Green.

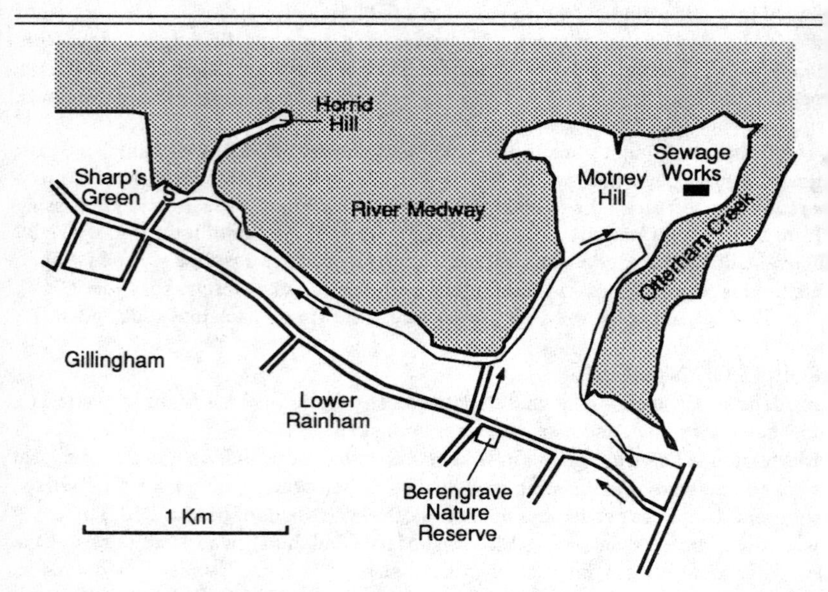

From the car parking area, face the river and follow the path going right. On occasions, the path will be marked with the **Saxon Shore Way** motif, a horned helmet on stone markers. Very soon you will reach a concrete path leading out to the promontory known as **Horrid Hill**. This is not on the route, but if you follow the detour, at the outermost end there are broad views across and along the Medway Estuary.

Continue along the riverside path to reach an industrial breakers yard. There, follow a path along the inner wall, going past the entry gate, continuing along it to return to the riverside. Continue along the river to reach the old dock at Motney Hill, which is where material from the pit which is now **Berengrave Nature Reserve** used to be shipped out. Take the path to the left out to Motney Hill. Although the walking is easy, this area can be bleak and cold in winter as it is very exposed to the elements.

When the path and the shoreline bear to the left, go down on to the parallel road and follow it towards the entrance of the sewage works. Just before the entrance there is a signed stile to the right: cross the stile and follow the line of the fence to reach a a footbridge over a ditch. Cross and go up on to the sea wall. Turn right and continue along the wall, with Otterham Creek on your left.

Eventually you will reach an industrial complex: skirt around the outside edge of this complex to reach a road. Turn right to a junction and turn right again along Lower Rainham Road, taking great care as this can be a busy road. After about $^3/_4$ mile the road reaches the Berengrave Nature Reserve, on the corner of Berengrave Lane, with a garage opposite.

Just after this, on the right, Motney Hill Road is signed as a public footpath. Go along the road to reach the old dock area and turn left there to retrace your steps along the riverside to Sharp's Green.

POINTS OF INTEREST:

Saxon Shore Way – This ancient long distance route was originally used by the Romans moving armies to defend against Saxon invaders. Today the 140 mile route from Gravesend to Rye is taken by more peaceful walkers.

Horrid Hill – This delicately named hill is a promontory out into the Medway, offering excellent views. It is also the site of a former rubbish dump (hence the name ?) and so of interest to collectors and diggers.

Berengrave Nature Reserve – This site of a former chalk pit is being sympathetically managed by the local council. Birdwatchers will find plenty to enjoy in the reed beds and mudflats of the Reserve and the river, particularly in winter.

REFRESHMENTS:

Army & Navy, Lower Rainham.
Hastings Arms, Lower Rainham.
Three Mariners Inn, Lower Rainham.

Walk 46 St Margaret's and Kingsdown $5^1/_2$m ($8^3/_4$km)

Maps: OS Sheets Landranger 179; Pathfinder 1232.

A walk through open fields then back along the clifftop.

Start: At 369445, St Margaret's at Cliffe car park, by the shore.

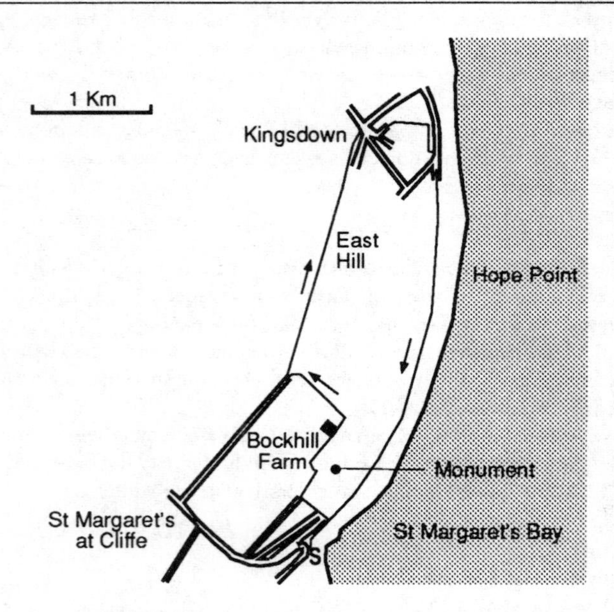

Go to the back of the car park and up the steps that are set into the cliff. At the top, turn right and walk straight on, ignoring the sign for 'The Leas'. After the last house the path divides: go left to reach a road. Turn right along the road to reach the **monument** on the hill. There, go left along a track, heading in the direction of Bockhill Farm. Shortly before the farm, bear right, and then cross the track leading to it.

Now go straight downhill to reach a road. Turn left to reach a junction. There, double back to the right, and then take the clearly defined track on the left. Go diagonally up the slope, and when the track divides, at a row of houses, keep right to go along a bridleway. Follow the bridleway across open country for about $^1/_2$ mile to reach a road. Turn right to reach a junction. Turn left and walk to another junction. Keep left at the next junction. The road now bears right: follow it past a Scout camp and then take the clearly defined path on the left. Follow the path towards the cliff-top bearing right with it to reach steps which descend to Undercliff Road.

Turn right, heading southwards and eventually going up a path to the top of the cliff. Now follow this cliff-top path for $1^1/_2$ miles, taking due note of the edge, but enjoying the superb seaward views. When you reach the point where, on the outward journey, you turned left to go inland, keep left along the coastal path. From here, the return to the car park in **St Margaret's at Cliffe**, where the walk began, is straightforward.

POINTS OF INTEREST:

Monument – The obelisk was raised as a memorial to those members of the Dover Patrol who gave their lives during the First World War. Prince Arthur of Connaught laid the first stone in 1919 and the memorial was completed in 1921.

St Margaret's at Cliffe – This fine cliff-top village is worth visiting for its weather-boarded houses, fine Norman church, parts of which date back to the 12th century, with ships carved on to some of its pillars and the splendid Pines Gardens. St Margaret's Bay, below the village, is the arrival point for many cross-Channel swimmers.

Kingsdown – The white cliffs, of Dover fame, actually begin here and the cliff top part of this walk follows them.

REFRESHMENTS:

The Hope Inn, St Margaret's at Cliffe.
Cliffe Tavern Hotel, St Margaret's at Cliffe.
The Rising Sun, Kingsdown.

Walk 47 **Ivychurch** $5^1/_2$m ($8^3/_4$km)

Maps: OS Sheets Landranger 189; Pathfinder 1272.

A pleasant walk, mainly on quiet country roads.

Start: At 028276, the church at Ivychurch.

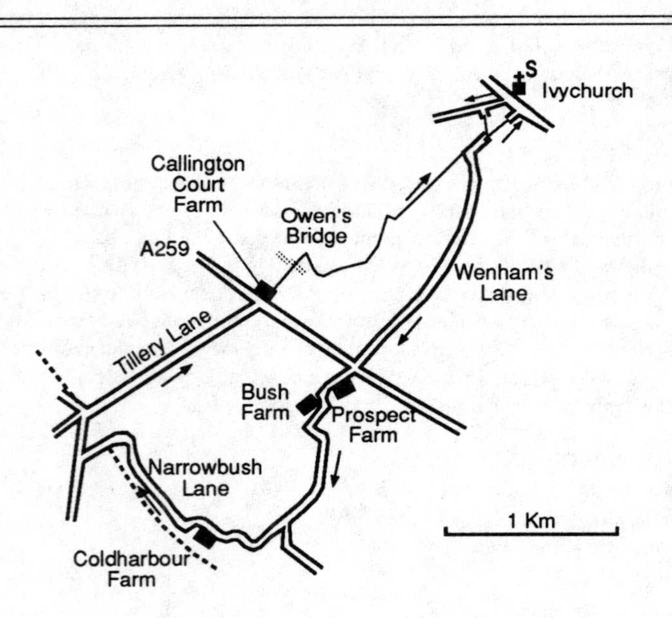

From the church, turn right along the main village street to reach a road junction Turn left, and then next left to go along Wenham's Lane. At first the lane meanders but then runs straight for nearly a mile. Cross Yoakes bridge and continue to reach the A259. Go straight over, with great care, and follow the minor road opposite (Beggarbush Lane), going past Prospect Farm, to the left. The road bears left to pass Bush Farm, to the right, and, eventually, meanders around Coldharbour Farm, to the left, to become Narrowbush Lane, running parallel to the railway line.

Follow the lane as it swings left and crosses the railway, and then continues to meet Barnhouse Lane. Turn right and follow the road to reach a cross-roads. Turn right, crossing the railway line again and going past Barnland Farm into Tillery Lane Follow this to once again meet the A259, directly opposite Callington Court Farm

Cross, with great care, and go through the farmyard on a track that soon becomes a path. Continue along the path to Owen's Bridge. Cross and turn sharp right to walk alongside a ditch.

When you reach the corner of a field, cross a stile into the next field and head diagonally right to the far corner. Cross another stile and bear right along the field boundary to reach a ditch. Turn left and follow the ditch, eventually turning right to cross it. Now head left towards the houses in view in the distance, and pass to the left of them to reach Wenham's Lane at the point at which it turns right. Go along the lane in the direction of Ivychurch, retracing the outward route, but when the road bears left, cross to go along a path that runs straight between houses to reach the main village road in **Ivychurch**. Turn left to return to the church and the start of the walk.

POINTS OF INTEREST:

Ivychurch – The village has one of the finest churches on Romney Marsh, parts of it dating from the 14th century. The tower is nearly 100 ft high. Unfortunately the fine box pews – so popular in Marsh churches – have been removed.

The village stands at the edge of Romney Marsh, a huge expanse of flat marshland that has been turned into grazing land by the excavation of a vast array of dykes. The area is famous for its sheep, for being the only British home of the marsh frog, and for Dr Syn the smuggler-parson. The fact that the latter is fictional does nothing to dampen the enthusiasm with which the name is used throughout the area.

REFRESHMENTS:

The Bell Inn, Ivychurch.

Walk 48 **Waltham and Sole Street** $5^1/_2$m ($8^3/_4$km

Maps: OS Sheets Landranger 189; Pathfinder 1231.

A walk through two small hamlets and across isolate countryside.

Start: At 109486, the Lord Nelson Inn, Waltham.

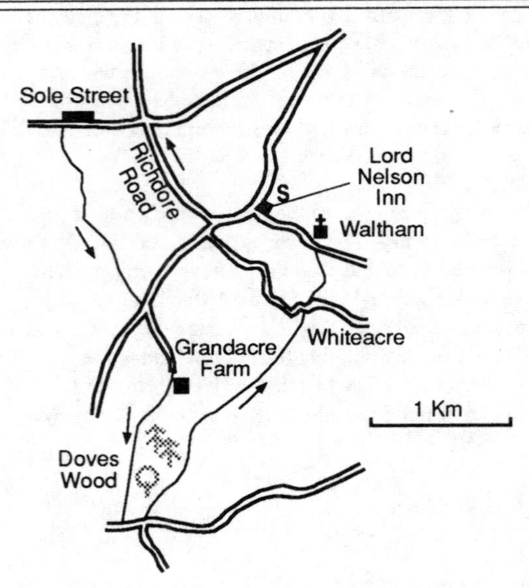

From the inn, turn right, very soon reaching a junction of roads. Turn left and wal through **Waltham** village to reach a road fork. Take the right-hand branch (Richdor Road), following it gently uphill to reach a cross-roads. Turn left and follow the roa soon reaching Sole Street, a tiny hamlet. Walk through the village and just beyond th last house, go over a stile on the left and follow the path beyond along the left-han boundary of a field into the corner. Cross into the next field and again follow the le boundary.

Continue along the path to reach a junction of paths. Turn left, crossing into th next field when you reach the corner. The path now divides into three: follow th central route, heading uphill, gradually at first, then more steeply. Maintain directio when another path crosses, continuing to reach a road. Cross and go through a gat directly opposite. Follow the farm road beyond the gate, going through the buildings of Grandacre Farm. Stay on the farm road for a few hundred yards, then take a path going off to the left. The path goes gradually downhill to reach a stile. Cross into another field, and maintain direction as the path runs beside Doves Wood and then continues to reach a road.

Turn left along the road to reach a turning on the right. Directly opposite this, on the left, turn along a path that runs along the outer boundary of woodland (Doves Wood) on the left. Stay on the path as it bears left and goes into the woods. The path now bears right to emerge from the woods, and then follows the woodland's right-hand edge. When the woodland boundary turns right, cross into a field and walk to the far left-hand corner. Cross a stile into the next field and maintain direction, following the path leads into the next field, and on into the next. The path reaches a road near Whiteacre.

You join the road at a turn: go straight on then, when the road turns right, go straight on again, along a path. When another path joins from the right, go left along the new, single route, following it uphill to reach a road near Waltham church. Turn left and follow the road back to the start of the walk.

POINTS OF INTEREST:

Waltham – This little village is typical of many North Downs villages – quiet, pretty and with little to detain the visitor apart from its sense of rural peace. Nearby, the town of Wye, itself a typical North Downs market town, is a more robust place.

REFRESHMENTS:

The Lord Nelson, Waltham.
The Compasses Inn, Sole Street.

Walk 49 **HASTINGLEIGH** $5^1/_2$m ($8^3/_4$km

Maps: OS Sheets Landranger 189; Pathfinder 1231.

A walk along quiet country roads and public byways.

Start: At 095449, the Bowl Inn, Hastingleigh.

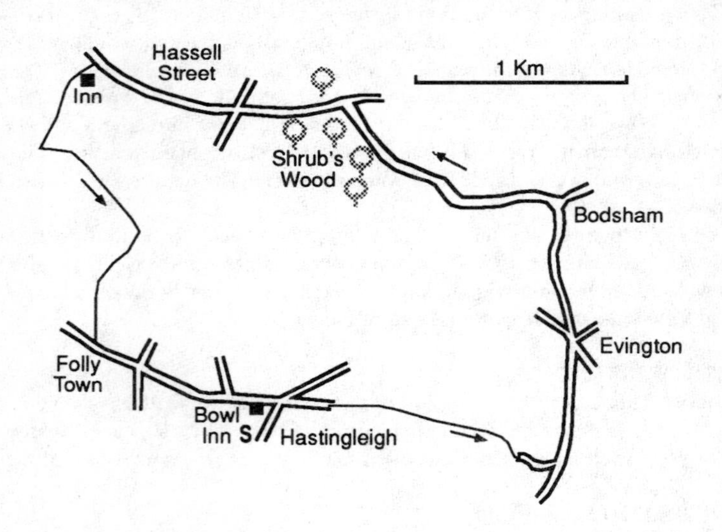

Turn right from the inn and walk through Hastingleigh to reach a cross-roads. G straight across and follow a track which soon becomes a byway. Follow the bywa downhill through open fields to reach a road just as it bends. Turn left, and follow th road downhill. Continue along the road as it bears left to reach a cross-roads, on turning of which is the entrance to Dawlton Farm. Turn left and follow the verg alongside the road to reach another cross-roads at Evington. Go straight across an stay with the road as it heads into Bodsham.

Walk through Bodsham, continuing along the road as it goes left. Eventually th road reaches the edge of Shrub's Wood. Continue along it, with the wood on your le to reach a T-junction. Turn left, and follow a road, initially with woodland on eithe side, to reach a cross-roads. Go straight across and follow the road into the hamlet c Hassell Street. When you reach the hotel, on your left, take the byway that runs besid it, following it across a field where it interconnects with another byway. Turn left along the new route and follow it to Little Coombe. There you will find a track: take this track, following it through the buildings of Smeed Farm and staying with it when it bears right. Now, when the track turns left, go right along another byway, following it along the edge of a field to reach a stile. Cross and continue along another field edge to reach a road at Folly Town.

Turn left along the road, following it to reach a cross-roads. Go straight across and follow the road as it goes gradually downhill and back into **Hastingleigh**.

POINTS OF INTEREST:

Hastingleigh – Despite appearances, the village name is pronounced with a final 'lie'. The village lies just below the high ridge taken by the North Downs Way. The Downs here are superb, home of the lady orchid, or Maid of Kent, some 30 species of butterfly, several rare moths, a good number of birds and the occasional adder. A mile or so to the west of the village a Nature Reserve has been set up on the Downs to protect this rare habitat. Close to it is the Devil's Kneading, a curious dry valley cut through the chalk, probably at the time of the last Ice Age.

REFRESHMENTS:

The Bowl Inn, Hastingleigh.

Walk 50 **DEAL AND SANDWICH BAY** 6m ($9^1/_2$km

Maps: OS Sheets Landranger 179; Pathfinder 1212.

Following two ancient routes that ran between Deal an Sandwich and, along the sea front.

Start: At 375543, the northern end of Deal sea front (on roa parking).

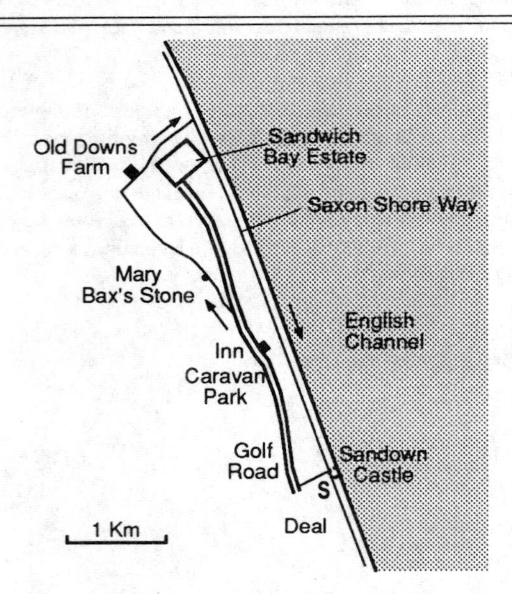

The walk starts at **Sandown Castle**, of which only a fragment remains. Where th Deal sea front ends, take the footpath on the left leading to Golf Road. Turn righ here, and go past the clubhouse. Do not follow the road around to the left: insteac take the grassy track ahead, signposted 'Ancient Highway'. In inclement condition you may wish to use the made-up footpath on the right. When the track ends at th Chequers Inn, follow the road for a while until it veers left, then right. The publi right of way is now along the top of the bank on the left. On the right-hand side ar reclaimed lands, called polders by the Huegenots who settled in the area.

Also along this path is **Mary Bax's Stone**. The stone is on top of the bank an will be found just before you reach a red cottage. Go over the stile and continue alon the top of the bank, which is signed as a 'White Cliffs Country Trail'. When the bank veers away to the left, keep straight on, crossing a ditch and walking down the edge of a field. Pass a pumping station on the right, then cross two stiles to arrive at a farm drive. Turn right here, walking past Old Downs Farm to reach a road. There is a stile opposite: cross the road and go over. Follow the waymarked footpath beyond, going through a meadow and across the **Royal St George's Golf Course**. When the path meets the sea road, turn right towards the Sandwich Bay estate. This is a private estate with some fascinating and diverse architecture.

This stretch of the walk is on the right of way which runs below the sea wall and is part of the Saxon Shore Way, a long distance route which follows much of the coast of Kent. You may wish to walk along the top of the bank, from where there are excellent views towards Deal. In clear weather you may even be able to see waves crashing on the **Goodwin Sand**, notorious for being the watery grave of many sailors and ship over the centuries.

Continuing along the Shore Way, you will eventually return to Deal and the starting point.

POINTS OF INTEREST:

Sandown Castle – The castle was built by Henry VIII at the same time as those at Deal and Walmer. After the Restoration it was the prison of Col. Hutchinson, one of the judges of Charles I. The conditions were so appalling that Hutchinson died after 6 months. Seeing him just after his death his wife claimed he looked "as he used to do when best pleased with life". Perhaps he was happy to have been set free from the place.

Mary Bax's Stone – The stone is purported to mark the place where Mary Bax was murdered by one Martin Lash, over 200 years ago.

Royal St George's Golf Course – This superb course is occasionally home to the British Open Championship.

Goodwin Sands – About 4 miles out to sea, these sandbanks have claimed at least 50,000 lives since records began. At certain low tides it is possible to visit the sands, and it has even been known for cricket matches to be played there.

REFRESHMENTS:

The Chequers Inn, on the route.

There are also various inns and cafés in Deal.

Walk 51 **HADLOW** 6m ($9^1/_2$km)

Maps: OS Sheets Landranger 188; Pathfinder 1209 and 1229.

A pleasant walk through Kentish countryside and villages.

Start: At 634497, St Mary's Church, Hadlow.

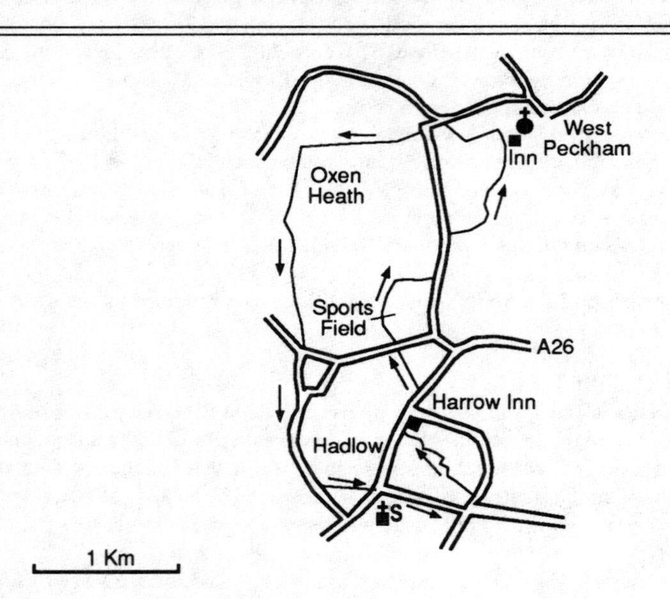

From the church, go along Church Street and turn right along the main road. Turn right again into Court Lane, and when you reach a cross-roads turn left. Now, opposite a house on your right, turn left again, crossing a stile. Walk straight on, with orchards on either side, until you reach another stile. Cross it and follow the edge of the field beyond around to the right. When you reach a corner where you can see the cemetery over on the right, keep straight on across a field. To the left now you will see oast houses. Walk past the end of a hedge and turn right, then left, with a wire fence on your right. Continue to reach a road (the A26) and turn right, soon reaching the Harrow Inn.

Continue along the road, with care, to reach a signposted footpath on the left. Take this path, following it to another road. Cross and take the footpath opposite. When you arrive at a sports field, turn right, following the edge of the field, then bearing left across a grassy track. Turn right along a track with a hedge on the right and a fence on the left, continuing along the track when it becomes a made-up lane and following it to a road.

Turn left along the road and, just before a house, cross a stile on the right. Follow the edge of the field beyond, then cross another stile on the left. Now walk with enclosed woods on the right, crossing a small stream to arrive at a hut on the left. Here the track veers right: follow it to some farm buildings. Continue on, passing an oast house to arrive at the village green of West Peckham. Across the green is the Swan Inn and **St Dunstan's church**.

If you visit the church, you must turn right on leaving and cross the green to reach a kissing gate. Go through and follow the track beyond, passing a bungalow, on the left. Turn right, then left at the top of the field. Cross a stile on to an enclosed footpath and follow it to a road. Turn left and after passing a cottage on the right, turn right along a signposted track. When this track eventually turns left, continue straight on through the gates of the Oxenhoath Estate. Go past the main house on the left and ornamental gardens on the right, continuing between gate posts. Leave the track to walk down and across a field to reach a stile next to a gate. Go over and walk downhill along a grassy track from which there are excellent views, including a sight of **Hadlow Castle**, a Victorian folly.

Cross a stile on to a road, reaching it at a junction. Go along the road opposite (heading south). At the next junction, ignore the turning on the left, continuing along the road, through Hadlow village, to reach its junction with the main A26. Turn left, with care, to return to the start.

POINTS OF INTEREST:

St Dunstan's Church, West Peckham – This fine church is also an interesting one, parts of it dating from the 11th century.

Hadlow Castle – This extraordinary, 170 foot high tower, is also known as May's Folly, after William Barton May who built it in 1840.

REFRESHMENTS:

The Swan Inn, West Peckham.

The Harrow Inn, Hadlow.

There are also other possibilities in Hadlow.

Walk 52 **IDE HILL** 6m ($9^1/_2$km)

Maps: OS Sheets Landranger 188; Pathfinder 1208.

A pleasant walk through open woodland and fields, with excellent views.

Start: At 486518, the car park to the rear of Ide Hill village hall.

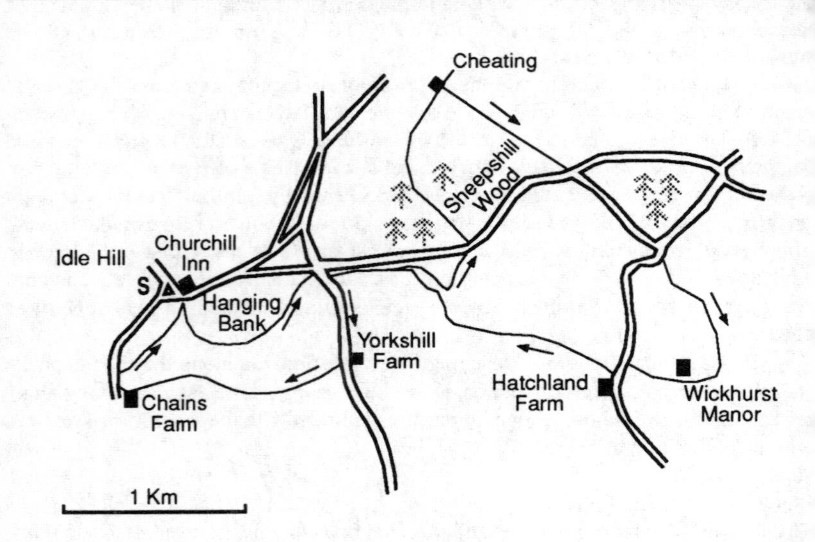

From the car park, go left along the B2042 towards the Churchill Inn, but before reaching it, turn right along a side road. Of the two paths now on offer, take the left-hand one which leads around **Hanging Bank** to reach a junction of paths. Take the second path on the left, keeping right at two forks. Keep to the left as the path ascends to a crossing track. Turn right, and walk to the car park at the Yorkshill cross-roads. Cross Yorkshill Road and maintain direction, walking through woodland, parallel with the road on the left. Eventually you veer away from the road, but soon turn sharp left to return to it. Cross and go along the footpath opposite, into Sheepshill Wood, a conifer plantation. The path zig-zags to reach a wider track which turns to the left. Go downhill for a while, then cross a track and continue uphill. On reaching the top of the hill, head straight on to reach a large clearing in which there is a junction of paths.

Turn along the path immediately to the right. The path eventually goes downhill: keep to the right and go over a stile. Walk past a cottage and then take the small footpath on the left, following it to emerge on to a track in the woods. Turn right and go downhill to a road. Turn left and, shortly, at a junction, turn right along a narrow road. Go past a house called Everlands, turn right into the drive of a red brick house and immediately turn left along a footpath which leads down to another road. Turn right along the road to reach another downhill path on the left. Take this, following it to a gate. Go through and bear left. After passing the second entrance to **Wickhurst Manor**, turn right along a made-up path. Pass in front of the manor house and some farm buildings, then, opposite the barn, cross a stile on to a signed footpath and follow it around the edge of a field to reach a road.

Turn left, but very soon right over a stile and follow a path with Hatchlands Farm on your left. Cross a plank bridge and bear left to cross a stile into a field. Turn right, and after 200 yards cross diagonally left over the field to reach a stile amongst trees. Go over, walk through a small wood and continue uphill. Go over two more stiles to reach an enclosed footpath, following it until another path crosses. Turn left to reach the outward route. Retrace the route, walking parallel to the road, to reach Yorkshill Road again. Turn left along it to reach Yorkshill Farm, on the left. Take the signed footpath opposite, crossing a stream and continuing with a hedge on your right. Cross a stile to reach a driveway. Turn sharp left, go over a stile at the side of the garage and walk across the field beyond. Bear left to cross a ditch, then go through a gate to arrive at Chains Farm. Turn right up a driveway to a road. Turn right along the road to reach a signed footpath on the right. Take this, crossing a field to a stile just beyond a telegraph pole. Cross the stile and go left, uphill, to reach another stile. Go over and walk up a fairly steep path to reach a drive on the left. The drive takes you back to the road near the Churchill Inn, from where it is a short step back to Ide Hill village hall.

POINTS OF INTEREST:

Hanging Bank – Situated in nearly 100 acres of mixed woodland, this viewing station offers excellent views across the Weald.

Wickhurst Manor – This beautiful manor house dates from the 15th century.

REFRESHMENTS:

The Churchill Inn, Ide Hill.

The Cock Inn, Idle Hill.

Walk 53 **IWADE** 6m ($9^1/_2$km)

Maps: OS Sheets Landranger 178; Pathfinder 1179.

A walk along bleak estuary banks, following part of the Saxon Shore Way.

Start: At 901679, the car park beside the Woolpack Inn, Iwade.

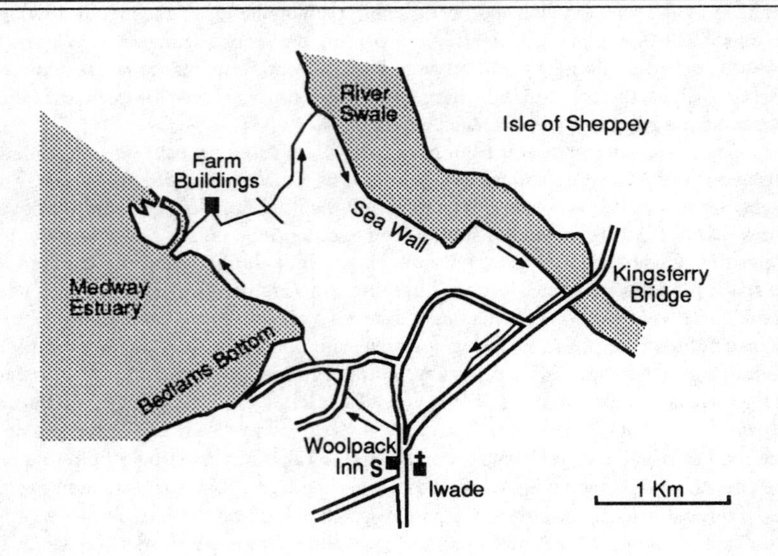

From the car park, opposite the Church of All Saints, turn left along the main road (the A249) in the direction of the Kingsferry Bridge. You will soon reach a small path running parallel to the road: take this, following it to Old Ferry Road. Turn left, and after about 100 yards go through a gate on the left into a field. Be warned: in the summer this field is used on Sundays for a car boot fair and can be very crowded.

Cross diagonally towards the centre of the field, keeping to the footpath as cattle usually graze here. At the far end of the field, go through a gate into another field and bear left to the far corner, crossing a small lane on the way. Go through the gate at the corner and turn left along a road. After just a few yards, go over a stile, on the right, sporting a yellow **Saxon Shore Way** marker. Follow the marked path beyond the stile across a series of further stiles to reach the raised wall that runs beside the estuary.

The estuary is part of the **River Medway**, and to your left is the strangely named mudbank of Bedlams Bottom. Stay on the path, which is still marked as the Saxon Shore Way, along the top of the raised wall for about 1 mile. Early parts of this section may be muddy after rain. You will see many abandoned barges in the river mud to the left: at one point there are several together. Eventually the path turns sharp left on to a small rectangular spit of land jutting out into the estuary. Follow the edge of the rectangle, staying with the path as it heads inland. Cross a stile, skirt some farm buildings, go over another stile and continue along the signed path.

This section of the walk is through open, bleak countryside, with the Chetney Marshes on the left and rough grazing on the right. After $^1/_2$ mile, cross a farm road via two stiles, and continue to reach the estuary of the River Swale. Turn right and follow the water's edge, heading in the direction of the towers of the Kingsferry Bridge in the distance. The path ends in a fenced area which is actually the parking place for a local water skiing club. Leave this through a narrow, fenced exit to reach a lorry park. Now leave along the path that runs parallel to the main road (the A249). The path reaches a road going right: follow this, but soon turn left through a gate into a field. Walk straight ahead along a footpath that stays close to the fence on the left. Go through a series of gates, reaching the main road through one final gate. Now walk beside the busy main road, with great care, to return to the starting point in Iwade.

POINTS OF INTEREST:

Saxon Shore Way – This ancient long distance route was originally used by the Romans moving armies to defend against Saxon invaders. Today the 140 mile route from Gravesend to Rye is taken by more peaceful walkers.

River Medway – In addition to Bedlams Bottom, many more of the creeks and mudbanks along this part of the Medway Estuary have strange names. Others include Slaughterhouse Point and Deadmans Island. It is thought that the names are possibly due to the fact that prison hulks, and hospital and asylum ships used to be moored in the middle of the wide reaches of the river.

REFRESHMENTS:

The Woolpack Inn, Iwade.

There is a snack bar in the lorry park beside the Kingsferry Bridge.

Walk 54 **CONYER ROUTE 1** 6m ($9^1/_2$km)

Maps: OS Sheets Landranger 178; Pathfinder 1194.

A pleasant walk along the Swale estuary and through fields and orchards.

Start: At 963646, the centre of Conyer.

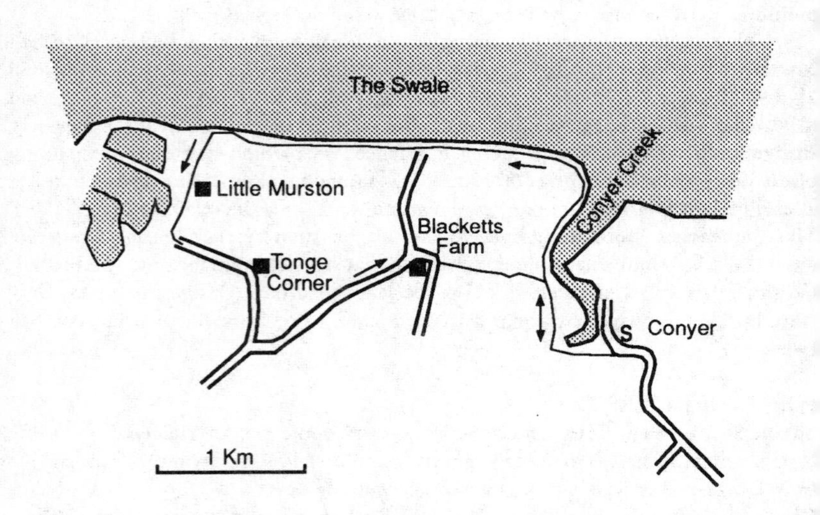

From the centre of the village of Conyer, go south past the terrace of houses in the direction of the main road. When the road turns left, turn right, along the main (right-hand) track of the two options. Follow this track past a row of warehouses to reach **Conyer Creek**. Go past a boatyard, and follow the track as it goes up on to a dyke.

Turn right here and walk to a footbridge over a stream. Cross to reach a point where the track divides. Follow the left-hand route across a spit of land formed by the creek, instead of going around it on a muddy path. The two options rejoin and then divide again: this time follow the right-hand branch, continuing along the side of Conyer Creek. Eventually, after about $^3/_4$ mile, the path swings to the left so that you are walking alongside the **Swale**, the channel that separates the Isle of Sheppey from the mainland.

When the path on the dyke ends, take the track on the left. Soon you will see some large lakes through the trees on your right. Continue along the track to its end, where it meets a road. Turn left, along the road, bearing right to pass Tonge corner, and continuing to reach a junction. Turn left and follow the road to Blacketts Farm. This section of the walk takes you through fields and orchards before the farm is reached.

Now take the track that goes around and behind a large barn, and then follow it to the left as it heads across open country. Follow the track to return to the bank of Conyer Creek. Here, turn right and retrace the outward route back the start point in **Conyer**.

POINTS OF INTEREST:

Conyer Creek – As the walker will soon realise, the Creek is of particular interest to boat lovers, with not only the boatyard, but numerous craft adding interest to the waterside section.

Swale Shorline – For bird watchers, binoculars are a must along this part of the walk. The area has large flocks of waders, including bar-tailed godwits and sanderling, with Brent geese and divers in winter.

Conyer – This attractive little village, grouped around its inn, was once the haunt of smugglers.

REFRESHMENTS:

The Brunswick Arms, Conyer.
The Ship Inn, Conyer Quay.

or 9m (14¼km

Maps: OS Sheets Landranger 188; Pathfinder 1228 and 1229.

A walk from the interesting town of Tonbridge, alongside th River Medway.

Start: At 588461, Tonbridge Railway Station.

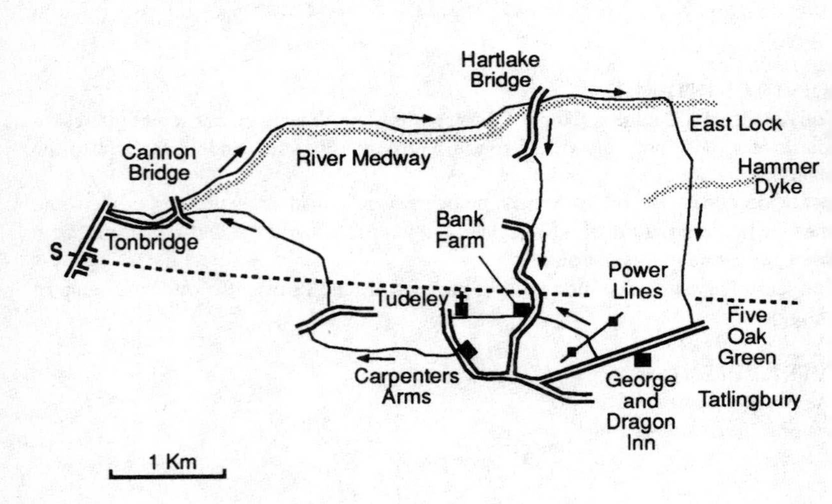

From the Station – there is parking nearby – go left and along the High Street for ½ mil then turn right along Medway Wharf Road. After 300 yards, turn left to reach th River Medway. Follow the towpath to Canon Bridge, using it to cross to the left ban of the river. Now follow the riverside walk for about 2½ miles, passing Edridge's an Porter's Locks. About 250 yards after Porter's Lock, you reach Hartlake Bridge.

The shorter walk crosses the bridge and follows a road away from the rive When the road bears right, cross a stile on the left and continue along a path th eventually leads to an orchard. Go into the orchard, continuing to reach a path fro the left. Turn right along this, very soon reaching a road. Go left, following the road reach Bank Farm, on your right. The longer route is rejoined at this gate.

The longer walk continues beside the river to reach East Lock. Cross the river by way of a footbridge and head across a field towards a gap in the hedge ahead. In the next field, head for a plank bridge across a ditch, then follow a path to another bridge. Cross and head towards three oast houses, soon crossing Hammer Dyke. Continue to reach two stiles. Go over the right-hand one and bear right across a field to a concrete bridge. Cross the bridge and go through the field beyond to reach the right-hand corner of an orchard. Cross two stiles and follow the left-hand boundary of a field, eventually going under the railway and continuing into Five Oak Green. When you reach Five Oak Green Road, turn right towards Tatlingbury. Beyond Tatlingbury you will reach the George and Dragon Inn, on the left. Take the footpath opposite the inn, and follow the left edge of a field. Just beyond the end of the field, go through a gate on the left, and cross the field beyond, going beneath power lines to reach a gap in the hedge. Go through and follow the left-hand edge of the field beyond to reach a track that reaches a road opposite Bank Farm. The shorter route is rejoined at this point.

The shorter route continues along the road, the longer route turns right along it. Just beyond Bank Farm, turn right through a gate and follow a path through a field to reach a farm track. Follow the track to a road at Tudeley Church. Turn left and follow the road towards the Carpenters Arms. Just before the inn, turn right along a path signed for Vauxhall Lane. Follow the path over a brick bridge and across the field beyond, heading to the right of the farm buildings ahead. Cross a farm road and continue along the left edge of a field and then a wood. Continue along the path to a driveway. Turn right to reach a road. Turn right again, and then left along a lane with a 'Private Road' sign. The lane crosses the railway and then turns left. Continue along it to reach Cannon Bridge, and from there retrace your steps back into **Tonbridge** and the start of the walk.

POINTS OF INTEREST:

Tonbridge – This pleasant market town lies on two rivers, the Medway, whose valley the walks follow, and the Tun, which names the town. The town's famous school was founded in 1533 and claims Jane Austen's father as a former teacher. The castle was built in 1070 by Richard de Clare, a kinsman of William the Conqueror. It was destroyed during the Civil War. The church is also Norman, but was substantially rebuilt in the 14th century.

REFRESHMENTS:

The Carpenters Arms, Tudeley.
The George and Dragon, Capel.
There are also many inns, cafés and restaurants in Tonbridge.

Walk 57 **NEW POUND AND SHIPBOURNE FOREST** 6m (9½km)

Maps: OS Sheets Landranger 188; Pathfinder 1209.

A walk entirely on forest tracks and paths, so best avoided after continuous rain when it can be muddy.

Start: At 648547, the Beech Inn, New Pound, on the west side of the B2016.

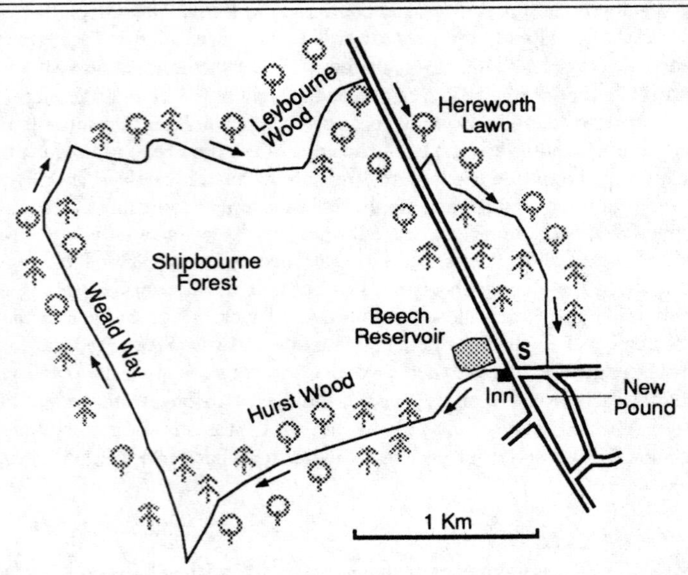

Go to the rear of the inn and take the track that heads westwards, away from the road. Go past Beech Reservoir and bear left, with the track, into the forest. Initially the walk is through a conifer plantation, but eventually emerges into the mixed woodland of Hurst Wood. There are a large number of paths in the forest but it is unlikely that you will get lost if you follow the directions.

Continue along the track as it goes deeper into the forest, ignoring a path that goes off to the left. When your track gradually bears left, do not join the path that leads off sharp left. Then, when another track crosses, continue straight on. The next track to cross is the **Weald Way**, which is well signed. Turn right along this new route

There are now many paths leading from the Weald Way which you may wish to use to explore the forest, but you should always return to the waymarked Way.

Follow the Weald Way for about 2 miles: it eventually becomes a public byway and then runs alongside the forest boundary. When the byway bears away from the woodland, it is crossed by a path: turn right along this path, following it as it runs to the south of some works. Soon after returning into the forest, turn left along a path, staying with it when it runs right and heads back into the woods. Continue along the path to reach the outer fence of an enclosed area of woodland. Now follow the fence for a short time to reach a crossing path. Turn left along this, maintaining direction when another path crosses. Continue through Leybourne Wood and bear right to reach a road (the B2016 again).

Turn right and follow the road, with great care, to reach **Mereworth Lawn**. Now take the second track on the left. At the end of the buildings of Mereworth Lawn, turn right and follow a path as it skirts the edge of woodland on the left. Now, at the corner of a field, the path leads back into woodland. Maintain direction as the path meanders through the wood to emerge into a field. Continue to reach a track and follow that to a road at New Pound. Turn right to return to the start of the walk.

POINTS OF INTEREST:

Weald Way – This long distance footpath links Gravesend with the South Downs Way, joining the latter to the north of Eastbourne.

Mereworth Lawn – The name derives from the village just a mile or so south-east of the walk, and is pronounced *Merryworth*. Mereworth is also the name given to a section of woodland traversed by the walk. The village is well worth visiting, especially if you are interested in military history as Admiral Lucas, the first recipient of the Victoria Cross is buried in the church. The medal was awarded in 1854, for bravery during the Crimean campaign.

REFRESHMENTS:

The Beech Inn, at the start.

It also worth taking a picnic and stopping in the woods.

Walk 58 **Hogben's Hill** 6m ($9^1/_2$km)

Maps: OS Sheets Landranger 179; Pathfinder 1211.

A walk through woodland and orchards and along quiet country roads.

Start: At 032568, in the main street of Hogben's Hill.

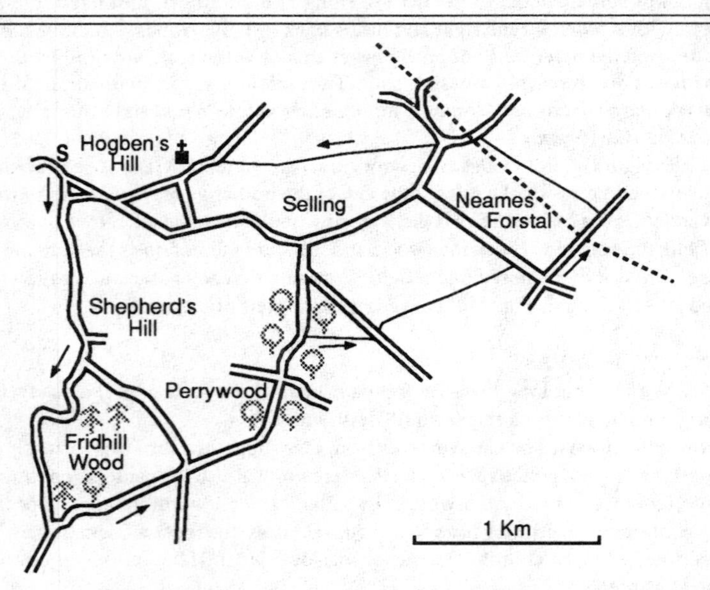

From the inn, turn right, and when the road forks take the minor road on the right. Follow this road past the reservoir at Shepherd's Hill and past two turnings on the left. The road bears to the left, and then follows the boundary of a wood. Next it turns sharp left and leads into the wood, which, at first, is known as Step Wood but soon becomes known as Fridhill Wood. Stay with the road as it continues through the wood then, when it emerges, immediately turn left along another road.

This road leads gently uphill to a cross-roads. Go across and very soon you enter more woodland and continue on uphill, passing the Rose and Crown Inn on your right. Stay on the road as it bears left through Perry Wood and continues to reach another cross-roads. Again, go straight across. On your right is the **Perry Wood** Nature Reserve. When the road emerges from the woodland it bears right, and very soon meets the corner of another patch of woodland. Here, turn right along a signed footpath which runs close to the edge of woodland to reach another road. Turn right and follow the road as it bears left. At a bend where the road bears right, cross a stile on the left and follow the path beyond for a short distance to reach an orchard. Turn right along a path that runs through the orchard to reach another road. Turn right and walk to a cross-roads, with Rhode Court, on your right and Rhode Farm opposite, on the left.

Turn left and follow the road over the railway line. Very soon after, turn left through a gate and go along a path that runs parallel to the railway line. Go through an orchard and continue to reach another road. Turn left, go under the railway line and continue to the outskirts of Neames Forstal. At the T-junction, turn right and then almost immediately left along a path that runs beside houses. At the corner of the buildings, cross into an orchard and maintain direction, following the boundary of a field. When another path crosses, go into a field and follow the left-hand edge to reach a road.

Turn left and follow the road past **Selling Church** and on to a T-junction. Turn right and follow a road back into Hogben's Hill and the start of the walk.

POINTS OF INTEREST:

Perry Wood – This large area of unspoilt woodland was once owned by Corpus Christi college in Oxford. There are two mesolithic sites, circa 1800BC, in the woods.

Selling Church – This remote church is particularly notable for its fine stained-glass windows.

REFRESHMENTS:

The Rose and Crown, Perry Wood.

There are also inns at Hogben's Hill and Neames Forstal.

Walk 59 **Elham** 6m ($9^1/_2$km)

Maps: OS Sheets Landranger 189; Pathfinder 1231.

A walk, almost entirely on country roads, from this pretty village through isolated farmland.

Start: At 177438, Elham Church.

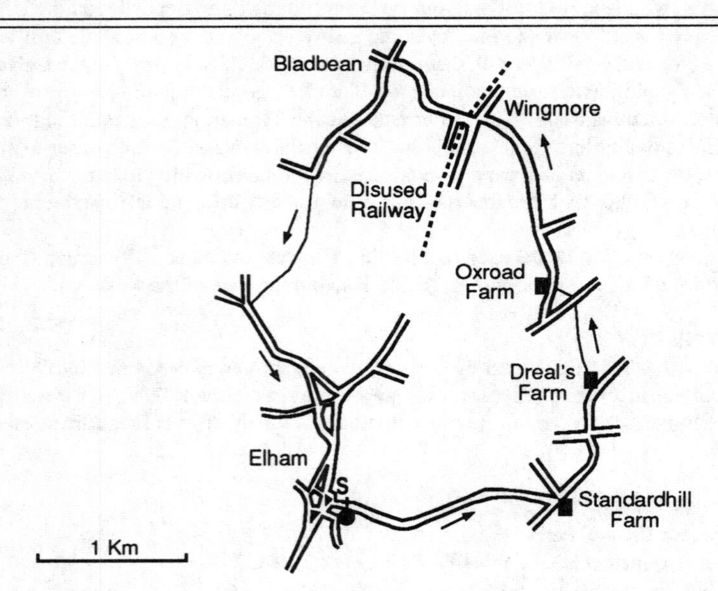

There is limited parking in the village of Elham, so please park tidily.

Leave the church and turn right along the road that leads away from the village. Stay on this road as it goes uphill and bears left, then right, to reach a junction near Standardhill Farm. This is the first of a series of isolated farms that you will pass on this walk. Ignore the two left turns just past the farm and continue on, following the road as it bears left and reaches a cross-roads.

Go straight across, continuing along the road as it begins to bear to the right. On the right is Henbury Manor, while on the left is Dreal's Farm. Turn left along a path that leads through the farm buildings and then go through a gate into a field. Follow a path as it bears to the right, and then bears right again to reach a road at Beam End. Go straight across the road to reach another path, following it as it bears left to the corner of the field. Cross into the next field and maintain direction to reach a road opposite the entrance to Oxroad Farm.

Turn right, and follow this road for about $^3/_4$ mile, ignoring a road going off to the right to reach Wingmore. At the staggered cross-roads cross to the road opposite and follow it across a dismantled railway and on past Grove House Farm. The road goes uphill and crosses the Baldock Downs to reach a cross-roads at Bladbean. Turn left and follow the road across the top of the Downland.

When the road turns sharply right, take the path straight ahead, following it to a stile. Cross into a field and continue along the path to reach another stile. Cross and bear right across the next field to reach a road. You reach the road where two forks join: turn left along the single road, following it downhill to reach a fork. Take the right-hand branch and continue to reach a cross-roads. Go straight ahead, following the road into **Elham**. Turn left along the main village street, bearing left at a fork to continue along it. Now turn left to return to the church.

POINTS OF INTEREST:

Elham – This very pretty North Downs village has a church dating from the 13th century with some fine art treasures. There is an alabaster Beckett triptych depicting the murder in the cathedral and extraordinary stained glass windows featuring Thomas Carlyle and the opera singer Mme Patti as David and Saul. In attendance are Gladstone, Disraeli and three of Queen Victoria's daughters no less!

Of the many fine 16th- and 17th-century buildings, the Abbot's Fireside pub is exceptional. Once used by the Duke of Wellington as a headquarters, it is a huge half-timbered building with an overhang supported on beams with grotesque carvings.

REFRESHMENTS:

The Abbot's Fireside, Elham.
The Rose and Crown, Elham.
The King's Arms, Elham.
The Palm Tree, Wingmore.

Walk 60 LITTLE CHART AND WESTWELL LEACON 6m ($9^1/_2$km)

Maps: OS Sheets Landranger 189; Pathfinder 1230.

A walk between villages, across open country and through a nature reserve.

Start: At 944458, Little Chart Church.

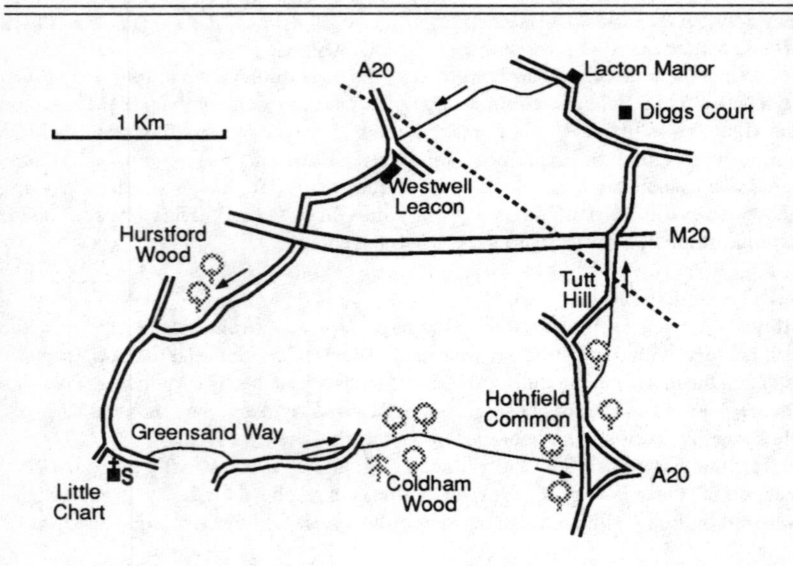

From the church, turn right and follow the road leading away from the village. Very soon, take the path on the left signed as part of the **Greensand Way**. Follow the path as it goes gradually uphill to reach a junction of paths. Turn right, soon reaching a road (Ram Lane). Turn left and follow the road until it bears away to the right. There, go left along a path, following it to meet Ram Lane again. Cross the road and maintain direction along a path into Coldham Wood. Continue along the path, going past a reservoir and then on to **Hothfield Common,** a designated Nature Reserve. There is plenty of opportunity to explore the Common or to stop off for a picnic.

The route continues along the path to reach a road. Turn left along the road. Shortly, the road joins the A20. Turn left along the main road, with care, but soon cross, with even greater care, to turn right along a path. The path soon bears left, and then goes to the rear of the hamlet of Tutt Hill. Just past Tutt Hill Farm the path reaches a road. Go ahead, along this, crossing a railway line and then the M20 motorway.

Stay with the road as it goes gently downhill to reach a T-junction. Turn left and follow this new road past Digges Court, on the right, and Lacton Manor, also on the right. About 50 yards past Lacton Manor there is a sheep wash on the left. Beside it is a path heading off south-westwards. Turn left along this path, following it as it bears first to the right, then to the left. Follow the edge of a patch of woods, then maintain direction, still on the path, to go under the railway line and into Westwell Leacon to reach the main A20. Cross, with great care, and take the road opposite. Follow the road past houses, on your right, and then bear right to reach a turn on the left (Hurstford Lane). Take this, following the road past Hollybush Farm and across another bridge over the M20.

Stay with the road, going downhill. Go past Hurstford Wood, on the right, then Calehill Farm, on the left, to reach a T-junction. Turn left and follow the road back into **Little Chart**. When the road forks, take the left-hand branch to return to the church and the start of the walk.

POINTS OF INTEREST:

Greensand Way – This fine long-distance footpath has Kent and Surrey sections, the whole linking to create a superb 100 mile route from Haslemere to Yalding.

Hothfield Common – This managed area of 250 acres of open land and woodland is a Nature Reserve, preserving the flora and fauna of this unique greensand area of the Vale of Kent, which lies between the North Downs and the Weald.

Little Chart – This hamlet, on the outskirts of Ashford, has one of the largest Forstals, where cattle were penned, or 'forestalled', before being driven to market.

The writer H E Bates lived in the village and it was here that he created the Larkin family of *Darling Buds of May*.

REFRESHMENTS:

The Swan Inn, Little Chart.
The Olive Branch, Westwell Leacon.
The Woolpack Inn, Tutt Hill.

Walk 61 EGERTON 6m ($9^1/_2$km)

Maps: OS Sheets Landranger 189; Pathfinder 1230.

A field and woodland walk, with occasional steep ascents.

Start: At 908475, Egerton Church.

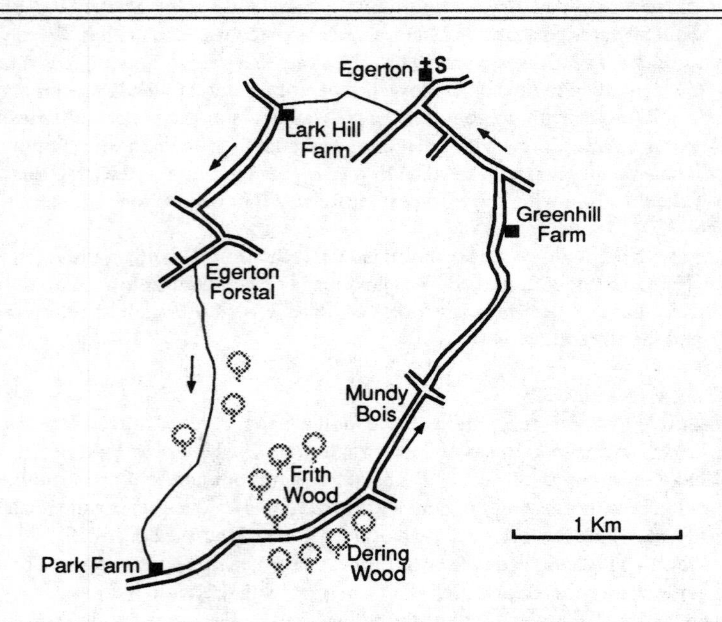

From the church, turn right and walk through the village. Just after passing the school, turn right along a footpath, following it as it leads to, and then runs beside, the boundary of a field. Continue along the path to reach a road near the buildings of Lark Hill Farm. Turn left along the road, following it downhill to reach a T-junction. Turn left and walk along a road for about 200 yards to reach a turning on the right. Take this, following the road into Egerton Forstal.

Opposite the Queen's Arms inn, in the village, turn left along a track which is also the driveway to both Forstal Farm and Poplar Farm. Maintain direction along the track, passing the farm entrances. The track then becomes a path: continue along it for just over a mile, ignoring various paths that lead off on either side. Cross several stiles and go through gates that link fields, following, at first on your left, and then on your right, patches of woodland. Continue along the path, eventually going through the buildings of Park Farm to reach a road. Turn left and follow the road as it meanders through Frith Wood. Just as the road emerges from the woodland, it forks. Take the lesser road on the left, following it to the cross-roads at Mundy Bois.

Go straight across to reach Greenhill Lane. Follow the lane past the entrances to Little Mundy Bois Farm and Oak's Farm. The road now bears left and runs parallel to the Greensand Way for a short while. After it bears left again, you pass the entrance to Greenhill Farm and climb steeply to reach a T-junction.

Turn left along New Road, following it along the top of the ridge that leads back into **Egerton**. At the T-junction in the village, turn right to return to the church.

POINTS OF INTEREST:

Egerton – This is another delightful, Vale of Kent village, surrounded by orchards. The village church, built in the 14th century, has a fine 15th-century tower built with local ragstone. The tower is a good example of the 'Kentish' style.

REFRESHMENTS:

The George Inn, Egerton.
The Queen's Arms, Egerton Forstal.
The Rose and Crown, Mundy Bois.

Walk 62 **FRITTENDEN** 6m (9½km)

Maps: OS Sheets Landranger 188; Pathfinder 1230.

A pleasant walk across open countryside.

Start: At 813409, Frittenden Church.

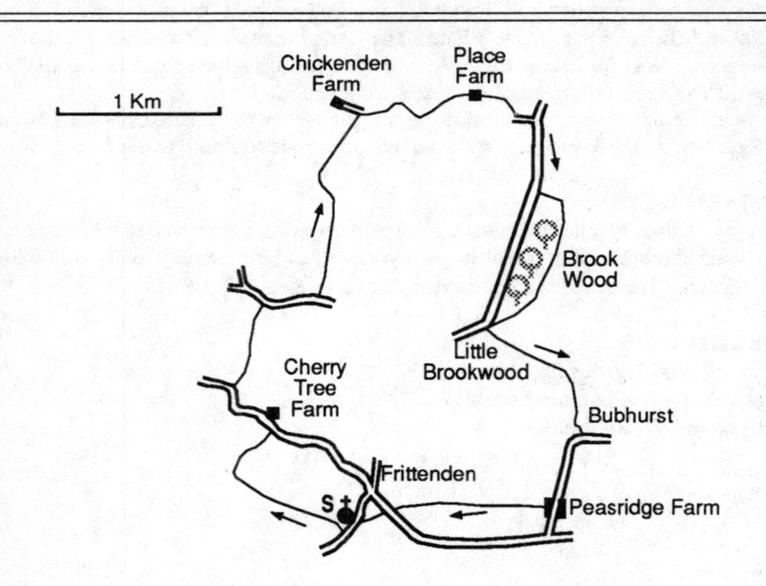

Go to the rear of the churchyard and take the path that leads away from the church and the village. Follow the path along the right-hand boundary of a field to reach a stile. Cross into the next field and walk beside the patch of woodland to your right. Continue to reach a crossing track. Turn right and follow the track as it first bears right, then left and continues to reach a road.

Turn left and follow the road round past Cherry Tree Farm, on your right, where the road bears left. Continue along the road as it bears right, then go through a gate on the right. Take the path that begins in the corner of the field and follow it diagonally to the centre of the field boundary ahead. Cross a stile into the next field and follow the left-hand boundary to reach the corner. Cross and continue along the right-hand edge of the next field. The path then leads between houses to reach a road. Turn right and follow the road for 200 yards, to reach a stile on the left. Cross and follow the path beyond for about 800 yards, crossing several fields to reach a track near Chickenden Farm.

Turn right, away from the farm buildings, following a path as it meanders very gently uphill. Cross a stream and go past Place Farm and Headcorn Place. Just past the latter you continue along a track, staying with it to reach a road. Turn right and follow the road for 250 yards to reach a track, on the left, which is the drive for Brook Wood Farm. Take this, but just before the farm buildings, turn right along a path that runs beside Brook Wood. At the end of the wood, cross into another field and bear right with the path to reach a minor road at Little Brookwood. Do not follow the road: instead, turn left and follow a path that goes through several fields. After passing Little Hungerden Farm you bear right, then left, to reach a road at Bubhurst.

Turn right and follow the road until you pass Peasridge Farm on the right. Now go through a gate on the right and follow the path beyond. Very soon the path joins a track running alongside an orchard. Follow this track through the buildings of Manor Farm and on to reach a road. Go straight across and continue along the track, following it to Frittenden. When you reach the next road, turn left and you will soon arrive back at the **church**.

POINTS OF INTEREST:
Frittenden Church – Although substantially rebuilt, the church retains its fine 15th-century tower.

REFRESHMENTS:
The Bell and Jorrocks, Frittenden.
The Knoxbridge Inn, Frittenden.

Walk 63 **RUCKINGE AND HAM STREET** 6m ($9^1/_2$km)

Maps: OS Sheets Landranger 189; Pathfinder 1251.

A walk between two villages, across isolated countryside and alongside the Royal Military Canal.

Start: At 025335, Ruckinge Church.

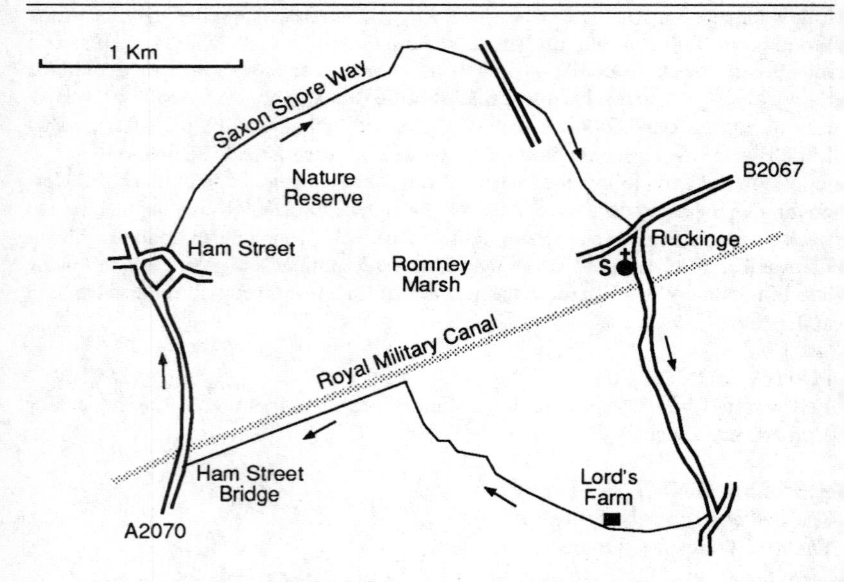

From the church, turn right along the road, following it through the village to reach a road on the right. Turn along this, following it out of the village and soon crossing the disused **Royal Military Canal**. Continue along the road through isolated farmland on the edge of **Romney Marsh**. When a road turns off to the left, turn right along the lane to Lord's Farm. Go past the farm buildings, staying with the track (Kitsbridge Lane) which eventually runs parallel to Sedbrook Sewer. When you reach a bridge (Kits Bridge) use it to cross the drain on to another track.

Follow this new track along the boundary of a field to reach the Royal Military Canal again. Turn left and walk along the canal for $^3/_4$ mile to reach Ham Street Bridge. Go up on to the bridge, using it to cross the canal. Now follow the road (the A2070), with care, to Ham Street. Follow the road through the village, continuing along it as it bears round to the left and reaches a cross-roads. Turn right along the B2067, again with great care, until it begins to bear right. Here, turn left up a street that leads past houses to woodland. Cross a stile into the woods, signed as part of the Saxon Shore Way and follow the path beyond until it forks. Take the right-hand branch and continue into the heart of the woodland, which is also a Nature Reserve.

When you emerge from the wood, continue with the woodland boundary on your right to a point where your path joins another coming from the right. Turn left along the new single route, following it to reach a track on the right which leads to Gill Farm. Take this track, going past the farm buildings. Stay on the track as it becomes a path and bears around to the right to reach a road. Cross diagonally on to a continuation of the path on the opposite side, entering a field at its corner. Head diagonally towards the middle of the boundary ahead to reach a stile. Cross into the next field and continue along a path. Go through several more fields, heading towards Ruckinge. Go past houses to reach the main road. Turn right and follow the road back to the **church**.

POINTS OF INTEREST:

Royal Military Canal – The canal was built during the Napoleonic Wars as both a defence and to transport troops and supplies.

Romney Marsh – A huge expanse of flat marshland that has been turned into grazing land by the excavation of a vast array of dykes. The area is famous for its sheep, for being the only British home of the marsh frog, and for Dr Syn the smuggler-parson. The fact that the latter is fictional does nothing to dampen the enthusiasm with which the name is used throughout the area.

Ruckinge Church – This 14th-century building, with a Norman tower, has a curious grave in its churchyard. A rough-hewn plank with three iron supports marks the grave of two members of the Bourne gang, who ran smuggling across the Marsh during the late18th century. The gang was eventually arrested and the leaders, the Ransley brothers were hanged near Maidstone. Many years later, an old man arrived in the village from Australia. A well-to-do old chap, he was soon liked by everyone, and when he died the village turned out in force to attend his funeral. Only then did they discover that his wealth was based on a pension from the government in exchange for his betrayal of the Ransleys. The government had organised his escape to Australia, from where, disguised by age, he had returned to live out his years in the village. As almost everyone attending the funeral was related to a member of the Bourne gang, and none of them saw smuggling as particularly dreadful, the funeral ended in a near riot.

REFRESHMENTS:

There are possibilities in Ruckinge and Ham Street.

Walk 64 **Bilsington** 6m ($9^1/_2$km)

Maps: OS Sheets Landranger 189; Pathfinder 1251.

A walk through woodland and across open farmland.

Start: At 039345, the White Horse Inn, Bilsington.

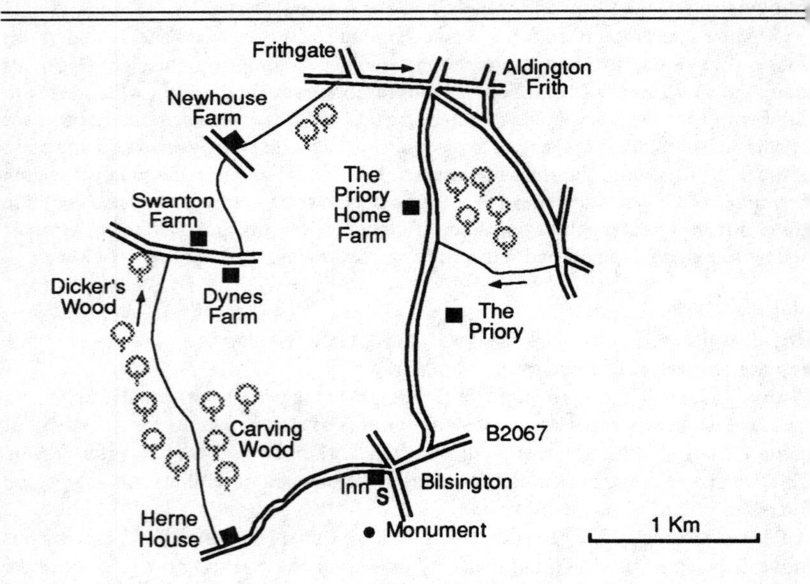

From the inn turn left along the main road (the B2067), heading away from the village. Follow the road, with care, past Herne House to reach the buildings at Herne Hill. Just past the last house, turn right along a track, following it along the boundary of a field, going uphill towards woodland. At first, walk with woodland on your left, then follow the track into Carving Wood. Stay on the track as it bears away to the left, ignoring all turnings, to either side.

When the track emerges from the woods into a field, continue with the woodland boundary on your left. When the woodland turns away to the left, maintain direction towards the corner of the patch of woodland ahead. When you reach this continue straight on, again with the woodland boundary on your left, to reach a road. Turn right, and walk past Swanton Farm, on the left, and then Dynes Farm, on the right. Just past the buildings of the latter, turn left along a path that leads through a field and then continues to the corner of the second field. Go through into a third field, and turn right along a path that heads diagonally right to the opposite corner. At the corner, cross on to a road. Go straight across the road and take a path that runs alongside Newhouse Farm. Cross a stream and follow the left-hand edge of a field to reach a stile in a corner. Cross and follow the right-hand edge of the next field, with woodland on your right.

When you reach the boundary of the field cross over and maintain direction towards the buildings of Frithgate ahead. Just to the left of the buildings you join a road: turn right. Walk along the road to reach the cross-roads in Aldington Frith. Turn right, then almost immediately left along Bourne Road. Follow this road for nearly a mile, to a point just after a turning on the left. On your right, here, is a path signed as part of the Saxon Shore Way. Take this path, following it through woodland. On emerging from the wood, continue with the woodland boundary on your right to reach a road opposite the entrance to The Priory Home Farm.

Turn left along the road, going past the entrance to the remains of **Bilsington Priory**. Continue to reach a T-junction. Turn right and follow the road back into the village of **Bilsington**. When you reach a cross-roads, go straight over to return to the start of the walk.

POINTS OF INTEREST:

Bilsington Priory – The remains are those of an Augustinian Priory, founded in the 13th century. Rumour has it that the remains are haunted by a number of ghosts, most notably by the wife of a man who murdered her for having dropped a tray of his best china, and by a disembodied head trailing scarlet ribbons.

Bilsington – Close to the village, but not on the line of the walk, is a monument erected by grateful villagers in memory of Sir William Cosway. Sir William, who was killed in a coaching accident in 1835, was a local landowner who was held in high esteem for his fairness and philanthropy. Sadly, the monument has been struck by lightning several times and is in a poor state of repair.

REFRESHMENTS:

The White Horse Inn, Bilsington.

The Good Intent, Aldington Frith.

Walk 65 **LADDINGFORD** 6m ($9^1/_2$km)

Maps: OS Sheets Landranger 188; Pathfinder 1229.

A walk from this village, mainly alongside the Rivers Medway and Beult.

Start: At 691481, the Chequers Inn, Laddingford.

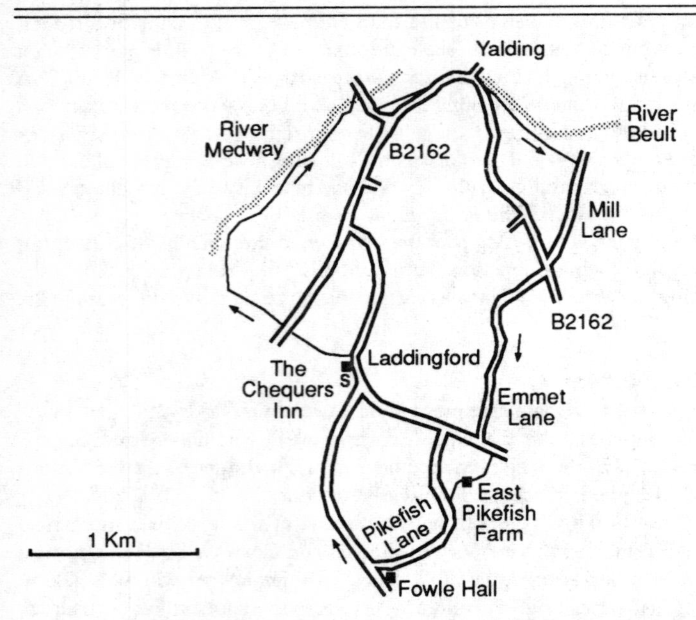

From the inn, turn left and walk for about 50 yards to reach a track on the left. Take this, following it through a field and on into an orchard. Go through the orchard to reach a road. Go straight across and follow the track opposite. The track crosses a small stream and then continues towards the **River Medway**. Go past a lake, on your right, continuing to join the riverside path. Turn right along this path. The walk now follows the river, which flows most enjoyably through open country. Eventually the path runs to the rear of a car park near Twyford Bridge to reach a small bridge.

Cross this bridge to reach a road at the other side of the river and turn right to cross back over. Very soon you will reach, on your left, a path signed as part of the Greensand Way. Take this, following it away from the river to reach a road (the

B2162, as travelled, briefly, before). Turn left and follow the road, with care, through the southern tip of **Yalding**, a village that spans the River Beult, a tributary of the Medway. Stay with the road as it bears round in a loop to the right and joins Benover Road. After a row of houses on the left, take a track that leads to the bank of the River Beult. Turn right along the riverside path, following it for several hundred yards. Just after you walk alongside a patch of woodland on the left, the path reaches a road (Mill Lane). Turn right and follow this road for $^1/_2$ mile through open countryside.

When you reach a road junction, turn left, and then very soon right along Emmet Lane. Follow this minor road as it meanders between fields and orchards to reach a T-junction. Turn left, then cross over and go along a track on the right. Stay on this track until it ends, then turn right along a path that soon bears left and runs between the buildings of East Pikefish Farm. Go past the farm buildings, cross into a field and head diagonally left towards the far corner. Cross a stile into the next field and bear right towards the road in the distance. When you reach the road (Pikefish Lane), walk parallel to it for a while, then leave the path through a gate to join it.

Walk on this until you reach a junction where you turn and follow this road as it leads back into Laddingford. You again have open fields and orchards on either side. When another road joins from the right you continue on, following the single route and eventually returning to the start of the walk.

POINTS OF INTEREST:

River Medway – The river has played a very important part in the history of Kent, carrying timber and iron from the Weald downstream and, later, supplying water for the hop growers to make beer. So important was it that it is the traditional barrier between the Men of Kent, to the east, and the Kentish Men, to the west.

Yalding – The medieval bridge at Yalding is the longest in Kent. An exceptional view over superb Kentish landscape can be had from the tower of the church of St Peter and St Paul.

REFRESHMENTS:

The Chequers Inn, Laddingford.
The Swan, Yalding.
The Two Brewers, Yalding.

Walk 66 **Shadoxhurst** 6m ($9^1/_2$km

Maps: OS Sheets Landranger 189; Pathfinder 1250.

A mainly woodland walk around this small village.

Start: At 971381, the King's Head Inn, Shadoxhurst.

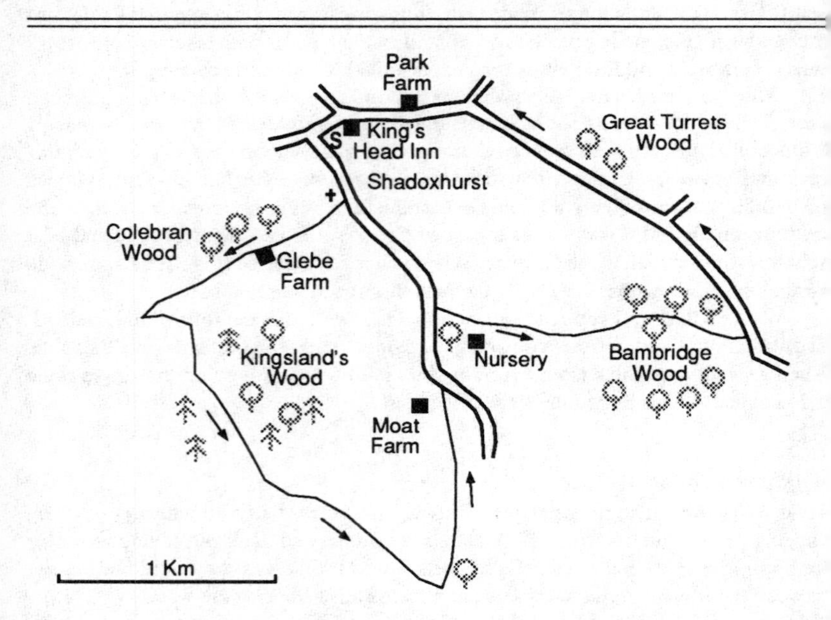

From the inn, turn left along the main village road. Very soon the road forks: stay o the left and follow that road to reach a turning on the left. Take this, following th road past houses, on your left, and then the church, on your right. Just past the church turn right along a track which is the drive to several farms. Stay with the track to reac Glebe Farm. Here the track turns to the left: cross on to the path directly ahead an continue along it, with Colebran Wood on your right. At the end of the woodland, g over a stile into a field, and head diagonally towards the centre of the boundary ahead Go through a gate into the next field and head straight on towards the track in th distance. When you reach this track, turn left along it.

Very soon the track leads into Kingsland's Wood. There follows a pleasant wal of nearly a mile through mixed woodland. When the track divides, take the left-han branch and continue through Courthope Wood East. When the track emerges from the woodland, continue ahead until the track turns to the left. Here, turn sharp left and take a path that bisects the right angle of the track. When the path is crossed by another, continue straight on, following your path through several fields, eventually reaching a road next to the driveway leading to Moat Farm. Turn left along the road, following it as it swings around to the right. Soon, you reach a small patch of woodland, on the right. At the end of this, turn right along a track.

Follow the track past a nursery, on the right, and back into the woodland of Bambridge Wood. Stay with the track to cross a stream, continuing through the wood. When the track emerges from the wood, you soon turn right to reach a road. Turn left along the road, following it for just over a mile and going past Great Turrets Wood, on your left. Go past Woodside Farm and Menilworth Farm, both on the left, to reach a road on the right. Do not take this: instead, continue along the road you are on as it swings left and back into Shadoxhurst. Go past Park Farm, on the right, and continue to reach the King's Head, the start of the walk.

POINTS OF INTEREST:

There is nothing specific about this route, yet it is a fine one, enjoying extensive areas of mixed woodland. In all seasons the walk is excellent, and is especially good for birdwatchers.

REFRESHMENTS:

The King's Head Inn, Shadoxhurst.

As an alternative, take a picnic and enjoy it somewhere along the route.

Walk 67 **EAST MALLING** $6^1/_2$m ($10^1/_4$km

Maps: OS Sheets Landranger 188; Pathfinder 1209.

A gently sloping walk through woodland and across farmland

Start: At 703571, East Malling Church.

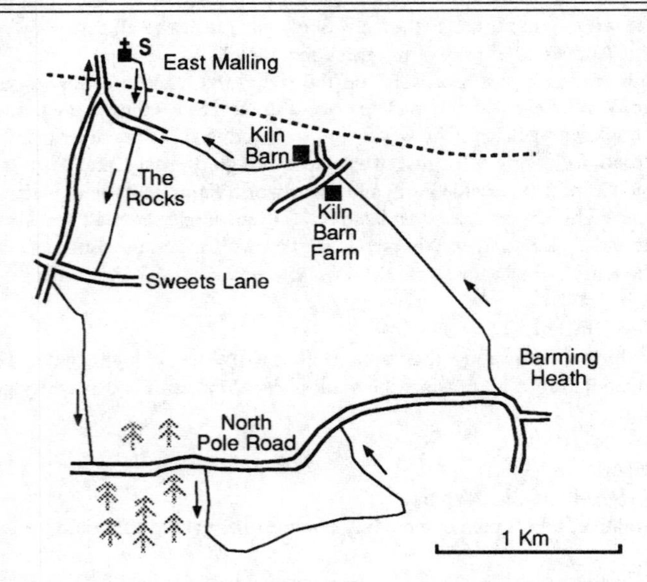

Go to the rear of the churchyard and take the track that leads away from the villag Now turn right along a track which leads across the railway line to reach a minc road. Turn right, and then very soon left along a street and, ignoring a turning on th left, continue straight on as the road becomes a track. Follow the track through sever fields, crossing a series of stiles as you go along the field edges. Maintain directio when the track becomes a path, following it to reach a road, Sweets Lane. Turn rig and walk to a cross-roads. There, turn sharp left along a path, following it into coppice woodland and then taking a path that leads diagonally away from the cross-roads.

The path leads past the edge of the woods: follow it first to the left, then to th right, to reach a farm building on your right. Here, follow a path that bears left an leads gently uphill to go through the heart of the woods. Maintain direction when yo reach a field, keeping the field boundary on your right, until you reach a road, Nort

Pole Road. Turn left and follow the road for nearly $^1/_2$ mile to reach a signed footpath on the right. Follow this back into the woods, continuing to emerge into a field. Stay on the path as it meanders gently downhill, then turn left along another path, following it along the edge of woodland. Stay with the path, going along field edges to reach Hall Place Farm. Go past the farm buildings to reach the farm track and turn left. Follow the track as it bears left, and at the corner of a field cross over and bear left and gently uphill to rejoin North Pole Road.

Turn right and follow the road to **Barming** Heath. When the road swings round to the right, go left along a byway, following it past a water tower and through woodland to reach Kiln Barn Farm. Go through the farmyard and on to a road. Take the road directly opposite and follow it to reach a track on the left, just before Kiln Barn. Take this track, skirting the edge of Four Acres and passing Paris Farm. The track leads back into **East Malling**: when you reach the main road through the village, turn right, go under the railway line and continue to reach a path, on the right, that leads back to the church, or, as an alternative, leave the road on the right to retrace the outward route back to the church.

POINTS OF INTEREST:

Barming – This hamlet, a short detour from the walk, still has a wooden bridge that carries traffic across the Medway. It's church has a mounting stone for horse riders at the gate and carved oak choir stalls from Flanders.

East Malling – The fine church dates from the 14th and 15th centuries, with a tower that is part Norman. The Research Station, close to the walk, is housed in a fine Queen Anne mansion and can be visited, by appointment, by those interested in horticulture.

REFRESHMENTS:

There are several alternatives in East Malling and Barming Heath.

Walk 68 **CHILHAM** $6^1/_2$m ($10^1/_4$km)

Maps: OS Sheets Landranger 179; Pathfinder 1211.

A walk from an historic village, mainly through orchards or along country roads.

Start: At 069536, Chilham village square.

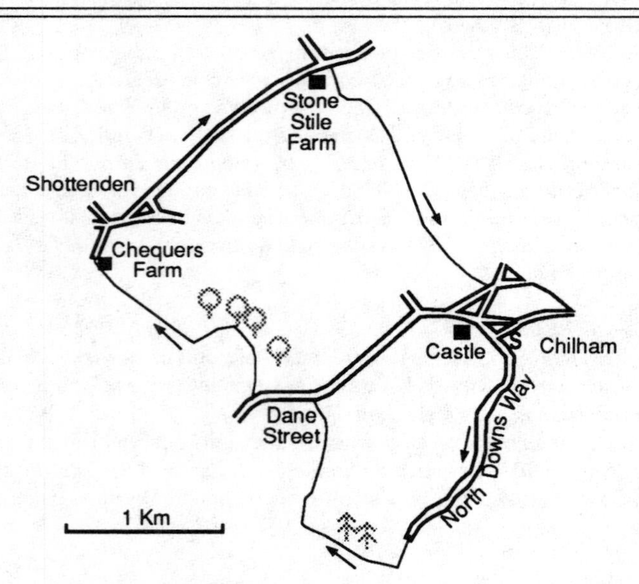

From the **village square**, facing the **castle** entrance, take the road on the left, which is signposted as the North Downs Way. Follow this as it leads away from the village and goes past a small patch of woodland, and a lake on the right. As the road goes past Mountain Street it starts to go gently uphill: keep along it as it becomes a byway. About 200 yards after the byway begins, it turns right: follow this new route, which is still part of the North Downs Way, going uphill and into woodland.

Once in the heart of the woods, the path bears away to the right and leads downhill. Emerge from the woods and cross into a field. Now, ignoring the path on the left, continue straight on and downhill to soon reach a road (the A252) in the hamlet of Dane Street. Turn left and walk carefully along the main road for about 200 yards, then cross, even more carefully, to turn right along a byway. Follow this as it swings ight along the boundary of a field, and then crosses towards woodland. The path now follows the left-hand edge of the woods, turning left, and then right to emerge into an orchard. Soon the path becomes a track that goes across the front of Chequers Farm to reach a minor road. Turn right and follow the road into the village of Shottenden.

When you reach the main village road, turn right and continue until the road forks. Take the left branch and follow it for just over a mile. This is a quiet country road, running between orchards, and in summer is a haven for all kinds of wildlife. Eventually you reach Stone Stile Farm, on your right, opposite a road going left. Turn right along the track that runs through the farm buildings and then goes along the edge of an orchard. When the track forks, take the left branch and follow the left-hand edge of a field. At the corner, where a track goes left, cross into another field and continue, with an orchard on your right.

Cross another track and follow a path that runs through orchards to emerge, finally, at the corner of a field. Maintain direction along the path to reach a road (the A252). Cross, with great care, and go along the road opposite, very soon turning left to return to the start.

POINTS OF INTEREST:

Village Square – Chilham is a very pretty village with several well preserved half-timbered houses set around the square. The excellent church is 15th-century: inside is the superb white marble monument by the sculptor Sir Francis Chantrey whose bequest for the founding of an art collection in London led to the establishment of the Tate Gallery.

Castle – Chilham Castle is a Jacobean mansion built, in 1616, to a design said to have been of Inigo Jones. The gardens were laid out by Capability Brown and in them are the remains of a Norman castle built on Roman foundations. Open to the public.

REFRESHMENTS:

The White Horse, Chilham.

The Woolpack, Chilham.

Various tea rooms in Chilham.

Walk 69 **RHODES MINNIS** 6 1/2 m (10 1/4 km)

Maps: OS Sheets Landranger 189; Pathfinder 1231.

A field and woodland walk, on gently slopes.

Start: At 152428, the Gate Inn, Rhodes Minnis.

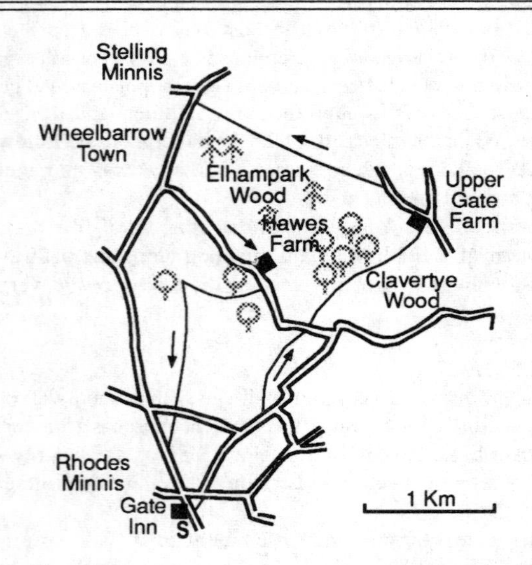

Take the path directly opposite the inn, heading diagonally left to reach another road. Turn right, and then immediately left along another road. Follow this road past a turning to the left and then another to the right. Just past this second turning, go over a stile on the left and follow the path beyond as it bears away to the right. When you reach the corner of the field, follow the left-hand boundary, then cross into another field and continue to reach a road.

Cross straight over and go along a byway that leads past Clavertye Wood, to the left. Go through a gate and on through the buildings of Upper Park Gate Farm to reach a road. Turn left, and follow the road until, after about 200 yards, it bears right. Now cross a stile on the left and follow the path beyond. Go through an orchard, continuing along the path into Elhampark Wood, which is mainly coniferous. When you emerge from the woods, cross into a field and maintain direction, staying with the path as it heads for the centre of the far boundary. Cross into the next field, then go through two more fields to reach a road near Boormanhatch Farm, at the edge of **Stelling Minnis**. If you are looking for a refreshment stop, take a short detour into the village which has several inns.

The walk turns left along the road, following it to reach a turning on the left, near to the wonderfully named Wheelbarrow Town. Take this turning, following the road for $^3/_4$ mile to a point just past the entrance to Hawes Farm, on the left. Now turn right along a path heading into woodland. Go through the wood to emerge into a field and bear diagonally right to reach the boundary of another patch of woodland. There, turn left, and then very soon right, over a stile into the woods.

Soon you will arrive at a crossing of paths: turn sharp left and follow a path out of the woods on to an area of open Downland. Follow the path as it gradually descends to reach a road. Cross straight over and follow the path opposite, soon reaching another road. Turn left and follow the road into Rhodes Minnis, going straight ahead at the cross-roads to return to the start of the walk.

POINTS OF INTEREST:

Stelling Minnis – As well as possible refreshment stops, the village has a splendid smock-mill, which was originally built in 1866. Though now disused, the windmill has been restored and is open to the public.

REFRESHMENTS:

The Gate Inn, Rhodes Minnis.

There are also several possibilities in Stelling Minnis.

Walk 70 **Boughton Lees** $6^1/_2$m ($10^1/_4$km

Maps: OS Sheets Landranger 189; Pathfinder 1231.

A Downland walk, following part of the North Downs Way.

Start: At 022473, the Village Green, Boughton Lees.

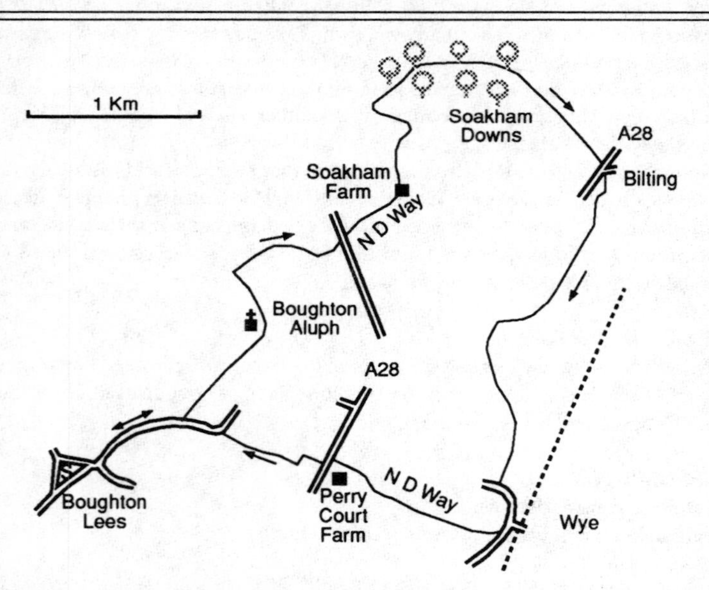

From the Flying Horse Inn, on the Green at Boughton Lees, turn left and go to th corner of the Green. Now take the turning on the left, signed as part of the **North Down Way**, and follow it as it leads away from the village. Ignore the byway that goes off t the left, continuing until you can turn left along a path that is also signed as part of th North Downs Way. Stay with this path as it leads through fields to the hamlet o **Boughton Aluph**.

Turn left along the minor road that runs through the village, going past the church Now bear right as the road becomes a track. Follow the track uphill, and just beyon Forstal Cottages, on your right, take a path that initially runs beside the cottages, the bears right across open country heading to the centre of the field boundary. Cross stile and maintain direction, then, when another path joins from the right, go left on t the new, single route. This new path soon reaches a road. Cross and go along th byway opposite. This byway is also the driveway for Soakham Farm and a part of the North Downs Way.

Follow the byway past the farm buildings. Stay with it as it bears left and goes uphill on to Soakham Downs. The path turns right and reaches the edge of woodland. Turn left and follow the woodland edge. When this boundary turns left, cross a stile and maintain direction, going into the woods. Soon you will emerge from the woods: turn right, following the woodland boundary. Go back into the woods when your path turns right, and continue for about 50 yards to a point where the byway bears left. There, take the path going off to the right.

Follow the path gradually downhill. The path turns left, then very soon right and leaves the woods to reach a track. Now follow the track, continuing to descend, to reach a road (the A28) at Bilting. Go straight across, with great care, and follow the road opposite, but almost immediately turn right along a footpath between houses. Follow the path across delightful Downland for 1½ miles, eventually reaching a road opposite Bramble Farm house. Turn left and follow the road in the direction of **Wye**. At the staion, do not cross the railway: instead, walk parallel to it for a short distance to reach a path on the right, signed as part of the North Downs Way. Take this path, going uphill to reach the A28 (the main Ashford-Canterbury road) near the entrance to Perry Court Farm.

Cross over, with great care, and take the path opposite, but almost immediately turn left, then right on to another path. Follow this path to reach a junction of paths. Turn left and follow the edge of an orchard. Turn right with the orchard boundary and continue to reach a road. Turn left and follow this road back to the Village Green at Boughton Lees.

POINTS OF INTEREST:

North Downs Way – As with all National Trails, the Way is waymarked by an acorn symbol. The Way links Farnham, in Surrey, with Dover, a distance of 140 miles.

Boughton Aluph – The village church, dating in part from the 13th century, is now only used irregularly for worship, but is a focal venue during the annual Stour Music Festival.

Wye – A short detour would take the walker to this delightful market town, home of a famous agricultural college. The college was originally for priests, but was dissolved by Henry VIII. It then became a grammar school, becoming an agricultural college in the late 19th century and part of London University in the early years of this century.

REFRESHMENTS:

The Flying Horse Inn, Boughton Lees.

Walk 71 SISSINGHURST CASTLE $6^1/_2$m ($10^1/_4$km)

Maps: OS Sheets Landranger 188; Pathfinder 1250.

A walk from the tiny hamlet of Three Chimneys past Sissinghurst Castle and through woodland.

Start: At 826387, the Three Chimneys Inn, Three Chimneys.

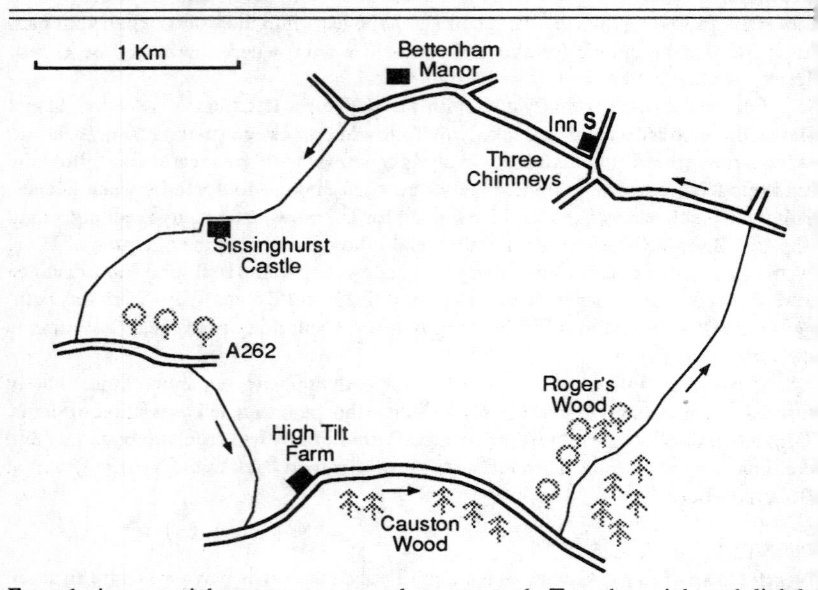

From the inn, turn right to, very soon, reach a cross-roads. Turn sharp right and slightly back from the main junction, and follow this minor road past the entrance to Little Bettenham. Continue to reach a T-junction. Turn left and follow this new road past the entrance to **Bettenham Manor**. Continue along the road until it turns to the right. There, take a track, on the left, that continues straight ahead. Initially, the track goes downhill. Then, after crossing a field boundary it goes gradually uphill. Follow the boundary of the field to reach a stile, and cross into the next field. From this field, the track goes through the buildings of Sissinghurst Castle Farm, skirting the boundary of **Sissinghurst Castle** and its gardens. A visit to this world-famous sight is a must, and you can easily detour from the walk to reach the main entrance.

The track merges with the castle path near a car park: follow the castle's approach drive to reach a road (the A262). Turn left and follow the road, with great care, for about 300 yards, passing woodland, on your left. At a slight curve in the road, cross, with even greater care, to reach a signed footpath on the right. Follow the path as it bears diagonally downhill. At the foot of the slope, cross Crane Brook and bear right. Ignore the track leading to High Tilt Farm, on the left, continuing to reach a road. Turn left and follow the road for about a mile as it goes past the substantial Causton Wood on the right.

Go past the entrance to kennels, on your left, and about 200 yards after this, go left along a track that leads into woodland. Follow the track through the mainly coniferous woodland and up a gentle slope. On emerging from the woodland, cross a stile and turn right, staying with the track. Very soon, the track becomes a path: follow it along the left-hand boundary of a field to reach the corner of that field, where the path reverts to a track. Continue through several fields, always following the left-hand boundary, to reach a road at a T-junction.

Turn left and follow the road, passing the entrances to Great Bachelor's Farm, on the left, and Holden Farm, on the right. Continue to reach the cross-roads at Three Chimneys. Take the turning on the right to return to the start of the walk.

POINTS OF INTEREST:

Bettenham Manor – The Baby Carriage Collection, a unique collection of Victorian and Edwardian carriages, is housed in an oast house next to the Manor.

Sissinghurst Castle – The Manor House was built in the late 15th century, but had later additions. It needed extensive restoration work after having been used as a prison during the Napoleonic Wars. The French prisoners nicknamed it the *Château*, and the name stuck, the manor having been Sissinghurst Castle ever since. The main restoration was carried out by Vita Sackville-West and Sir Harold Nicholson, whose home it was in the mid-War years. The Nicholsons were responsible for the magnificent gardens, which are quite rightly world famous and still the centrepiece of the Castle. Inside, Vita's work room can still be seen. The buildings and gardens are now managed by the National Trust.

REFRESHMENTS:

The Three Chimneys Inn, Three Chimneys.

Tea Rooms, Sissinghurst Castle.

Walk 72 **CONYER ROUTE 2** 7m (11km

Maps: OS Sheets Landranger 178; Pathfinder 1194 and 1195.

A walk alongside Swale, then across fields, occasionally on quie public roads.

Start: At 963646, in the centre of Conyer.

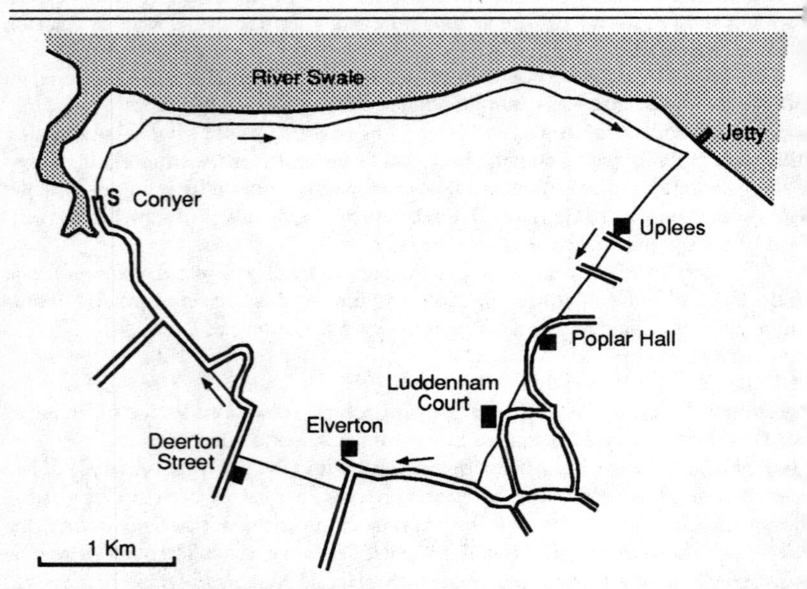

From the centre of **Conyer**, continue northwards along the main village road, wi Conyer Creek on your left. Very soon the road becomes a track and bears right an away from the creek-side: stay with the track, passing some industrial works on you left and eventually climbing on to a dyke which runs alongside the **River Swale**. Nov to your right, are a series of water-filled ditches and, on your left, in the River Swal is Fowley Island. This Swale side route is part of the **Saxon Shore Way**.

Continue walking along the dyke for about $2^1/_2$ miles, then, by a disused jett take the path on the right, heading inland. Follow this path down to a group bungalows, continuing on when the path becomes a road to reach a T-junction. G over, cross a stile, and continue down the side of an enclosed wooded area, with fence on your left. Continue to reach a minor road. Cross over and follow a path as bears slightly to the left. Continue along the path to reach the driveway that runs in front of Poplar Hall.

Follow this drive for 300 yards, then take a track on the left, following it as it goes diagonally down to Luddenham Court. Just past the church, bear right along a made-up path that soon becomes a track. Go through the middle of a field to reach a minor road. Turn right and follow the road to the hamlet of Elverton. At a junction, turn left and then go over a stile on the right and follow the track beyond. This bears slightly right, crosses a farm road and continues to reach a road. Follow this to a T-junction in Deerton Street. Turn right and follow the road around a sharp left bend.

Now, when the road goes to the right, keep straight on along the edges of three fields, regaining the road at the end of the third field. The remainder of the walk is on public roads and, although they are usually quiet, it is important to take care. Follow the road to a junction. Continue straight on, going past Banks Farm on your right, and following the road back to Conyer.

POINTS OF INTEREST:

Conyer – This attractive little village, grouped around its inn, was once the haunt of smugglers.

River Swale – The river is the channel that separates the Isle of Sheppey from the mainland. It is a haven for water birds, especially in winter.

Saxon Shore Way – This ancient long distance route was originally used by the Romans moving armies to defend against Saxon invaders. Today the 140 mile route from Gravesend to Rye is taken by more peaceful walkers.

REFRESHMENTS:

The Brunswick Arms, Conyer.

The Ship Inn, Conyer Quay.

Walk 73 **KESTON, DOWNE AND FARNBOROUGH** 7m (11km)

Maps: OS Sheets Landranger 187 and 188; Pathfinder 1192.

A walk through the rural area outside Bromley.

Start: At 419639, the car park at Westerham Road, Keston.

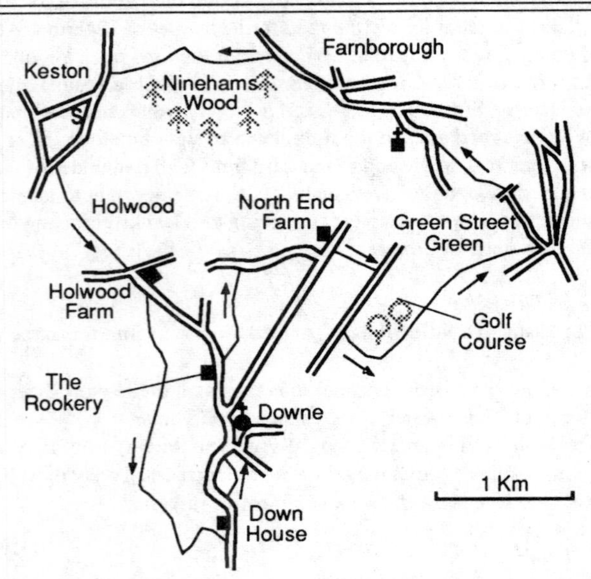

Leave the car park into Westerham Road, cross and turn right. Follow the road to reach a stile and a signed footpath on the left. Cross and follow the path through the estate of Holwood Park and along the boundary of a field to reach a road junction. Follow the road directly ahead, with Holwood Farm on your left. Just past the last of the farm buildings, turn right along a fenced footpath.

Go past a riding centre and cross over a stile. Now follow the side of a valley, where there is a golf course, and take a footpath to the left. Next, turn right to walk beside woodland. At the end of the wood, turn left along a track, following the new boundary to reach a junction of tracks. Turn left, but almost immediately right through a gate. Follow the footpath beyond across a field, with Down House on your left, to reach a road (Luxted Road). Turn left along the road to reach the entrance to **Down House**. Turn right, opposite the house, along a signed footpath, following it through a field. Cross a stile and a fence, and bear left to reach a road on the outskirts of Downe.

Turn right to reach a cross-roads. Turn left and walk through the village, passing close to the church and the Queen's Head Inn. When you reach the Rookery, on your left, turn right along a footpath, following it along the right-hand boundary of a field. Cross a stile and, with a hedge on your left, continue to reach another stile on the left. Cross this, and soon after another stile, then follow the edge of a field to reach a junction of lanes. Take the route directly ahead, following it to reach another junction. Turn right along a bridleway, passing a picnic site to reach a road.

Turn left and walk to North End Farm, on the left. Turn right, opposite the farm, along a signed footpath, following it into woodland and then across a golf course to reach a road. Turn right and follow the road to the edge of Cuckoo Woods. There, turn left along a path that follows the edge of the woods for some distance. Maintain direction when another path crosses, and then, when another goes off to the right, continue along your path through a section of woodland and out into a field. Cross diagonally to the centre of the far boundary. Cross into the next field and continue to reach a road at Green Street Green.

Turn left and follow the road to reach a T-junction. Cross and follow the path opposite which leads diagonally across to another road, joining just as it bears left. Go ahead along this road, following it as it skirts Farnborough village, and continuing to reach woodland on the left. When the wood ends, and houses begin, go left along a path. Follow the path, with houses on your right, and Ninehams Wood, and then Lake Wood, on your left. Eventually the path reaches Westerham Road: turn left and retrace your steps to the car park.

POINTS OF INTEREST:

Down House – The house was the home of Charles Darwin for the last 40 years of his life. Here he wrote *The Origin of Species*. It is owned by the Royal College of Surgeons and can be visited. The grounds are preserved as the Darwin Memorial Garden.

REFRESHMENTS:

The Queen's Head Inn, Downe.
The Crown Inn, Keston.

Walk 74 HOLLINGBOURNE 7m (11km)

Maps: OS Sheets Landranger 178 and 188; Pathfinder 1210.

A walk from the village of Hollingbourne across the surrounding downland.

Start: At 834551, Hollingbourne Railway Station.

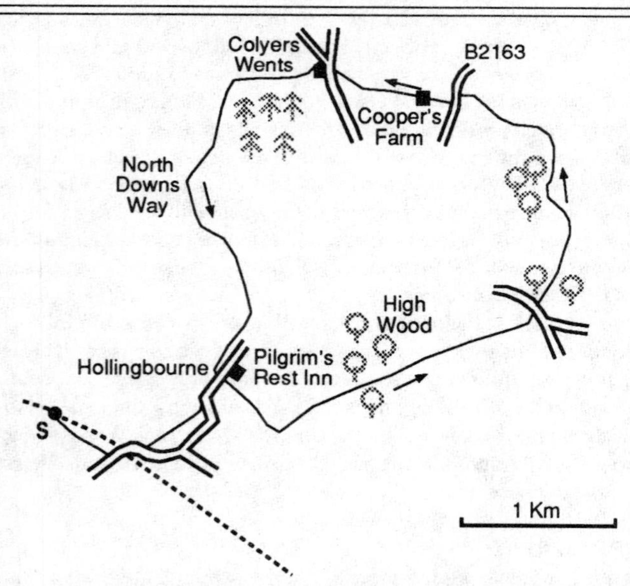

From the station, turn left into Station Road and then left again into the village street, crossing the railway line. At the village school, take the path on the left, following it across a meadow and past the church to reach the road again. Walk ahead to reach the Pilgrim's Rest Inn and turn right there, along the **Pilgrim's Way**. After $^1/_4$ mile, turn left along a cart track, following it to reach a track on the right. Take this, going uphill to the corner of the field. On the hill ahead, follow the left-hand boundary to the top, from where there are excellent views.

Take a path on the right which initially follows the edge of woodland, then leads into and through the trees. On emerging from the woodland, bear diagonally right across a field to its far corner where you will reach a small road at a junction. Turn left, then, when the road bears left, you will reach a barn in a farmyard. Go to the left of the barn, through a gate and cross a field towards the middle of the hedge opposite. There, cross a stile and head towards the corner of the field beyond to reach an old trackway, Drake Lane. Walk ahead, along this track, staying with it when it turns left through woods and then returns to open Downland. Now continue along it as it turns right and, eventually, leads into another clump of woodland.

When you emerge from the woods turn left through a gate and follow the woodland edge. Cross two stiles and head for the far left-hand corner of a field. Cross another stile on to a road (the B2163). Cross, with care, and follow the drive to Cooper's Farm. Go through the farmyard and into the field beyond. Cross the field to a wood and follow a track through the wood and on to a road. Turn right to reach a cottage called Colyers Wents, on the right. Bear left, then left again along a track beside the cottage. Follow the track for about a mile, going through woods, then when you reach the end of a field on your right, turn left through a gate and follow the track beyond on to a concrete platform at the edge of the Downs.

Turn left along the North Downs Way, following the ridge top of the Downs. The track gradually leads downhill and then to the far corner of a field, with a road visible beyond the hedge. Turn right into the next field and follow its edge until you find a way out on to the road, reaching it close to the Pilgrim's Rest Inn. From there, retrace your steps to the railway station.

POINTS OF INTEREST:

Pilgrim's Way – Although there is no evidence of its ever having been used by pilgrims, this evocative name has been given to a long distance footpath from Winchester Cathedral to Canterbury Cathedral. The route can be seen as a southerly variant of the North Downs Way, with which it co-incides for several sections, but is worthwhile in its own right. From cathedral to cathedral is about 115 miles.

Hollingbourne – This village, nestling in the shadow of the North Downs, has many fine period houses. It's 15th-century church has a chapel devoted to the Culpeper family. The red brick Tudor manor of the Culpepers is next to the church.

REFRESHMENTS:

The Pilgrim's Rest Inn, Hollingbourne.
The King's Head Inn, Hollingbourne.

Walk 75 PENSHURST AND CHIDDINGSTONE 7m (11km)

Maps: OS Sheets Landranger 188; Pathfinder 1228.

A walk between two historic villages and through parkland.

Start: At 519465, Penshurst Railway Station.

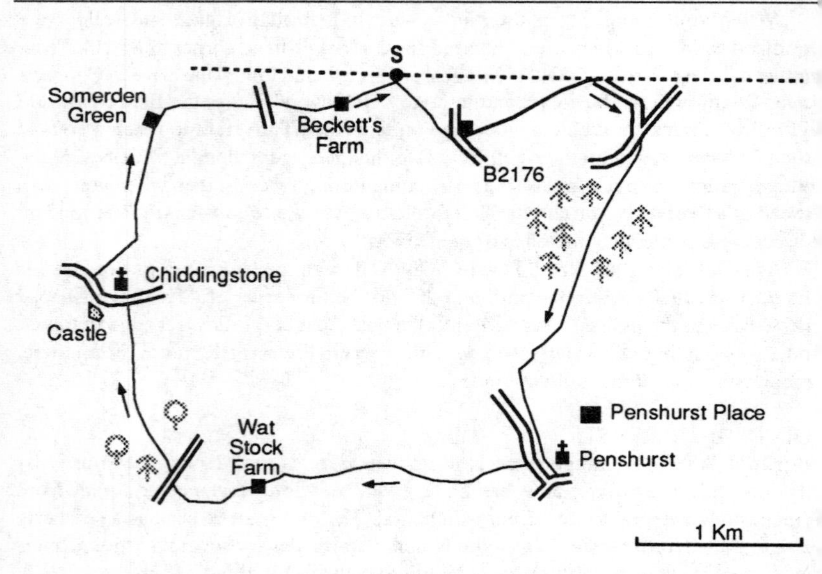

Leave Penshurst station, on the side opposite the Little Brown Jug, and go along the station approach to reach a road (the B2176). Turn right, then very soon, cross, with care, and turn left along a farm drive. Turn left into a farmyard and follow the track beside the farm buildings. Maintain direction, with woods on your right, then follow the boundaries of several fields to reach a road, with the railway line to your left. Bear right and follow the road as it bends around the boundary of Roundabout Wood to arrive at a junction. Turn left, and then almost immediately right along a track. Cross a stile and go along a path marked for Penshurst Place. Cross another stile and continue along the path, going into woods, over a stile and then uphill along a drive. At the end of the drive, cross a stile, turn right and then, very soon, turn left along a track into woodland. Go through an avenue of trees to reach a stile next to a gate. Go over and continue to the next gate. Do not go through: instead, turn right and follow the fence on your left to reach a stile. Cross and follow the edge of a field. On your left, through the trees, is a lake known as Lancup Well. When you reach the corner of the field, turn right, cross a stile on the left and follow the path across the open parkland of Penshurst Park. Cross several stiles, then a drive and continue along the path to reach the churchyard at Penshurst, passing, on the way, the great mansion of **Penshurst Place**.

Go through the churchyard and out into Leicester Square. Turn right along a road to reach a junction. Turn right and, very soon, left along a farm road. Follow this across a bridge over the River Eden. Just beyond the bridge the road forks: go right, uphill, for about a mile to reach the buildings of Wat Stock Farm. Go past a pond on your right, then bear right to a gate on to a road. Cross, go through a gate and follow the path beyond into woodland. You will soon reach a drive: follow it to just beyond the edge of the woods, then go through a gate on the right and follow the path beyond to a road in **Chiddingstone**. Go left along the village street, passing the Castle Inn and the church. On your left is a lake, with a fine view across it to Chiddingstone Castle. Go through a gate on the right, opposite the lake, and follow a path along the right side of a field, then cross to a stile in the bottom corner of the next field. Go over and turn left along a more substantial path, following it over the River Eden and continuing to walk beside the buildings of Somerden Green. At Rectory Cottage, turn right, cross a stile and go across the corner of a field to a gate. Go through and turn right to the corner of the field beyond. Now go left to reach another gate. Go through and cross diagonally to a stile. Cross and go along a drive to a road.

Turn left, then right through a gate and cross a field to another gate. Go through and follow the right-hand boundary of a field to reach Beckett's Farm. Go past the farmhouse and, once past the buildings, bear left to follow the right edge of two fields. When you enter a third field, turn left, and then soon bear right and go diagonally to reach a stile. Cross and follow a path beside an orchard to return to the start.

POINTS OF INTEREST:

Penshurst Place – The Mansion House of Lord de Lisle, part of which dates from the 14th century, is the former home of the Sidney family, one of whom, Sir Philip Sidney, was a famous Elizabethan poet. Queen Elizabeth I herself once danced here.

Chiddingstone – Chiddingstone has a strong claim to being the prettiest village in Kent. The National Trust owns a row of the best of the houses, fine buildings dating from the 16th and 17th centuries. The Chiding Stone of the name is a sandstone rock where nagging wives were taken to be nagged at by the whole village.

REFRESHMENTS:

The Castle Inn, Chiddingstone.

Walk 76 **Lympne and Royal Military Canal** 7m (11km)

Maps: OS Sheets Landranger 189; Pathfinder 1252.

A fascinating walk along, and around, the disused canal, with many historic sites.

Start: At 125350, Shepway Cross, Lympne.

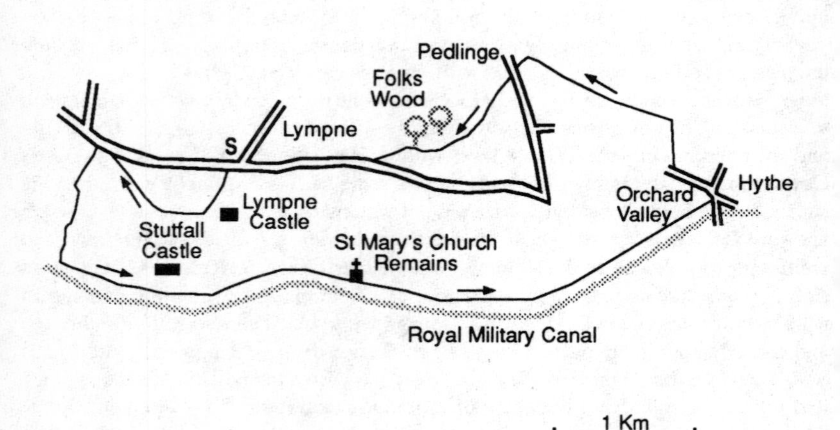

From the cross-roads, head south, then turn right along the Saxon Shore Way, following it past a church and on through the buildings of **Lympne Castle**. Continue along the Way, going along the top of the escarpment. The route swings right, goes behind Lympne Place and eventually leads to a road. Do not go along the road: instead, turn sharp left to continue along the Saxon Shore Way as it leads down the escarpment to reach the **Royal Military Canal**.

Turn left along the path that runs beside the canal for an exciting walk of just over 3 miles. Go past the remains of **Stutfall Castle**, where you may wish to detour, continuing through West Hythe and then on to reach the remains of St Mary's Church. Eventually the path leads to the area known as Orchard Valley. When you reach the road (the A261) near the railway station, turn left and follow it as it bears left. At the end of a row of four houses, cross, with care, and go right along a footpath through a built-up area, bearing left at first, and then right. Just after the path bears right, take the second of two paths going left. Follow this path uphill, cross a stream and then pass along the bottom boundary of woodland.

Cross into a field at the corner of the woodland and follow the left-hand boundary. Now go across the corner of Harp Wood, and when you emerge, follow the left-hand boundary to reach a stile in the corner. Cross and turn left, soon reaching a track and following it to reach a road (the A261 again) at Pedlinge. Go straight across, with great care, to join another section of the Saxon Shore Way. Follow the Way past Oxenden Farm, maintaining direction as the path runs for a short way alongside Folks Wood to eventually reach a road.

Turn right and follow the road back to Shepway Cross.

POINTS OF INTEREST:

Lympne Castle – The castle is actually a fortified manor house, built in the 14th century. It is sited on former 'cliffs' and offers fine views across Romney Marsh and out to the Channel.

Royal Military Canal – The canal was built during the Napoleonic Wars as both a defence and to transport troops and supplies.

Stutfall Castle – The Romans called there settlement here Portus Lemanis. It was the only one of their forts on Kent's southern shore, which seems odd as that shore is the closest to the continent. The remains of the *castrum*, the Roman fortification, is now called Stutfall Castle.

REFRESHMENTS:

It is advisable to bring your own as the inns and cafés are some way from the route. However, they do exist in ample supply in both Lympne and Hythe.

Walks 77 & 78 **DUNGENESS** 7m (11km) or $11^1/_2$m ($17^1/_2$km)

Maps: OS Sheets Landranger 189; Pathfinder 1272.

Two solitary walks around the open expanse of Dungeness.

Start: At 091186, the Pilot Inn.

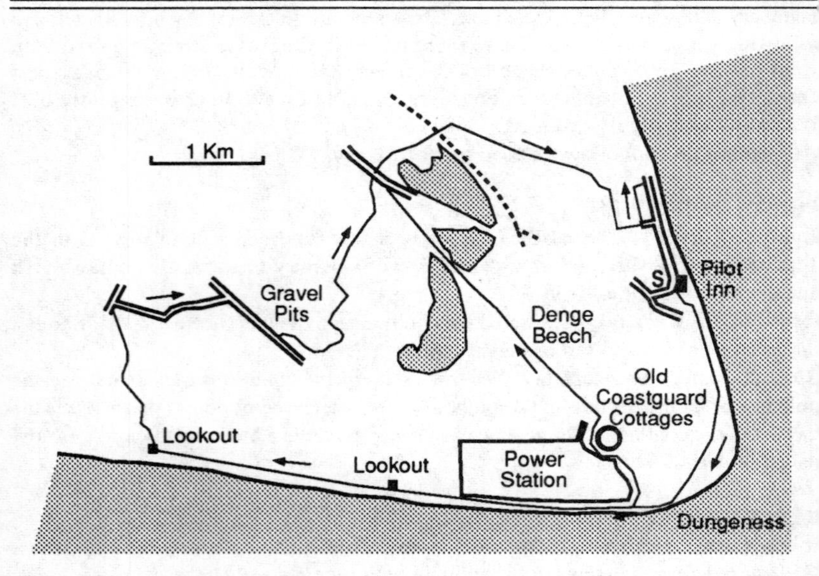

From the Inn, turn left along the road and, as it turns right, almost immediately, cross on to the shingle and follow the visible path that runs beside the road which leads to the power station. Follow the path, which is some distance from the sea, around the point at **Dungeness**.

The shorter route now goes right, with the road, as it turns in the direction of the **power station** entrance. Follow the power station boundary fence, then go left around a group of old coastguard cottages. At the front of the cottages take the path as it heads away from the sea across Denge Beach. Stay with this path as it leads between two large water filled gravel pits and on across Walkers Outland, a **bird reserve**. The path leads to Boulderwall Farm and, just beyond, reaches the main Dungeness Road. Here, the longer route is rejoined.

The longer route continues straight on towards a coastguard station. The path goes very close to the sea, offering a 3 mile walk along one of the bleakest parts of Kent. Go past another coastguard lookout, which is met by a road, and continue to reach a lookout tower. Turn right here, following a minor road away from the sea. To your left, and fenced off, is a military firing range. Follow the minor road to its junction with a more major one. Turn right to reach a T-junction. Turn right again, along Dengemarsh Road, following it for about 600 yards. Now turn left along a track. Cross a ditch and turn right to walk alongside a water filled gravel pit. At the corner of the pit, turn left and follow the path as it meanders around the edge of a field and then runs alongside another gravel pit. When the path bears right, away from the pit, it becomes a track: continue along this, passing the buildings of Boulderwall Farm to meet the main Dungeness Road where the shorter walk is rejoined.

The return route heads east from the road at Boulderwall Farm, following a path that very soon bears right between more gravel pits, then continuing to reach a railway line. Cross, and maintain direction to reach another path going off to the right. Take this, enjoying a walk of nearly a mile across the open shingle, until you reach a dismantled railway. There, turn right, and then, very soon, left to cross the railway. Now turn right again and walk parallel to the railway until it bears away to the right. There you turn left, follow the route of Kerton Road to reach some houses. Turn left and follow a route running behind the houses, then turn right and go between houses to reach the sea front road. Turn right to return to the Pilot Inn.

POINTS OF INTEREST:

Dungeness – This desolate, often austere place is a wonderful area for bird watching. Many of the 'houses' on the Ness are strange adaptations of other dwellings, including former railway carriages.

Power Station – There are two nuclear power stations here, with a visitors centre for those interested in the process of nuclear-generated electricity. The two stations are of the earliest 'Magnox' type and the later 'AGR – Advanced Gas-cooled Reactor' type.

Bird Reserve – The flooded gravel pits, gorse and seawater warmed by the outflow from the power station add up to an excellent habitat for all kinds of animals, but especially birds. Here, there are breeding terns, and flocks of migrants choosing the short way to the continent. In winter there are ducks, including smew, and hen harriers.

REFRESHMENTS:

The Pilot Inn, at the start.

Walk 79 **THE STOUR VALLEY WALK** 7m (11km)

Maps: OS Sheets Landranger 189; Pathfinder 1211.

A pleasant walk across farmland and along quiet country roads.

Start: At 067507, Godmersham Post Office.

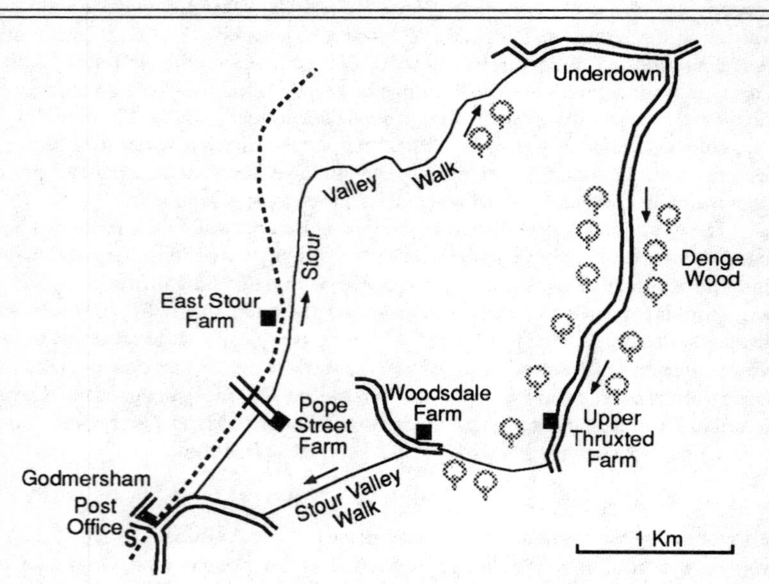

From the Post Office, turn right and cross the railway line. Immediately turn left along a road. When the road bears right, maintain direction along a path that runs parallel to the railway line. Follow the path across a road near Pope Street Farm, continuing to cross a track leading from East Stour Farm. Maintain direction to join a more substantial byway, the Stour Valley Walk, and follow this as it slopes very gently uphill and meanders across the Downland.

The byway bears right, and then soon runs alongside woodland. Cross another track and continue to reach a road. Follow this across a junction, continuing as it bears right and goes through Underdown. About 250 yards after passing Underdown, turn right along a road, following it for nearly 2 miles. Go through the hamlet of Thruxted and follow the road into Denge Wood, where there are many opportunities for exploration and picnics.

After emerging from the wood you soon pass Upper Thruxted Farm and then reach more woodland, on your right. Now when the road bears left, turn right along a byway, following it into woodland. The byway emerges from the wood and goes gradually uphill to meet a road near Forest Farm. Continue along this road for a short distance to reach a stile, on the left, opposite the entrance to Woodsdale Farm. Go over and follow a path signed as part of the Stour Valley Walk.

Stay with the path as it goes down and then continues to reach a minor road. Turn right and follow the road as it bears left to run alongside the railway line. Turn first right to go under the railway and return to **Godmersham**.

POINTS OF INTEREST:

Godmersham – The church, to the south of the village, has a Norman tower and a 13th-century chancel, although it was mostly restored in 1865. On the chancel wall is a 12th-century bas-relief of St Thomas à Becket. Jane Austen frequently stayed at Godmersham Park, to the north of the village, which was owned by her brother. She used the area as the background for her novel *Mansfield Park*.

REFRESHMENTS:

None on the route, so take your own and enjoy a picnic somewhere in the woods, or drive to nearby Chilham or Wye.

Walk 80 **Grafty Green and Boughton Malherbe** 7m (11km)

Maps: OS Sheets Landranger 189; Pathfinder 1230.

A walk between two villages, mainly on country roads.

Start: At 873489, the Post Office, Grafty Green.

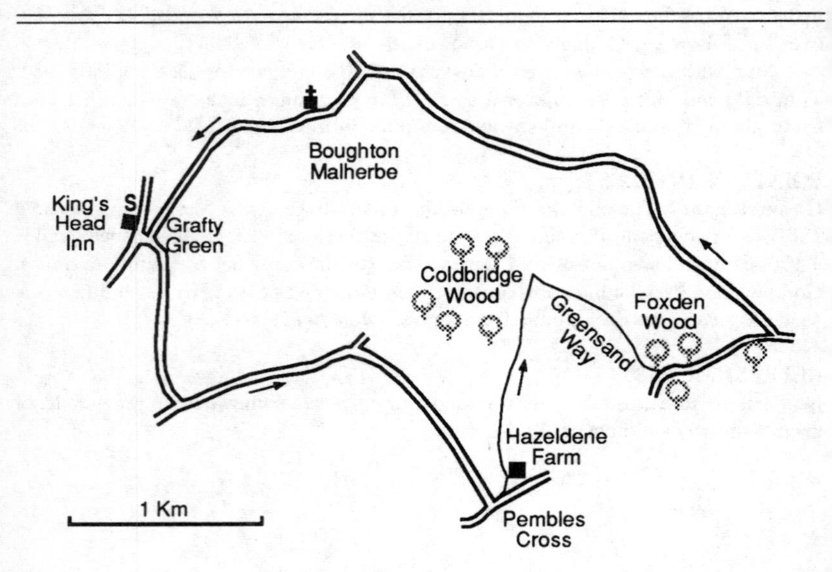

Turn right outside the Post Office, and then, very soon, turn left into Woodcock Lane. Go past Ash Tree Farm, on the left, Woodcock Farm, on the right, and to reach Judge House Farm and, just beyond, a T-junction. Turn left along Coldbridge Lane, following it for about $1^1/_2$ miles as it wends its way through isolated countryside. Eventually the road reaches another T-junction, at Pembles Cross.

Turn left, and very soon turn left again to go along a public byway. Follow the byway through the buildings of Hazelden Farm. Stay with the byway beyond the buildings, ignoring various paths going off in either direction. As you go uphill, you reach Coldbridge Wood, on the left. Continue along the byway beside the woodland edge. When you reach the end of the woodland, the woodland edge turning left, away from you, the **Greensand Way** crosses the byway. Turn right along this new path, following it as it goes uphill and leads through small clumps of woodland to eventually reach a road opposite the entrance to Egerton House.

Turn left and follow on the road as it winds through woodland (Foxden Wood). Just as the road emerges from the woodland, it reaches a turning (the first turning) on the left. Take this road (Coach Road), following it as it bears left, then right, and eventually leads into **Boughton Malherbe**.

Walk through the village, going past the church, and staying with the road as it swings first left, then right. The road now descends quite steeply into Grafty Green. When you reach a T-junction, turn right to return to the Post Office and the start of the walk.

POINTS OF INTEREST:

Greensand Way – This fine long-distance footpath has Kent and Surrey sections, the whole linking to create a superb 100 mile route from Haslemere to Yalding.

Boughton Malherbe – This is one of the many Boughtons in Kent, others including Monchelsea, Aluph and Lees. The name derives from Beech Town, descriptive of the wooded nature of this local area of Kent, though most of the beech woodland that inspired the name has now gone. The village church contains some fine monuments to the Wotton family who lived locally. Boughton Place was the home of Sir Henry Wotton, a 16th century diplomat, poet and scholar. Unfortunately it is not open to the public.

REFRESHMENTS:

The King's Head, Grafty Green.

Walk 81 **PRESTON AND THE STOUR RIVERS** 7m (11km

Maps: OS Sheets Landranger 179; Pathfinder 1196.

A walk around this village, mainly alongside the Great Stou and the Little Stour.

Start: At 228631, the Post Office, Preston.

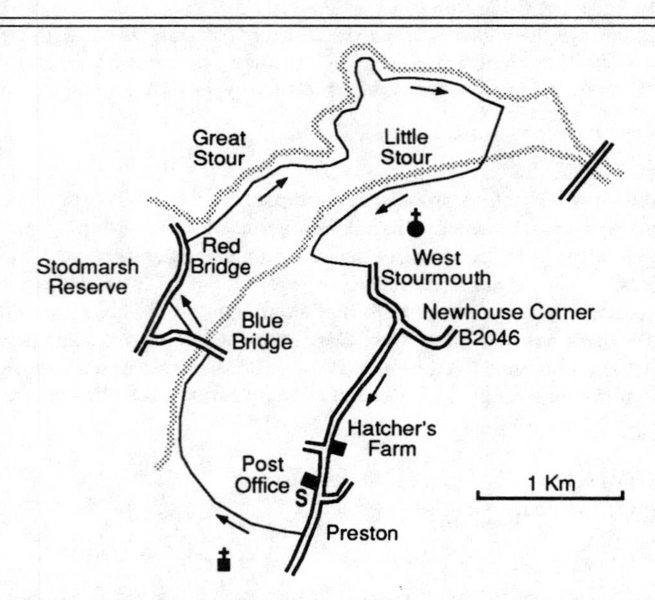

Turn right along the road in front of the Post Office and walk through the village. G straight over at a small cross-roads and then turn right along a signed footpath tha runs between houses. Once past the houses you will emerge into an orchard. Cross stile into open fields. The path now becomes a track: follow it through several field to reach a path that runs alongside the Little Stour. Turn right along the path, followin the river for about $^1/_2$ mile to reach a bridge known as Blue Bridge. Cross the bridge but do not follow the road: instead, go down right, beside the bridge to reach a pat that bears diagonally away. Follow the path to another road (Grove Ferry Road).

Turn right and follow the road as it bears left to run alongside the Great Stour To the right here is the **Stodmarsh National Nature Reserve**. When you reach Re Bridge, turn right along the footpath beside the river. You now enjoy a meanderin riverside walk of some 2 miles through open, flat country. At one point the river runs very close to the railway line on the far bank. The river then bears right, away from the line. Further on the path turns right, away from the riverbank. Follow the path, soon crossing a small bridge back over the Little Stour. Turn right and follow the path beside the smaller river for about a mile, ignoring two tracks leading away from the river. Now, when your path is crossed by another, which goes on to cross a footbridge over the river, turn left along this cross path, heading away from the riverbank. Very soon the path joins a track that goes beside the buildings of Russell Farm and continues to reach a road near the small hamlet of West Stourmouth. Here, a detour left to visit the **church** is very worthwhile.

The route turns right along the road, following it past Dean Farm to reach Newhouse Corner. Here the road joins a more major road (the B2046) at a T-junction. Turn right, soon passing Oast House Farm. Continue along the road into **Preston**. Go past The Gables, on your left, and continue to reach the Post Office and the start of the walk.

POINTS OF INTEREST:

Stodmarsh National Nature Reserve – The wetland area protected by the Reserve is an accidental one, created by land subsidence due to coal mining. Because of the rarity of such habitats in northern Kent, it is an important bird nesting area, with both Cetti's and Savi's warbler present. Grasshopper and reed warbler also breed here, as do several species of ducks, waders and seabirds. In winter hen harriers will often be seen, and there have even been sightings of osprey.

West Stourmouth Church – Although mostly Norman, this most interesting church also has Saxon work in its structure.

Preston – Just to the west of the church, which lies a short distance outside of the village, is the site of a Roman burial ground.

REFRESHMENTS:

The Half Moon and Seven Stars Inn, Preston.

Walk 82 **Upstreet and Sarre** 7m (11km

Maps: OS Sheets Landranger 179; Pathfinder 1196.

A long walk through open marsh country between two villages
The walk can be muddy after wet weather.

Start: At 235632, the Grove Ferry Inn, Upstreet.

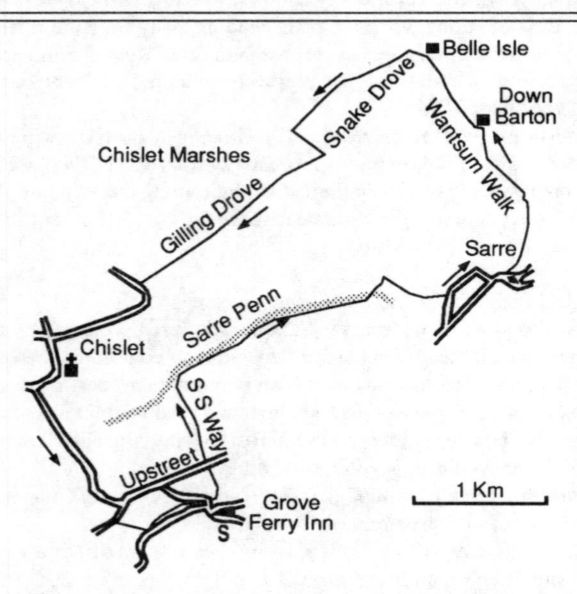

The Grove Ferry Inn lies to the south of the main village of Upstreet and on the othe side of the Great Stour. From it, turn right and cross the river and the railway line Continue along the road, but when it turns to the left, go right, along a path. The path is part of the **Saxon Shore Way**, and is signed with the Way's horned helmet insignia The path goes left, then continues to reach a road (Island Road). Cross and continu along the path, heading northwards, which soon becomes part of the **Wantsum Walk** When you reach the bank of the Sarre Penn, a substantial channel, turn right an follow the channel. After about $^1/_2$ mile, cross a footbridge to the other side, turn righ again and stay alongside the channel to reach a pumping station. Just beyond th station, there is a weir: here the path bears left, away from the channel, and then turn right, through a right-angle, to go alongside a section of a dike. Soon the path bears away to the left to join a track, following it to reach a road.

Turn left along the road, following it into Sarre. When you reach a T-junction, with the King's Head Inn opposite, turn left and walk to a road fork. There, turn left along a path beside the village Post Office. Follow the path into open country, staying with it when it bears slightly left. Continue along it to reach another path coming from the right. Turn left here, once again following a section of the Wantsum Walk. Continue along the path, going to the rear of Down Barton and then alongside Wade Marsh Stream, where the path becomes a track. When you reach Belle Isle, the track turns left, then left again. You are now walking along an old drover's route known as Snake Drove. Follow the drove to reach a bridge over Whitfield Sewer. Cross, turn left and walk alongside the sewer for about 250 yards to reach another, substantial drover's track, Gilling Drove, which goes off to your right.

Take this track, and enjoy a one mile walk through the bleak open spaces of Chislet Marshes before reaching a minor road. Turn left and follow the road as it swings around through Chitty and then reaches a cross-roads at Chislet. Turn left and follow the road through Chislet village to reach a turning on the left signposted for Upstreet.

Take this road, which is also part of the Wantsum Walk, and follow it across Nethergong Penn. Continue into Upstreet village. When you reach a T-junction, turn left and then turn left again along a track which runs past houses and continues to a railway line. Cross the railway and turn left to follow a path alongside the Great Stour, eventually reaching Grove Ferry. Turn right, cross the river and return to the Grove Ferry Inn.

POINTS OF INTEREST:

Saxon Shore Way – This ancient long distance route was originally used by the Romans moving armies to defend against Saxon invaders. Today the 140 mile route from Gravesend to Rye is taken by more peaceful walkers. On this walk it runs inland to follow the route of the former Wantsum Channel, which used to separate the Isle of Thanet from the mainland.

Wantsum Walk – The walk follows the route of the old channel from Reculver to Richborough.

REFRESHMENTS:

Grove Ferry Inn, Upstreet.

The King's Head Inn, Sarre.

Walk 83 BOROUGH GREEN AND BASTED $7^1/_2$ m (12km

Maps: OS Sheets Landranger 188; Pathfinder 1209.

A walk through orchards and farmland, offering expansive views

Start: At 609574, Borough Green Railway Station.

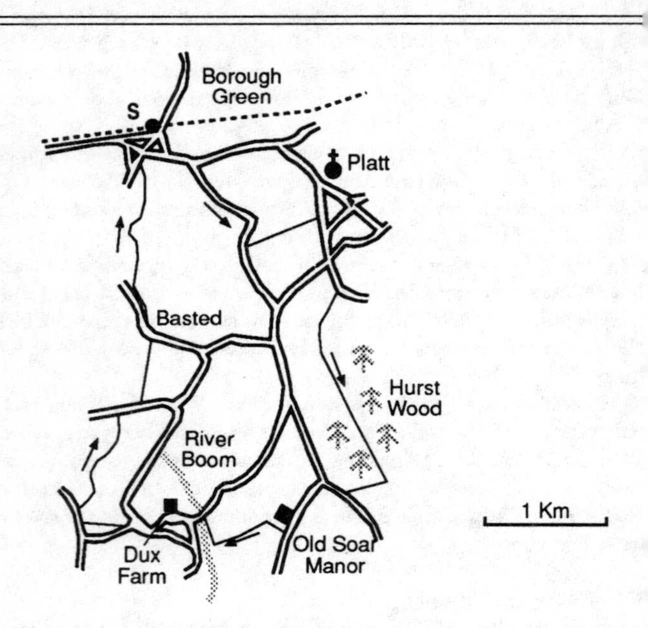

Parking is available in the car park adjoining the station, or the car park off nearby Western Road.

From Borough Green Railway Station turn right, cross the railway line, and immediately go left down Station Road. At the main A25 turn left and follow it to the bus station. Now turn right into Crouch Lane, following it for $^1/_2$ mile. Now turn left along a path and follow it to reach a road. Turn right, passing some houses to reach a cross-roads. Go over and follow the lane to where it bears left. There, go straight on along the second of two bridleways on the right.

Walk with wire fencing on your right to reach a corner. Turn right, cross a stile and walk towards a clump of trees. Go left through orchards, keeping the trees on 'our right, and eventually cross a stile on to a wide track. Go right, following the rack around the hillside, then turn right and go downhill to reach a road. Turn right, and then first left along a minor road, following it past **Old Soar Manor**.

At the bottom of the hill, turn right along a signed footpath and walk parallel to . small stream on your left to reach a bridge. Do not cross the bridge: instead, turn ight and follow the main stream as it goes between trees. Continue to reach a road. 'urn left, then right into Dux Lane. Walk to a T-junction and turn right to walk to nother T-junction. Here, go over and climb to a stile in the hedge. Go over and cross he field beyond to reach a road. Turn right, and then very soon right again along a rack, following it downhill. When the track ends, follow the fence on your left into voodland. Cross a stream and go over a stile into orchards. Turn right and keep ahead, oing under pylon lines to reach a stile in the boundary hedge. Cross into a lane. Turn ight, down the lane, cross a stream and then turn left along a signed footpath. Keep he hedge on your left until it bears away, and then continue along a well-defined rack that leads to the road at Basted.

Go left, downhill, then, at the bottom, turn right on to a private road (a right of vay for pedestrians). When the road bends left, follow the path on the right into trees. 'ross a stream and go uphill, continuing to reach a road. Turn right into **Borough Green**, cross the A25, with great care, and go along the High Street to return to the tart.

'OINTS OF INTEREST:

)ld Soar Manor – This solar block is all that now remains of a 13th-century manor ouse. It is now owned by the National Trust and is open to the public during the ummer months.

Borough Green – Well worth a visit is Great Comp Garden, a 7 acre plot with colour for all seasons'. Open April to October.

.EFRESHMENTS:

'here is a variety of inns and cafés in Borough Green and Basted.

Walk 84 **ALLHALLOWS MARSHES** $7^1/_2$m (12km

Maps: OS Sheets Landranger 178; Pathfinder 1178.

A walk through open marshland and along the shoreline.

Start: At 835775, the centre of Allhallows.

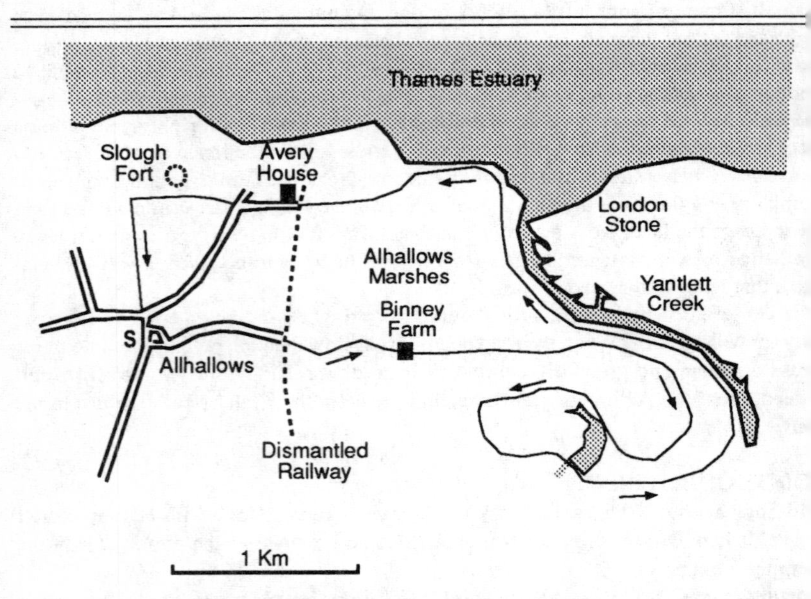

Street parking is available in Allhallows, but please park tidily.

From the centre of the village of Allhallows, take Binney Road, a right turn from th main road when facing north, and follow it to reach a dismantled railway line. Cros and follow the the track opposite. When the track divides, take the left branch an follow it past Binney Farm, continuing deep into Allhallows Marshes. When the trac goes left across a ditch, bear right and follow a path that loops around, with a series c ditches on your left.

Follow the path around a half-circle, then, at a gap between two ditches, clim up on to an old counter wall and follow this around to the right. Continue alongsid several ditches until the wall forks. Take the left-hand route, going away from th ditches and continuing to another fork. Go left again, following the wall along th ɔottom edge of a large expanse of water, and then going between ditches. Eventually he wall leads to the side of Yantlett Creek, which runs in from the **Thames Estuary**.

Walk along the wall, following the course of the creek on your right, for about 1½ miles. At the end of this section the wall runs alongside the Thames Estuary: about 400 yards along the Thames-side route a track goes off to the left, crossing the ditch and leading inland. Follow this track to reach a road at the end of the dismantled railway crossed earlier. Go straight on, passing Avery House, to the right. When the road turns left, go right, then immediately left on a track that leads to **Slough Fort**.

Go past the entrance to the fort and take a track on the left, heading southwards to reach a junction of roads. Take the road directly opposite and follow this back to **Allhallows** and the start of the walk.

POINTS OF INTEREST:

Thames Estuary – Close to the mouth of Yantlett Creek lies an obelisk which marks the limit of authority of the Port of London over the River Thames. Close by is an Elizabethan iron beacon erected when the possibility of invasion seemed very high.
Slough Fort – Excavations of this ancient fort have revealed Roman artefacts.
Allhallows – This pleasant village has been extended by the creation of Allhallows-on-Sea, the somewhat optimistically named resort to the north, on the estuary. Built when the boom in seaside tourism was at its height, the expected crowds did not materialise and the railway, built to carry them, was closed. Parts of the old village church date from the 12th century.

REFRESHMENTS:

The British Pilot, Allhallows.
The Rose and Crown, Allhallows.

Walk 85 **GRAVESEND AND SHORNE MARSHES** $7^1/_2$m (12km

Maps: OS Sheets Landranger 177 and 178; Pathfinder 1177.

A walk along the river front of Gravesend and out along the marshes.

Start: At 649741, Gravesend Railway Station.

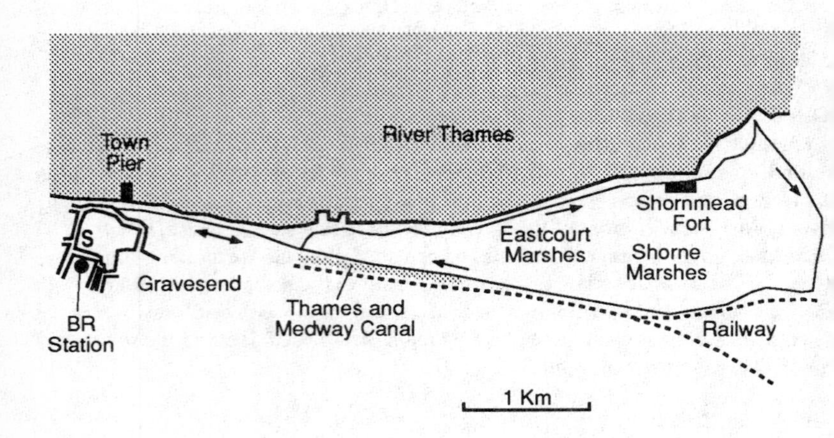

From the railway station, turn left, then right to head for the river. When you reach th riverside, turn right: you are now at the beginning of the Saxon Shore Way. Walk pas the town pier and two other piers to reach a riverside industrial works. There, take signed footpath, following it through the works, bearing left with it to return to th river.

Turn right and follow the Shore Way for about $1^3/_4$ miles to reach **Shornmea Fort**. Now do not follow the path going off to the left: instead, continue past the for To your right is the bleak expanse of Shorne marshes, while to the left there are view over the River Thames to Essex. The path meanders with the riverbank, but graduall moves away from the shore. Take a track going off to the right, following it dow hrough the heart of Higham Marshes. When the track goes right, maintain direction o reach the railway line. Turn right and walk parallel to the railway.

Eventually the path bears right, away from the railway, and then skirts the outside of industrial workings. Beyond, for a while, it runs parallel, and to the right, of a ection of the disused Thames and Medway Canal. Continue to a cross-paths. Go traight over, once again walking parallel to the railway line. After about $^3/_4$ mile nother, long, section of the disused canal appears on the left, separating you from the ailway line. To your right at this point are Eastcourt Marshes.

At the end of the canal section you will reach the outward route. Now retrace this ack to the start point in **Gravesend**.

)OINTS OF INTEREST:

hornmead Fort – Built during the time of Napoleon, when invasion was uppermost n the minds of the government, the squat remains of the fort are now romantically lad in greenery.

ravesend – With its industrial bustle, a bustle added to by the traffic on the Thames, t comes as something of a surprise to discover that the town is the resting place of the ocohontas, the daughter of a Red Indian chieftain who saved the lives of the settlers of Virginia in the early 17th century. She married one of the settlers, John Smith, and ame to England to live. Deciding to return to her homeland when she became ill, she mbarked at London, but was taken off the ship at Gravesend when her condition vorsened. The church in which Pocohontas was buried has long since gone. Today he site is occupied by the town's fine Georgian church.

REFRESHMENTS:

Every taste is catered for in Gravesend.

Walk 86 **GRAVENEY AND FAVERSHAM CREEK** 7½m (12km)

Maps: OS Sheets Landranger 178 and 179; Pathfinder 1195.

A walk across open country and alongside the Swale occasionally on public roads.

Start: At 053627, Graveney Church.

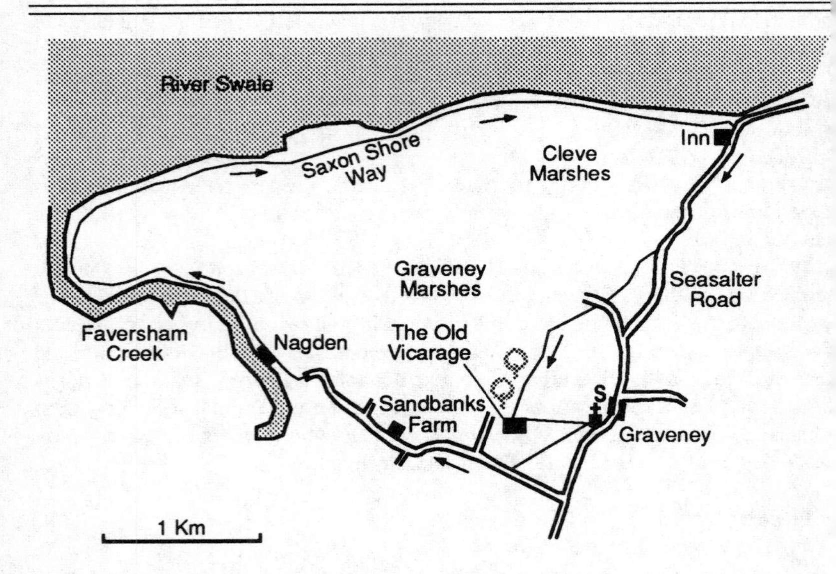

Go into the churchyard at Graveney and walk to the far left corner. There, cross ove on to a path that goes diagonally right across the middle of a field. Cross into the nex field and maintain direction to reach the far right-hand corner. Go out into Sandbank Road and turn right. Follow the road past Sandbanks Farm and Sandbanks Cottage to reach Nagden, passing splendid orchards on either side.

At Nagden, just past some cottages, you are faced with two paths: take the left hand one to reach **Faversham Creek**. Climb up on to the dyke that runs alongside th creek and bear right to follow it as it goes around to reach the edge of the River Swale This section of the walk follows part of the **Saxon Shore Way**, and offers a long an unencumbered walk alongside the Swale, with, for company, excellent views t Whitstable Bay.

When the riverside path joins the road that leads on to Seasalter, turn left and head back inland, going past the Four Horseshoes Inn, on the right. Continue along the road for about $^3/_4$ mile, then cross a stile on the right and follow the path beyond, going diagonally across a field into its far corner. Cross into the next field, staying with the path to walk down to the side of an orchard and then going along the side of the Old Vicarage. Now turn right and follow a path along the edge of fields, and then an orchard to reach a road just south of Graveney. This is the road used earlier in the walk: turn left and retrace your steps back to **Graveney Church**.

POINTS OF INTEREST:

Faversham Creek – The creek is named for the nearby town, an ancient place, both the Romans and the Saxons having had settlements there. If you have the time, it is worth visiting as the centre of the town has retained many of its old buildings, a number of them being of considerable architectural interest.

Saxon Shore Way – This ancient long distance route was originally used by the Romans moving armies to defend against Saxon invaders. Today the 140 mile route from Gravesend to Rye is taken by more peaceful walkers.

Graveney Church – This fine church has medieval origins, but has been substantially restored. Inside, there are some interesting brasses.

REFRESHMENTS:

Four Horseshoes Inn, on the route.

Walk 87 CLIFFE AND THE THAMES ESTUARY $7^1/_2$m (12km)

Maps: OS Sheets Landranger 178; Pathfinder 1177.

An isolated, but worthwhile, riverside walk.

Start: At 736766, Cliffe Post Office.

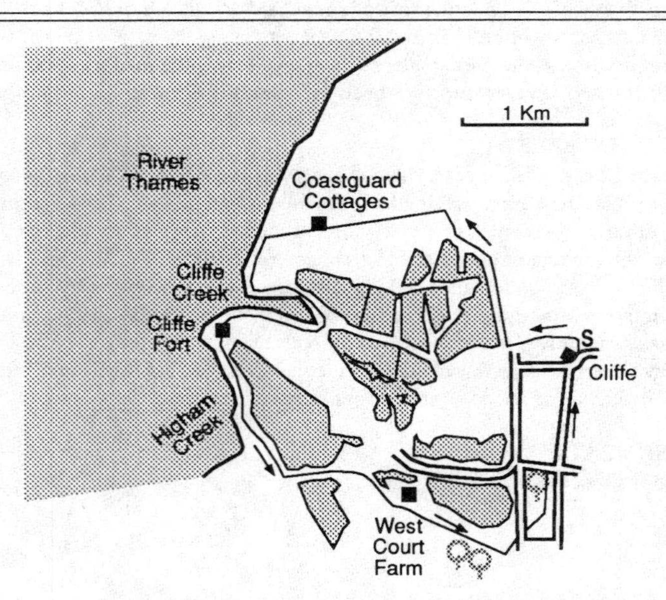

From the post office, turn left along the main road and follow this past the buildings to reach a track, Pickle's Way, on the left. Turn along this, following it to reach Allen's Pond. Here, turn right along the footpath that runs beside the pond. Stay with the footpath as it leads away from the pond and then turns left to head in the direction of the estuary. The footpath ends at a group of coastguard cottages, skirt these to reach the river's edge.

At the river, turn left and walk along the top of the embankment wall, with extensive views across the river to Essex. Bear left to follow the route along Cliffe Creek, going around its head and along the other side to reach the river's edge again. To your left now is **Cliffe Fort**. Continue past the fort, following the river's edge round into Higham Creek, a wide expanse of mud and water. Follow the Creek to its end, and where the shoreline goes right, go left, and then right, alongside a large pond.

On your left you will find an embankment wall running between two ponds: follow this to the edge of gravel works. Go across the top of the railway line that serves the gravel works, and then turn left to follow a path that runs parallel to the railway. When the path turns left to skirt West Court Farm, turn immediately right on to the path that runs below the farm. Go through a gate into an orchard and follow the left-hand boundary to reach a road.

Cross and go into another orchard. Now head diagonally left for the corner of the group of houses ahead. At the houses, continue straight on, with another orchard on your left, to soon reach a road. Turn right to a cross-roads at the major road in **Cliffe**. Turn left and follow the road, with great care, into Cliffe and take the short step back to the start of the walk.

POINTS OF INTEREST:
Cliffe Fort – This is another fort built to protect the Thames during an invasion. When it was built, it was decided that the estuary was so unhealthy that the men had to be billeted in Cliffe village.
Cliffe – During the 7th, 8th and 9th centuries, councils of the Saxon church were held in the village. Later, from medieval times until the 19th century, there was a beacon here to warn of the approach of enemy warships. During the Napoleonic Wars, when fears of a French invasion were at their height, a permanent watch of the Thames was maintained from Cliffe.

REFRESHMENTS:
The Six Bells, Cliffe.
The Evening Star, Cliffe.
The Staff of Life, Cliffe.

Walks 88 & 89 **EASTRY AND WORTH** $7^1/_2$m (12km)
or 11m ($17^1/_2$km)

Maps: OS Sheets Landranger 179; Pathfinder 1212.

Walks through the countryside around these villages, with an optional detour past a former colliery.

Start: At 311547, Eastry Church.

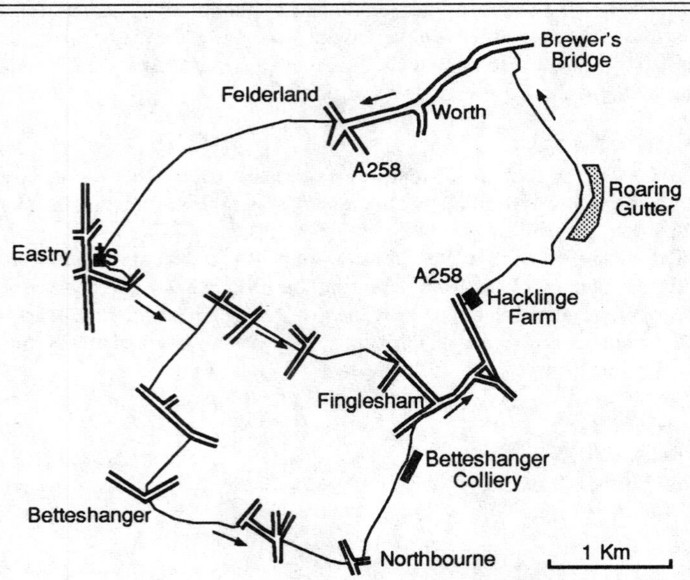

Enter the churchyard and follow the path to the right of the church. Exit the churchyard into a field, and continue to a path fork. Take the right-hand branch and go to the far right corner of the field. Cross and walk beside a house to reach a road. Go across to reach a stile into an orchard. Cross and follow the right-hand fence. Leave the orchard and bear right with the path to cross into the next field. Go ahead, ignoring a path off to the left. Follow the path through several fields to reach a crossing track.

The shorter route turns left here. Follow the path to a road, reaching it next to Cherry Trees Farm. Turn right to reach a T-junction. Go straight over and follow a path to another road. Cross and follow a track that goes downhill and then divides into two paths. Take the left-hand branch, continuing downhill until another path joins from the left. Turn right and follow the new single route, going to the rear of Westhill House and then bearing left to reach a road. Turn right and follow the road through the hamlet of Finglesham. At the next T-junction, turn left, rejoining the longer walk.

The longer walk turns right along the path, following it beside a field boundary to reach a road. Turn left and follow the road to reach a signed footpath on the right. Take this, following it to reach a road at Betteshanger, a former coal mining community. Turn right along the road for a short distance until it turns right. There, turn left along another path, following it past a school and continuing to Home Farm. Go along the farm drive to reach a road. Turn right to reach a junction of roads. Go along the track opposite, following it into Northbourne. When you reach the next road, turn right, and then, very soon, go left along a minor road. Shortly, turn left along a path, following it past the old colliery buildings of **Betteshanger Colliery**. Once past the colliery, maintain direction along the path, ignoring turnings to either side, to reach a road. Turn right and follow the road, rejoin the shorter walk at a junction on the left.

Follow the road to its junction with the A258. Turn left again, following the road, with great care, to reach the driveway leading to Hacklinge Farm on the right. Take the drive, following it through the farmyard and on to join a footpath that leads across open country, and then turns right to follow a dike. Soon you reach Roaring Gutter Dike: follow the path as it goes to the left and runs alongside the waterway. At the end of the dike, bear left with the path and walk along the top of Pinnock Wall. When you come down from the wall, at Fry Dike, maintain direction to cross Brewer's Bridge to reach a road. Turn left and follow the road into Worth. Go past the school to reach a road junction and go straight ahead along the main village street. Follow the road to its junction with the A258. Cross, with great care, and follow a track that leads off to the right. This track runs through Felderland and then continues parallel to a road that you can occasionally see on your right. Eventually the track becomes a path: maintain direction along it, passing alongside a nursery, and then the buildings of Staten Borough Farm. At the end of the farm buildings the path turns left, and then, soon, right. When you reach a field boundary, cross a stile and head diagonally left to reach a track. Turn left along this and follow it back into Eastry, arriving on a street by the village school. Go left at the next turning to return to the church.

POINTS OF INTEREST:

Betteshanger Colliery – The walk crosses an area that is at the centre of Kent's former coal field. The colliery remains are a reminder of this formerly important industry.

REFRESHMENTS:

There are many possibilities in Eastry, Finglesham and Worth.

Walk 90 **The Isle of Harty** 8m (13km

Maps: OS Sheets Landranger 178; Pathfinder 1179.

A walk across open marshland and along shoreline.

Start: At 044695, the car park near the drive of Muswell Manor just south of Leysdown-on-Sea.

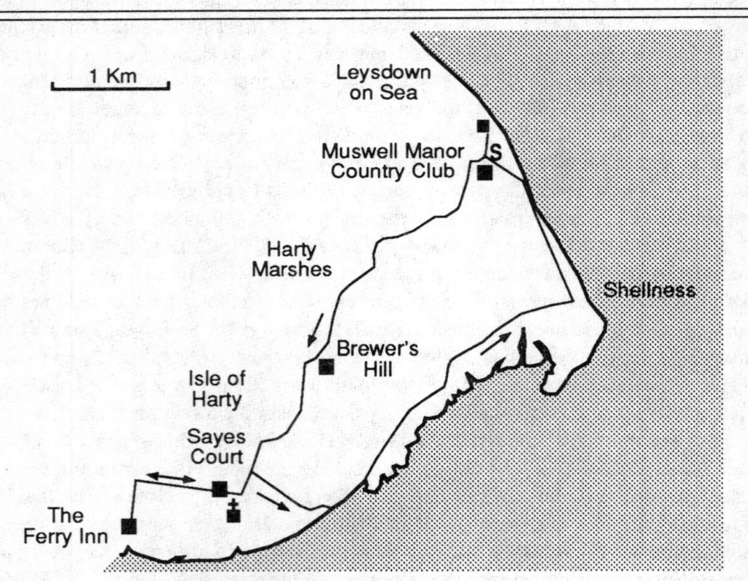

Leave the car park and turn left towards the drive for Muswell Manor. Follow th drive past a group of caravans, then keep left, heading towards the Manor. When th drive veers to the left again, heading towards the house itself, keep straight on. G over a stile by the cattlesheds and continue southwards along a track which, for pa of the time, runs parallel to a dyke.

The track leads deep into the bleak Harty marshes and gradually veers to the lef At a white house, Brewers Hill, the track turns to the right and goes around a group c trees. Immediately beyond these there is a private entrance, and then the official rig of way turns left into a field. Do not follow it: instead, continue along the farm trac to reach Elliots Farm. Go through the farmyard to reach a bridleway. Follow thi ignoring the footpath on the left which leads to the Swale shoreline, to reach a road. Turn right to reach Harty church, said to be Kent's most isolated church.

Continue along the road, passing the site of Sayes Court, the former great house of Harty, to reach a road junction. Turn left and walk to the Ferry Inn. There are excellent views from here across the Swale estuary. Suitably refreshed, retrace your steps back past Harty church to reach the footpath, ignored earlier, that leads to the Swale shoreline. At the end of the path, cross a stile into the Swale Nature Reserve. Now bear left to follow the yellow tipped post waymarkers on to the flood wall.

The long open walk that follows is a bird watcher's delight as the broad area around is home to many species. Eventually the houses at the isolated hamlet of Shellness comes into view. As this is a private hamlet, when the path reaches the road you must turn left, still walking along the top of the flood bank. Part of the beach here is for use by naturalists, although you may walk along it. Follow this route back to the starting point.

POINTS OF INTEREST:

Harty Church – Dedicated to St Thomas and dating from Norman times, the church has low walls topped by a tiled roof that, on one side, very nearly reaches the ground. The church is without electricity, being oil-lit, and has an intricately carved Flanders Kist (or chest), dredged up from the Swale.

Swale shoreline – For birdwatchers, binoculars are a must along this part of the walk. The area is one of the best bird watching sites in Kent, with large flocks of waders, including bar-tailed godwits and sanderling, and Brent geese and divers in winter. Other migrants include wheatears and whinchats, little and sandwich terns. There are also resident short-eared owls and, in winter, hen harriers and peregrines. Further out to sea, gannets and skuas can often be seen.

REFRESHMENTS:

The Ferry Inn, on the route.

Walk 91 **Wye and Crundale** 8m (13km)

Maps: OS Sheets Landranger 189; Pathfinder 1231.

Walking through woodland and farmland, and ending at a nature reserve.

Start: At 054469, Wye Church.

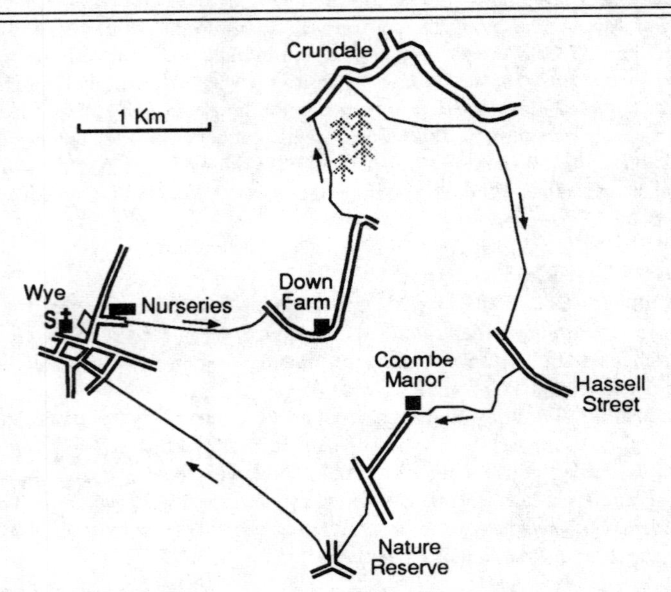

Go through **Wye** churchyard, passing to the right of the church and follow th churchyard path to a road. Turn right to a cross-roads. Go straight over into Occupatio Road. The road soon becomes a track: follow this into woodland and out to a lan Turn right and follow the lane to its conclusion at a farm. Go left on to the track whic runs alongside a hedge to reach another farm. Turn left along a path between hedge

When the hedges end at the edge of woodland, the main path goes left towards gate. Do not follow it: instead, take the lesser path to the right into the woods. Whe the path forks, take the right-hand branch and follow it to a road. Turn right along th road until it reaches the brow of a hill, just before the sign for Crundale. There, tak the path on the right into woods, continuing through the woods and beyond, ignorin various side turns, to reach a house on the left. Now keep straight on along the tarma track, then go straight uphill along a path through two gates. At the top of the ridge, cross a stile in front of **Crundale Church**.

Turn right through a gate on to a track which leads along the ridge of Crundale Down. Eventually the track bears left to a junction with another track: turn left and go uphill towards the hamlet of Hassell Street. The track becomes a road: go along this for about 50 yards, then turn sharp right along a path between fences and opposite a bungalow. At a junction of paths, bear right and go through a gate. Continue downhill towards a fence. Turn left at the fence and then immediately turn right through a gate on to a farm road. Turn left and follow the road to a T-junction. Directly opposite is a stile: cross into the **Wye Down Nature Reserve**.

Follow the path through the Reserve's woodland, leaving over a stile. Now head for the left-hand corner of the woodland on the right. Bear right along the wide grassy track, following it to a viewpoint. Now keep to the zig-zag path, going steeply downhill. At the bottom, leave the reserve over a stile and bear right over another stile on to a road. Turn right along the road for about 30 yards, then go over a stile on the left and turn right to follow the field as far as the fence at its end. Turn left and continue beside the fence to reach a stile on the right. Cross and follow the path beyond along the left-hand edge of a field. Go through a gate at the end, cross a track and change to the other side of the fence (that is, it is now on your right). Continue, ignoring all the side turns: the path eventually becomes a tarmac lane and leads back to Wye. Turn right past Wye College, then left, to return to the starting point at Wye church.

POINTS OF INTEREST:

Wye – This small town is full of interesting Georgian buildings. The college, now the Agricultural Department of the University of London, was originally founded in 1432AD as a college for priests.

Crundale Church – This beautiful little church dates in part from the 12th century, though there were additions and alterations through to the 14th century.

Wye Down Nature Reserve – The Reserve was established to preserve the flora and fauna of the uncultivated chalk downland. In addition to the wildlife, there are wonderful views all around.

REFRESHMENTS:

The Tickled Trout, Wye.

New Flying Horse Inn, Wye.

Walk 92 — Shorne Wood Country Park — 8m (13km)

Maps: OS Sheets Landranger 178; Pathfinder 117 and 1193.

A signposted route through, sometimes dense, woodland that lies mid-way between Gravesend and Rochester.

Start: At 687702, the main car park in Shorne Wood Country Park.

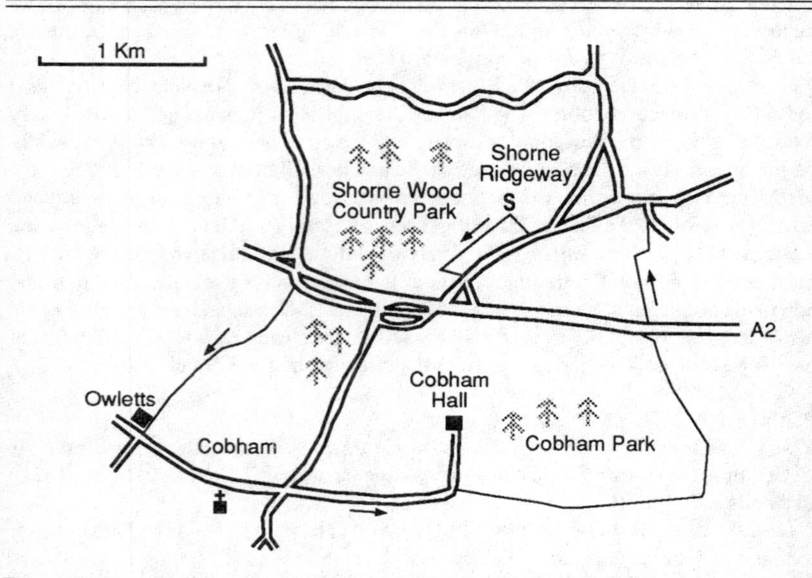

From the car park follow the signs for the Woodland car park to the south. Turn left out of this second car park, then go left again to cross the road bridge over the main A2. Go left, drop down and double back to take a road that runs parallel to the main road.

Follow the road to a cross-roads where you will find a yellow waymarker arrow which directs you to a path through the woods opposite. Walk ahead, then bear right when the path divides, following the road for a short while. At the next waymarker arrow, turn left and go back into the woods. There are a large number of paths in these woods but, although you may stray from the route, it is unlikely that you will go very wrong.

Head south-westwards through the woods to reach a road, near Owletts. Turn left into **Cobham**, walking through the village to reach a junction. Go straight to follow a well defined track. Ignore the road that goes to the right, to Lodge Farm, maintaining direction to the point where the main track turns left towards **Cobham Hall**. Here, take the rough path opposite, following it through woods.

After about $^1/_2$ mile you will pass a mausoleum on your right. Just after this take the path to the left and follow it back towards the main road. Cross the A2 by way of a small bridge and continue straight on in the direction of Shorne Ridgeway to reach a road. Turn left to reach a junction. Turn left again and follow the road back to the starting car park.

POINTS OF INTEREST:

Owletts – This fine Kentish farmhouse dates from the 17th century and has a contemporary staircase and plaster ceiling. There is also an excellent kitchen garden. The house is owned by the National Trust and is open to the public on Wednesdays and Thursdays during the summer months.

Cobham – The beautiful village church dates, in part, from the 13th century. The village has strong connections with Charles Dickens, who would go there as a boy whilst on country rambles with his father. The village is often recognisable in his novels.

Cobham Hall – Now a public school, this magnificent building is late Elizabethan. The grounds were landscaped by Humphrey Repton.

REFRESHMENTS:

The Leather Bottle Inn, Cobham.

The Darnley Arms, Cobham.

Walk 93 **East Farleigh** 8½m (13½km)

Maps: OS Sheets Landranger 188; Pathfinder 1209.

A pleasant walk, mainly alongside the River Medway.

Start: At 734534, East Farleigh Church.

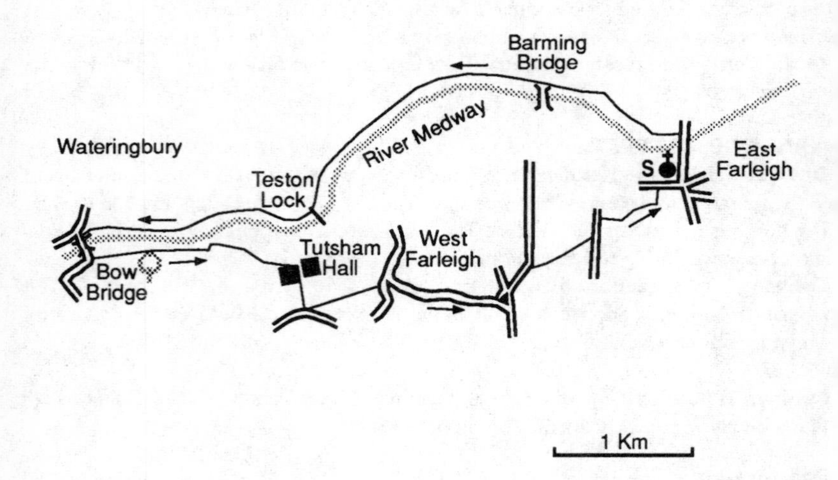

From East Farleigh church, turn left along a road in the direction of the river. Cross, and immediately turn left along the tow path that runs beside the river. You now have a long, but extremely pleasant walk beside this very pretty stretch of the **River Medway**. Understandably, the river hereabouts is a very popular place for pleasure boating.

Walk past Barming Bridge and Teston Lock, and about 3½ miles into the walk you will reach Bow Bridge, at the southern end of Wateringbury. Cross back over the river here, following the road for a short distance to reach a path on the left. In fact, the path goes left in two directions: take the one that goes directly left and then runs parallel to the river. Follow the path across several fields to reach Waregrave's Wood. The path skirts the top end of the wood and then runs alongside the river for a short time. When the river turns to the left, the path swings less sharply as you cross into another field. Soon you bear to the right and head for the far corner of a field. Cross into the next field and follow its right-hand boundary.

When you reach Tutsham Hall, follow the path that goes left, behind the buildings, and go along the left-hand boundaries of two fields to reach a road. Do not follow the road: instead, turn sharp left along a path that leads, eventually, to a track that is followed into West Farleigh. When you reach the road in the village, turn left, and then take the first turning right (Ewell Lane). Follow this relatively quiet road for about $^1/_2$ mile to reach a T-junction, with two turnings to the left. Take the second of these, going along a minor road that leads through woodland.

After about 400 yards, turn right along a path and follow it as it bears left through further woodland. Stay with the path as it swings right and continues to a road. Turn left, but after 200 yards, take a track on the right which leads to the corner of a field. Cross into the next field and head diagonally left to the centre of the boundary ahead. Go through a gate there, and straight across the field beyond to reach the centre of the boundary opposite. Turn left, keeping the boundary on your right, to reach a road. Turn right and follow the road back into **East Farleigh**. At the cross-roads turn left and you will very soon arrive back at the church.

POINTS OF INTEREST:

River Medway – The river has played a very important part in the history of Kent, carrying timber and iron from the Weald downstream and, later, supplying water for the hop growers to make beer. So important was it that it is the traditional barrier between the Men of Kent, to the east, and the Kentish Men, to the west.

East Farleigh – Cromwell's Roundheads crossed the Medway here following a bloody battle. In the church is a wooden cross made from an aeroplane propellor. This commemorates a young flier from the village who was killed in action over Ypres.

REFRESHMENTS:

The Bull Inn, East Farleigh.

The Victory, East Farleigh.

The Good Intent, West Farleigh.

Walk 94 **NEWENDEN** $8^1/_2$m ($13^1/_2$km)

Maps: OS Sheets Landranger 188 and 189; Pathfinder 1271.

A walk alongside the River Rother and through open countryside, mainly on quiet roads.

Start: At 834273, Newenden Church.

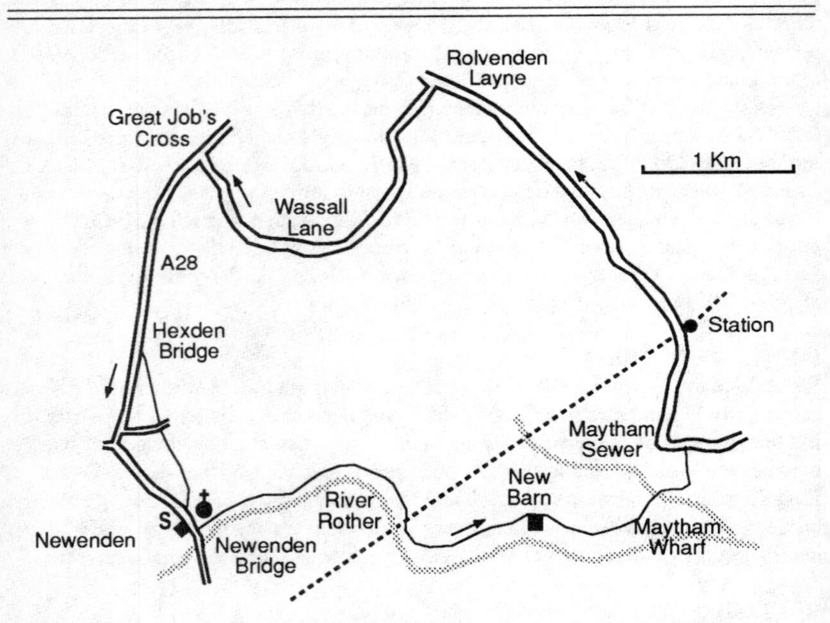

From the **church**, walk to the main village road and turn left to walk out of the village. When you reach the **River Rother**, at Newenden Bridge, do not cross: instead, go down to your left to reach the footpath that runs alongside the river. Follow this path as it runs parallel to houses on the left, and then goes past a sewage works. Continue along the path, which follows the river as it bends to the right, to reach a path fork. Take the left-hand branch.

The path still runs parallel to the river, on the right, but is now some distance from it. Stay with the path as it continues past New Barn, and then goes diagonally across a field to reach the Hexden Channel just as it emerges from Maytham Sewer, at Maytham Wharf. Cross the channel, and just before the buildings of Maytham Wharf, turn left along a road. You now have a long, pleasant walk along this quiet country road, going past a pumping station, on the right, and then Maytham Farm, on the left. Cross the **Kent and East Sussex Railway** at Wittersham Road Station, and then go past several farm entrances on either side of the road. The road eventually leads into the hamlet of Rolvenden Layne.

When you arrive at a turning on the right, with the village Post Office also on your right, turn left along a path that initially runs alongside some houses. Continue past nurseries, on the right, and then go past the buildings of Thornden Farm. Once past these buildings, go through a gate into a field, and head straight across. Now follow the edge of a small patch of woodland to reach a road (Wassall Lane). Turn left, going past Wassall House and Wassall Farm. Follow the road to reach the T-junction at Great Job's Cross. Turn left along the main road (the A28), with great care, following its left verge to reach Hexden Bridge.

The road here runs at right angles to Hexden Channel: take the path on the left that runs at about 45 degrees between the two. Follow the path through three fields and then into the left-hand corner of the third one. Cross a stile out of this field on to a minor road. Go straight across and maintain direction along the path as it leads very gently downhill to arrive at the rear of Newenden churchyard. From here it is just a short step back to the point where the walk began.

POINTS OF INTEREST:

Newenden Church – The building dates from the 14th and 15th centuries. Inside there is a fine Norman font, with grotesques from a medieval bestiary.

River Rother – Acting as a boundary between Kent and East Sussex, this river soon flows into the sea at Rye.

Kent and East Sussex Railway – A privately run service that operates steam trains down the Rother Valley, from Tenterden. The service runs from Easter onwards, mainly at weekends.

REFRESHMENTS:

There are possibilities in Newenden and Rolvenden Layne.

Walk 95 **Kent Water** 9m ($14^1/_2$km)

Maps: OS Sheets Landranger 188; Pathfinder 1228.

A walk across open country and along riverside paths.

Start: At 476410, Cowden Railway Station.

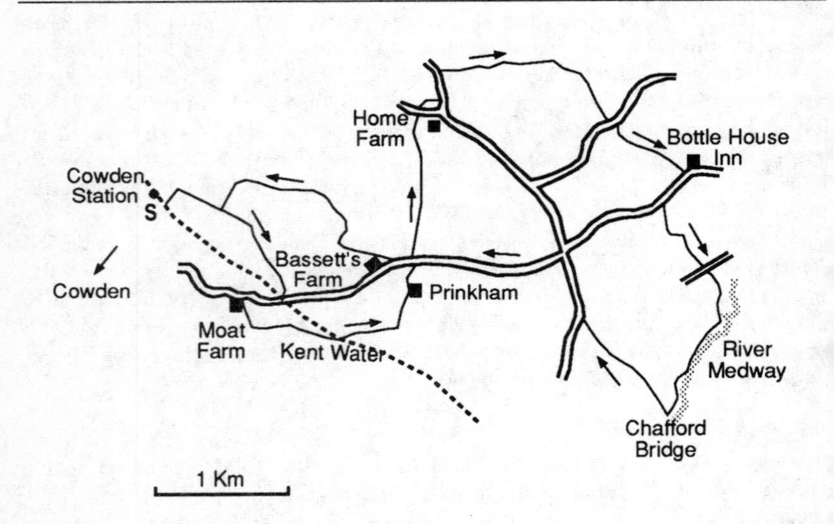

From the station turn left along a signed lane. Follow it to just past Wickens Farm, then turn right, over a stile, and go along a path into a field. Cross diagonally towards a telegraph pole, continue forwards, then turn right along a track. Go through a gate and a farm to reach a road. Turn right and, after about $^1/_4$ mile, cross a stile on the left and follow the fence on your right towards the bridge over Kent Water, which here forms the border between Kent and Sussex. Go over a stile on the left and walk beside the stream, going through trees and crossing three more stiles. Now turn left under the railway and then go diagonally right over a field, heading for the trees on your left. Cross a bridge under the trees and continue to a stile. Go over and pass a gated bridge on the left to reach another bridge further ahead. Cross this and the stile at the far end of the field. Go along the edge of the field, cross another stile and walk past Prinkhams, an old timber framed house, to reach a road. Turn left, then very soon right along a signed path to reach a gate. Go through and continue forward, uphill, across two fields. As the third field ends, bear right and cross a stile next to a gate. The path beyond goes through a gate on the right and then up a field. After crossing a stile on the left, keep the hedge on your right side until you reach the corner of the field. There, go over a stile and continue to reach a road. Cross and go along the path opposite, following it to reach a drive on the left. Turn along this to a road. Turn left, then right, over a stile. Follow the path beyond downhill and then along the side of a field. When the fence on the left ends, bear right, beside a hedge. Cross a stile and continue to a lane. Turn left, then right over a stile. Go down a field, keeping a hedge on your left. Go past a pond and through a small plantation. Now turn right along a gravel track. When the track goes left, continue along the path ahead. Cross the first of several bridges and go left to walk with a vineyard on your left and woods on your right. At the corner of the woods, turn right and continue, crossing two more bridges. Walk uphill, passing through some trees. Cross a stile and follow a steep path up to a road. Cross and take the stepped path opposite. Cross a stile and bear left through a field to reach a pond closed in by trees. Now follow the fencing until you reach a stile on the left. Cross and go right towards a gate. Go through and diagonally left to reach a stile. Go over and continue, then turn right along a track to a road.

Turn right, passing the Bottle House Inn, to reach a signed footpath on the left. Take this, bearing right, then going uphill and bearing left to reach a gate and another signed path. Go through and continue past some trees. Just beyond, turn right and descend to a bridge over a stream. The path here can be muddy, especially in winter and wet weather, so be prepared to take time. Cross the bridge and turn left, following the stream to reach a stile on to a road. Cross and go over the stile opposite. Head for the bridge ahead, cross and turn right, aiming for the left side of the line of trees seen in the distance as you walk beside the River Medway. When you reach the trees, cross a stile and follow the riverbank. Near the second of two weirs, cross a stile and continue to reach the road at Chafford Bridge. Turn right for about $^1/_2$ mile, and when the road turns sharp right, leave it over the stile on the left. Cross the field beyond, go through a gate and continue. Now turn left through a gate to reach a road. Turn right and walk to a cross-roads. Turn left for Bassetts and Cowden. Follow the road past the house called Bassetts, then turn right through a gate. Follow the edge of the field beyond to a corner. Now keep to the track, which soon veers right. Go through a gate and continue to the top of the hill, then head right, downhill, to the far right corner of the field. To the left of the corner is a cart track: follow it to open fields. Cross a stile and walk through a group of chestnut trees. Continue to the top of the hill and turn right, passing a cattle trough to reach a stile in the hedge. Cross this and then another stile, and walk down a track to a lane. Turn right and retrace your steps to the station.

Walk 96 **Markbeech, Hever and Penshurst** 9m ($14^1/_2$km)

Maps: OS Sheets Landranger 188; Pathfinder 1228.

Pleasant walking through woodland and across fields.

Start: At 476410, the car park at Cowden railway station.

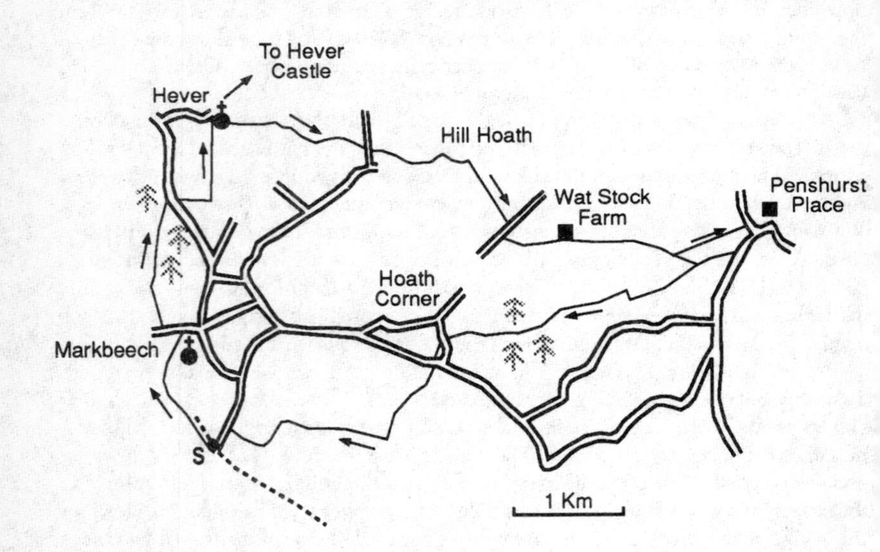

Cross the footbridge to the up platform and go through the gate into woodland. After 20 yards, turn right along a track. Ignore turns on either side to reach a stile into a field. Follow the left edge until, just before the corner of woodland, you cross to the other side of the fence, as marked. At the corner of the fence go forward to a stile into a churchyard. At the church, turn left to reach the road at Markbeech. Turn left and, just before the entrance to Bramsell's Farm, turn right through a gate on to a path between fences. (In summer this section of the walk can be overgrown with nettles: you can avoid it by turning right along the road, in front of the church, then left at the crossroads to rejoin at the Greyhound Inn.) When the fenced path ends continue, eventually entering woodland. Follow the path under the railway to reach a road. Turn right to the Greyhound Inn. There, take the path on the left, and at its end cross a double stile into a field. Ignore the hurdle on the left, going over the stile about

30 yards further on. Continue between fences to the end of the field. Go over the left-hand of two stiles into a field. At its end, bear right over a stile and go in and out of woodland to reach a road. Turn left, and then right along a path marked 'No Horse Riding' to reach a road in Hever village. Turn right, and right again into the churchyard (**Hever Castle** is further along the road). Take the path at the bottom right-hand corner, skirting the Hever Castle estate and cross a bridge over a driveway. At a gate by houses, bear right along a path beside the second house to reach a road. Cross, go over the stile opposite and cross a field. Go right, through a gate, cross a field and then a footbridge on your left into woodland. At the corner of the track go right, and after 20 yards, follow the track as it bears left and uphill to a junction. Go straight on, passing cottages in Hill Hoath.

In front of a farm is a turning area: turn left along a track to a junction. Turn right and walk to a road. Turn right, then left along the lane, passing Wat Stock Farm. A lane joins from the right: continue to reach a road and turn right into Penshurst. Go through the village, then, just past the school, turn right into The Warren. Go past a farm, cross a stile and follow a field's right edge to a stile. Cross a footbridge, a further stile, a field and another stile. Cross a lane and follow the path up the bank opposite. Go through the woods, avoiding a marked path to exit at a gate/stile. Follow a field's right edge, cross a stile in the corner and follow the path beyond. At a half-timbered house on the left, cross the stile on the left and follow a field's left edge to join a track through woods to a road. Turn right for 50 yards, then go left along a track. At a track junction, turn left and cross a field towards power lines. Cross a stile and go right, down through woods, to a road. Cross and follow the path opposite through two fields. Now do not cross a stile: instead, turn right and cross a barrier into woods. Just before a second barrier, cross a stile on the right and turn left along a field edge. Cross a stile to re-enter the woods. After 300 yards, turn sharp right at a track junction to go down to a footbridge. Cross and go up to a stile. Bear half-right up the field beyond and go right along the bottom of a bank of trees. Cross a stile and go through woodland to another stile. Maintain direction to a signed stile in a hedgerow. Go down to a gate at the left of some cottages and follow the track beyond to a made-up lane. Turn right to a junction, and go left back to the start.

POINTS OF INTEREST:

Hever Castle – This National Trust property was the home of Anne Boleyn, whose father, Sir Thomas Boleyn, is buried in the church.

REFRESHMENTS:

There are several opportunities in the villages passed on the walk.

Walk 97 **WESTERHAM AND TOYS HILL** 9m ($14^1/_2$km)

Maps: OS Sheets Landranger 187 and 188; Pathfinder 1208.

Rural countryside, with small fields, woodland and parkland.

Start: At 446542, Westerham village green.

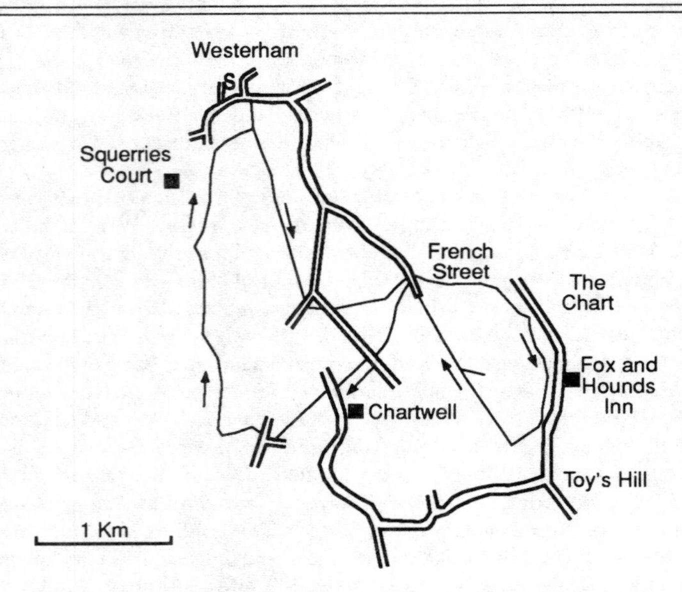

Go along Water Lane, and, at its end, cross a stile into a field. Go uphill to another stile, cross and bear left to reach a stile about 100 yards to the right of a house. Do not cross: instead, follow the left edge to a stile in the corner. Follow the path beyond uphill beside woodland to reach a road. Cross and follow the path opposite, ignoring a right-hand fork, to reach a road. Turn right, and then left along a path signed for French Street. Descend through woodland. The path is joined by a track from the right: continue past houses to reach a junction. Turn sharp right, downhill, and just after the burial ground on the left, cross a stile to Pipers Green and Brasted Chart. Go downhill, with a fence on the right, cross a footbridge and go through the gate to the left of French Street Farm. Follow the path beyond, crossing a stile and bearing right to another into woods. Keep the fence to your left to reach a road. Turn right, go past some cottages and turn right again at the sign for a National Trust horse track. After about 70 yards, turn left along a track, keeping left where it forks, to follow a blue marker on a tree. At the next track crossing, turn left (the horse track goes straight on) following waymarker posts. The track is joined by a wheelchair path: continue past an obelisk, cross the remains of brick parapets and swing left to a fork. For refreshments, bear left here, then left again at the road to reach the Fox and Hounds Inn.

The route takes the right fork, following the path to the National Trust car park at Toys Hill. Go through the car park and climb the steps on the left. At the top, bear left at the marker post along a path signed for French Street. At the next marker, bear left and follow the woodland path to reach a cross-path. Turn sharp right and follow blue markers, descending to the edge of the woods. Nurseries come into view on the left: take a left fork on to a signed bridleway. This becomes a track and then a road: follow it uphill to French Street. Turn left along a lane, passing signs to Mannings Wood. The lane becomes a track: follow it until the hedge on your left ends, then turn sharp left to reach a road. Cross and follow the path opposite, going left at a fork. The path goes left between fences and then steeply downhill, with the parklands of **Chartwell** on your left, to a road. Cross and climb the bank opposite, keeping to the main path, at the end of a steep slope, as it bends left. After 50 yards, turn right along a path across open land. Take the right-hand branch at a fork and continue to a lane. Turn right, passing a private road sign. Go down to a road, cross and follow the drive towards April Cottage, forking right when the drive goes up to the house. At the next fork, go left, uphill, towards an isolated house. Just before the house, turn right to reach a turning-circle. Now keep the house behind you, the turning-circle in front and a tarmac drive over to the left, and of the two woodland tracks, take the one half-right to reach a junction of tracks. Turn right, with a fence on your left, and go across open ground, crossing three stiles. Beyond the third, follow the track up to, then along, the left edge of two fields. Go ahead between fences, then uphill to reach a stile, on the right, marked 'All dogs must be kept on a lead'. Cross this and two further stiles, then go between fences, passing a cricket ground on the left. Go down to a stile near a cottage, cross and turn left. Just past a pond, go right, across a bridge, and walk beside the stream to reach a stile crossed on the outward route. Retrace your steps to the start.

POINTS OF INTEREST:

Chartwell – This is the former home of Sir Winston Churchill. It is now managed by the National Trust, as is Quebec House, Westerham, the family home of General Wolfe, of Quebec fame.

REFRESHMENTS:

The Fox and Hounds Inn, near Toys Hill.

Walk 98 RECULVER AND THE WANTSUM $9^{1}/_{2}$m ($15^{1}/_{4}$ km)

Maps: OS Sheets Landranger 179; Pathfinder 1196.

A fine coastal and marshland walk.

Start: At 227694, the car park at Reculver Country Park.

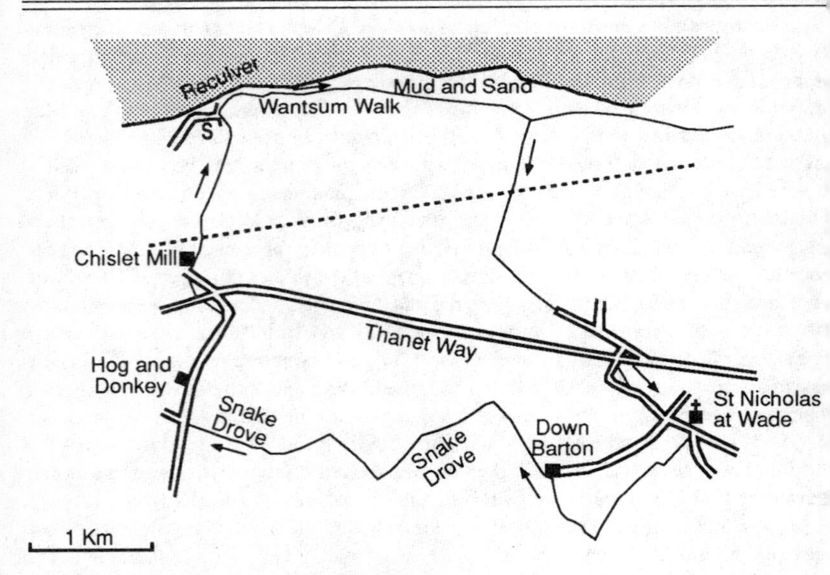

From the car park turn right (eastwards) along the sea wall: the path to the old Roman fort is to your right. Follow the sea wall path for about 2 miles. There are excellent seaward views to your left, but this part of the walk can be rather cold and windy in winter. When the wall reaches a lagoon it veers inland to skirt it. Follow the wall, but when it bears left to return to the sea, take the path on the right, marked as part of the Wantsum Walk. Follow this path along a reed-fringed dyke, go over the railway track with care, and follow the concrete track beyond towards the Church of St Nicholas at Wade.

Go through the farm at Chambers Wall to reach a lane. Continue along the lane to a junction. Turn right and climb up the ramp of a bridge which crosses the Thanet Way (the A299). Now follow the road into the village of St Nicholas at Wade, crossing over at a road junction and passing the church. Turn right at the Post Office, then when the road bears left, keep straight on past a half-timbered cottage, following the waymarker for the Wantsum Walk. Go along the left side of a recreation ground and walk across a field. Go past some houses, continuing along the tarmac path across open fields. At the bottom of the slope, ignore the kissing gate, turning right along a bridleway that runs beside a hedge and a dyke. At the farm at Down Barton, cross a track and a bridge to reach a concrete area with caravans. Head for the top left-hand corner and go through a gate to reach a track. Follow the track to meet another by a cottage. Turn left along this track (Snake Drove).

Go past a pond and, when the concrete ends, follow the continuation track along the edge of fields. At the end of the field beyond a concrete bridge, turn right and continue along the Wantsum Walk, following its waymarkers. When the Wantsum Walk divides, take the left-hand route, rejoining another part of Snake Drove and following it to a road. Turn right, passing the Hog and Donkey Inn to reach a new bridge over the Thanet Way. Cross and continue to a road junction. Cross and follow a track past Chislet Mill.

Continue along a path, heading northwards to pass under the railway line. Go through a gate and walk along the right-hand bank of a dyke, heading towards the twin towers of **Reculver**. The path ends at a farm track: turn left past caravan sites to return to the Country Park and the starting point of the walk.

POINTS OF INTEREST:

Reculver – Reculver is the site of the Roman town of Regulbium, a fort having been built here to protect this part of the coast from invasion. The town is now mostly undersea, but the walls of the fort can still be seen. They lie close to the twin towers of Reculver Abbey, a landmark for sailors for centuries. The abbey was founded in the 7th century by King Egbert, though the towers are Norman. Legend has it that they were erected by the Abbess of Davington to commemorate her escape from a shipwreck in which her sister drowned. Some locals still refer to the towers as the sisters.

REFRESHMENTS:

The Hog and Donkey, passed on the route.
The Bell, St Nicholas at Wade.

Walk 99 STONE-IN-OXNEY AND APPLEDORE $9^1/_2$m (15km

Maps: OS Sheets Landranger 189; Pathfinder 1271.

A walk between two fine villages, along the Saxon Shore Wa
and the Royal Military Canal.

Start: At 939278, the Crown Inn, Stone-in-Oxney.

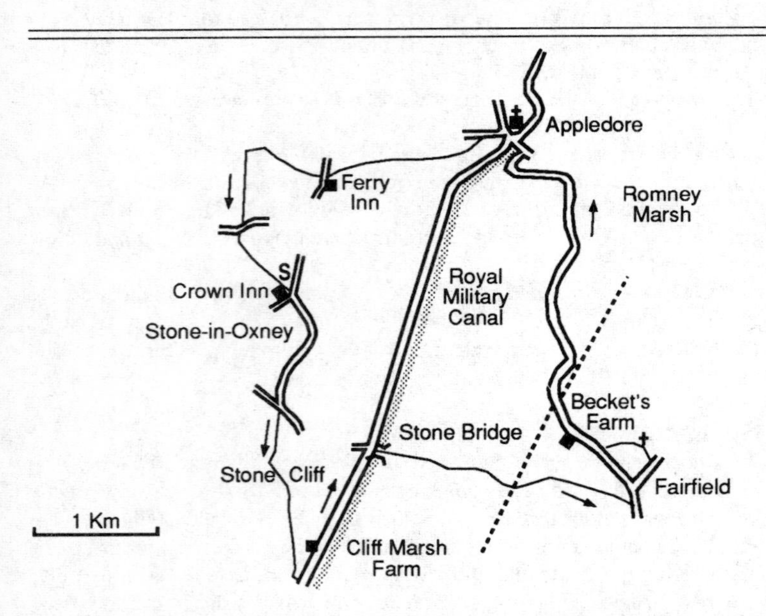

From the inn, turn left along the main village road, and then very soon turn right at sign for the Saxon Shore Way. Go through the village. The road becomes Churc Hill: continue past **St Mary's Church** and go uphill to reach a T-junction. Cross an go over the stile opposite. Now continue along the Saxon Shore Way, going throug a field and then through a gate to reach the buildings of Coldharbour Farm. Go pas these, following the path as it leads up Stone Cliff. The path descends the other sid and goes through a series of fields to reach Kent Ditch, the county boundary betwee Kent and East Sussex. Turn left along the ditch, very soon reaching a road that run beside the **Royal Military Canal**. Turn left along the road to enjoy a walk beside th canal. Go past Cliff Marsh Farm, on the left, continuing to reach Stone Bridge. Tur right and cross the canal. Now follow a grassy path that leads directly away from th canal. Cross Highknock Channel and then Five Watering Sewer, continuing to reach a railway line. Cross the line, staying with the path as it bears left. When the path forks, take the right-hand branch, following it to reach a road. Turn left and follow the road to reach a turning on the right. Take this, following the road towards Haywards Farm, on the right. Just before the farm entrance, go left along a grassy path which leads to the lovely, isolated **Church of St Thomas à Becket** at Fairfield.

Go past the church, continuing along the path to reach a minor road. Turn right. Go past Becket Barn Farm, on the left, re-cross the railway and continue to Becket's Bridge. Cross this, and Five Watering Sewer, and follow the road, initially close to the sewer, to pass Buss Barn and then Priory Farm. Stay on this minor road as it meanders through this open stretch of Romney Marsh, eventually arriving back at the Military Canal. Turn right and walk beside the canal to reach Appledore Bridge. Cross and follow the road towards Appledore village centre. To reach the centre, continue along the road. The walk does not go that far, taking the first turning on the left. Follow the road to Court Lodge, and just past the buildings, cross a stile on the left and follow the path beyond, which is signed as the Saxon Shore Way. Follow the path for about a mile through open country. It runs parallel to Reading Sewer and then continues to reach a road near the Ferry Inn. Cross and rejoin the path as it continues beside the sewer, this time on the right of the waterway. When the path forks, take the left-hand branch, which is still part of the Saxon Shore Way. Continue to reach a driveway and follow it to a road. Cross and follow the driveway of Luckhurst. When this bears away to the right, go left along a path, heading towards the corner of the field, where another path joins from the right. Follow the single path back into Stone-in-Oxney.

POINTS OF INTEREST:

St Mary's Church, Stone-in-Oxney – The church was rebuilt following a fire in 1464. Inside, under the tower there is a Roman altar to Mithras.

Royal Military Canal – Built during the Napoleonic Wars as both a defence and to transport troops and supplies, parts of the canal are now undergoing restoration.

St Thomas à Becket Church, Fairfield – This church is one of the most famous landmarks on Romney Marsh. Its isolation, there is no village of Fairfield, often meant that it was marooned by floods, the worshippers arriving by boat. Improved drainage means that this is now less frequent, though water or snow can still make it inaccessible.

REFRESHMENTS:

The Crown Inn, Stone-in-Oxney.

The Ferry Inn, on the route.

Walk 100 LYMINGE AND BRABOURNE 11m ($17^1/_2$km)

Maps: OS Sheets Landranger 189; Pathfinder 1231 and 1252.

A walk along part of the North Downs, offering expansive views.

Start: At 162409, the Coach and Horses Inn, Lyminge.

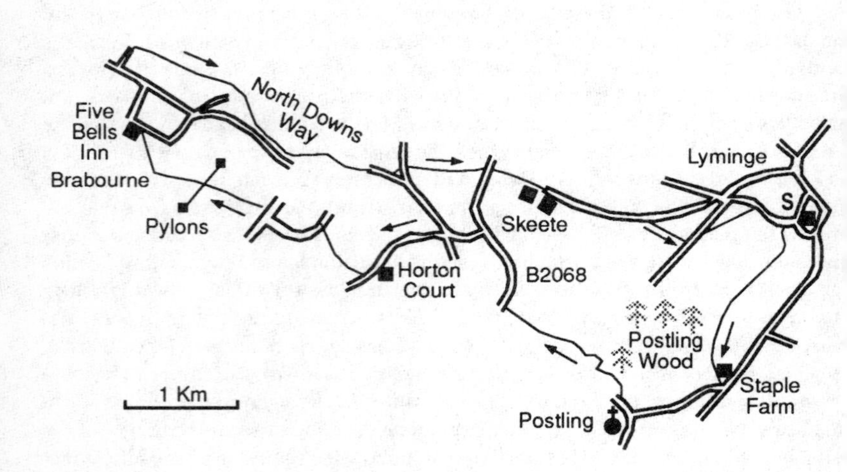

From the Inn, go westwards along the High Street until it turns sharp right. There, go through a wooden gate behind railings on the left, and follow an unmarked bridlepath uphill. At the top, cross a stile and go right along the hedgerow, ignoring the clearer path ahead. At the field end, cross the fence and continue along the right-hand fence to reach a road. Cross, go over the stile opposite and follow a fence past Postling Wood. When you meet a fence beside the wood, turn left and follow it downhill. Cross a stile, and continue to reach a road at Staple Farm. Turn right and follow the road to Postling. Turn right past the church to reach a footpath, on the right, marked by a stone plinth. Cross a stile and follow the right-hand hedge uphill. Walk along the hilltop, passing a stile on the right as you follow the fence around to the left. Now walk the open downland for about 1 mile to reach a stile with an acorn waymark (the waymark of the **North Downs Way**). Cross and follow the right edge of a field. When the hedgerow ends, maintain direction to reach a road, the B2068. Go right, with care, to reach a junction. Turn left for about 1 mile, and at the next junction take the road signed to Monk's Horton and Sellindge. Go past Horton Court, and cross the first stile on the right, after another 200 yards, and bear left across a field to another stile. Follow the edge of woodland to reach another stile, cross, turn right through a gate and go across a field in the direction of farm buildings to reach a lane. Turn left to reach a road junction. Cross to the stile in the fence opposite. Go over and bear right across a field to the far corner. Cross a stile and go along the right-hand hedge towards a row of pylons. Cross a stile and a footbridge, then follow yellow-topped posts across a field. Now ignore the marked footpath, continuing on to cross a ditch into the next field. Go along the hedge on the right to a gap into Brabourne churchyard. Leave by the front gate and go left along the road as far as the Five Bells Inn.

At the road junction by the inn, turn right to the next junction. Turn left, then first right along a road that goes up on to the scarp of the Downs. When the road goes to the left, take the track ahead, going through a gate and on to a track fork. Take the right-hand branch, go through another gate and walk below a wood to reach a road. Go straight across and continue to reach another road. Turn left. Walk past Water Farm, going uphill to reach the second footpath on the left, marked by a North Downs Way sign. Follow this path to a road. Cross, go over a stile and continue uphill along the right-hand hedge, which eventually becomes a fence. Cross the stiles at the top of the hill and go along the left-hand fence to reach another stile. Cross and go left to reach the next stile. Cross and go diagonally right to the bottom corner of a field. Cross a stile and continue to a road (the B2068). Cross, with care, and follow the track opposite to Skeete, where it becomes a road. Follow the road for $^1/_2$ mile to reach a house on the left. About 50 yards beyond the house, go through a gate on the right and diagonally across the field beyond to reach a stile. Cross and follow the left-hand fence to a road. Cross and go up a stepped path. Go over a stile at the top of the bank and cross a field to another stile. Go over and diagonally across the next field to reach a road at the edge of Lyminge. Now retrace your steps back to the start.

POINTS OF INTEREST:

North Downs Way – As with all official National Trails, the Way is waymarked by an acorn symbol. The Way links Farnham, in Surrey, with Dover, a distance of 140 miles.

REFRESHMENTS:

The Coach and Horses Inn, Lyminge.

The Five Bells Inn, Brabourne.

Titles in the Series

Cheshire

County Durham

Derbyshire

Dorset

Essex

Gloucestershire

Hampshire & the Isle of Wight

Hereford and Worcester

Kent

Lancashire

Northumberland

Somerset and Avon

Staffordshire

Surrey

East Sussex

West Sussex

Wiltshire

Yorkshire (Vols 1 and 2)